THE ROMAN LEGIONARY IN BATTLE

(Second Revision)

BY

JOHN PLANT

*Dedicated to the memory of
the 13th/18th Royal Hussars*

THE ROMAN LEGIONARY IN BATTLE

Preface

In a preface the author has an opportunity to comment on his work, and I will take advantage of this.

I have been fascinated by the Roman army for around 60 years. This fascination started when the class I was in at school read Macaulay's 'The Keeping of the Bridge'. Over the years I have read the majority of books on the Roman army, but as interesting as I found them I could not help noticing that the soldier's activity at the sharp end was either studiously ignored, or passed over with sloppy generalisations, and yet killing the enemy is the single most important military activity. It is only by understanding how the Romans went about it that Roman warfare can be fully understood, and this is what I have tried to do.

It remains to state that the opinions expressed here are purely mine. I generated most of them while running around Northern Ireland carrying a riot shield in the capacity of lance-corporal, and if sometimes these opinions are not capable of proof they are, at least, practicable.

Introduction

This study is an investigation into how the Roman legionary fought his enemies, which is to say what arms he carried, and what drills and procedures he followed on the battlefield when in contact with the enemy. However there are certain operational considerations that affect the legionary's battlefield performance, and to illustrate these brief accounts are given of the Battles of the Teutoburg Wald (The Varus Disaster), Philippi and others, and to do that, procedures for marching and constructing temporary marching camps must be considered. The study is restricted to the activities of the legionary, and light infantry and cavalry are only considered in the roles supporting the legionaries, or as enemies. Also the legionary took part in a wide range of activities other than set-piece battle, such as siege operations. These activities are not considered here.

What follows, then, is a cautious attempt to describe the legionary tactical system. Unfortunately due to this lack of evidence a series of sweeping deductions must be made and conclusions drawn that are open to argument. These deductions will be based on the historical trends described in the earlier chapters, the few useful literary sources available, archaeology and, it is hoped, common sense!

The sources used for this study are listed at the end of each chapter, as much as possible they are readily available Penguin or Loeb editions. There is a small number of references to various sculptures and similar sources. Pictures of all these are easily found on the internet.

While the greater part of this study describes legionary warfare at the height of empire, the first two chapters describe the development of the legion and legionary up to the time of Caesar. During this period, despite the scarcity of sources, it is certain that Roman warfare evolved from the heroic stage to the hoplite phalanx, then from the phalanx to the legion, so an attempt will be made to understand the Greek phalanx, particularly from the hoplite's point of view.

Chapter 1: The Greek Background

Heroic Warfare

In prehistoric times people naturally grouped together in their tribes and when the tribe went to war it was a matter of survival so the entire capable male population fought, and fought with great determination. The result of such a hurly-burly could well be the total extermination of one side. However as the tribes became settled geographically a social order emerged, as did a different and less lethal model of warfare. The reason for this change was that the cause of the war usually no longer involved the whole tribe, but increasingly became a matter for a small class of leaders, and the dynastic and personal conflicts of this class would little affect the mass of the people. This model is termed 'heroic warfare' and is the style described by Homer in the Iliad, which is an account of some incidents in a war fought over the abduction of a princess, not an event which would result in a mass of subsistence farmers rushing to arms.

This warfare was essentially a matter for aristocrats. In Homer there is a clear difference between the hero, such as Achilles, and his followers, in this case the myrmidons. Homer does mention masses of troops but the important fighting was done by the aristocrats supported, no doubt, with missiles and cheers by their followers.

The reason for the importance of the aristocrats was that, in primitive societies, they were the only ones able to afford the arms and armour required to be a hero, and the time to practice the required skills. They could arrive at the field of battle fresh, Homer says that they came by chariot, but by horse seems more likely. Retainers would carry their shields and heavy arms, and refreshing water or wine. Then after some strutting and fretting, a high-powered duel would decide the day.

The cost of armour was certainly high. Homer valued a set of bronze armour as being worth nine oxen, so naturally warfare was a rich man's sport. Also, naturally, the rich man was just as interested in keeping his retainers in their place as he was in fighting the enemy. This fact would have generated a feeling of reciprocity between the opposing heroes which would have evolved into a kind of chivalry. Warfare may well have become choreographed into duels in which aristocrats acted out cameos from the Iliad and their retainers stood by and cheered.

The Hoplite Phalanx

The classic age of Heroic Warfare was followed by a dark age, but after that Greece, during the 9th and 8th centuries BC, saw a steady increase in population and prosperity. These trends saw the growing importance of cities and the increase in size of armies. In battle the mass of retainers became large enough to eclipse the duelling heroes, and the fact that war was not a sport for them but a very serious business meant that they became more likely to demand a quick decision via hand-to-hand fighting with spears rather than by missile action.

The hero was not that well equipped for hand-to-hand fighting. The shield of the heroic age was a small buckler with a single central hand grip. This was good enough for warding off arrows, sling shot and light javelins, but not the eight-foot 'Dorian spear'. The new warfare demanded a serious shield, and this resulted in the invention of the *aspis*. The word *hoplon,* from which the word 'hoplite' is derived also refers to the shield, but its plural refers to all the hoplite's fighting equipment. It is interesting to note that the word 'panoply' is derived from the complete set of the hoplite's equipment. This shield, as opposed to the hero's buckler, was held at two points. There was a fixed loop in the centre for the elbow. The forearm was held horizontal and flat against the shield, and the hand held a grip on the shield's rim. The shield was round and about three feet in diameter. It was bowed outwards after the fashion of a very flat bowler hat, this was so that its considerable weight, around 15 lbs could be largely supported on the left shoulder. Being sturdy it could also be used as a sledge to transport its previous owner's corpse.

The size of the *aspis* meant that there was no longer the necessity for the expensive armour of the hero, all now that a man needed to take his place in the fighting line was a shield and spear. Consequently the widespread adoption of the *aspis* resulted in a dramatic increase in the number of infantry available for hand-to-hand fighting, and this had a profound effect on infantry warfare.

The Greeks knew that in the hoplite they had a fighting man ideally suited to their system of warfare. In 'The Persians' Aeschylus makes the chorus, after disdaining archery, say of the Greeks: '*They carry stout shields, and fight hand-to-hand with spears*'.[1] The importance of spears resulted in a reduced requirement for the long, and expensive, swords of the heroes.

The hero now, instead of riding to battle to duel with his opposite number, led a file of his retainers. He might still be resplendent in his gleaming armour, but his followers were equally capable of his style of fighting. They would all, of course, know each other and their leader. This knowledge strengthened unit cohesion. Also there were many more such heroes with their small bands of followers. These soon became the files of a phalanx. The leading men of society still led the phalanx, and they were still supported by their retainers, but the accent had changed. The duelling hero in his armour could fight, as it were, in any direction. The unarmoured, or lightly armoured, hoplite was only protected by his shield so could fight in one direction only. Consequently the hoplite was forced to fight in a line with other hoplites. The result of all this was that very quickly a distinct hoplite phalanx style of fighting developed. In his Iliad Homer makes Nestor say: '*Sort your men out, Agamemnon, into their tribes and clans, so that clan may help clan and the tribes support each other. Such dispositions, if the troops adhere to them, will show you what cowards you may have among the officers or in the ranks, and what good men. For each man will be fighting at his brother's side, and you will soon find out whether it is God's will that stands between you and the sack of Troy, or the cowardice of your soldiers and their incompetence in war.*'[2]

The order of the hoplites in the file could not be left solely to their station in civil life but, Xenophon recounts, as a young man said to Socrates: '*In war too you should post the best troops in front and in the rear, and the worst in between so that they may be led on by the one lot and pushed forward by the other.*' Socrates rather sourly asked '*how to distinguish the good from the bad*'.[3] That the order of the hoplites was important, particularly with reference to the rear man, is shown by the way that Greek armies would carry out the counter-march drill on the battlefield. This will be mentioned below.

In its early days, roughly up to the Peloponnesian War (431-404 BC) the manoeuvrability of the phalanx was limited and commanding it did not call for a professional. Once the commander had decided on a battle and got his phalanx facing that of the enemy, he took his place in the ranks as an ordinary hoplite, and lost all control of the battle. However as war became more serious so a system was developed for passing orders by trumpet. Such a system was very limited, but within its limitations, could be effective. For example as Xenophon recounts: *'But when the line of hoplites came up, moving at a quick pace, and at the same time the trumpet sounded and they sang the paean and then raised a shout as they brought their spears down for the attack, then the enemy stood their ground no longer, and took to flight'*[4].

The trumpet involved was the salpinx which seems to have been something like a coaching horn but was produced in a wide variety of shapes. It certainly made a loud sound, but probably not a very pleasant one, flutes were far more musical. From the earliest times some phalanxes had been accompanied by flute players, but these did not have a signalling function other than, perhaps, assisting those phalanxes that marched in step to do so. However it must be emphasised that throughout the classic age of hoplite warfare, the hoplites were part-time militia incapable of serious drill or manoeuvre. The exceptions were the Spartiates, the regular core of the Spartan army, who were superbly disciplined but were too few to alter the pattern of Greek warfare.

The depth of the phalanx, that is the length of the files, was not standard but seems to have averaged around eight men. After the Peloponnesian War, with the increasing employment of professional soldiers, this became standard.

The hoplite had to fight in a fairly restricted way. He did not have much space to move in. His left arm was fully occupied with his shield and his right hand held his spear five feet from its point. He gripped his spear with his thumb towards the point, usually he thrust underarm, but could thrust overarm. Usually he would aim at his opponent's eyes or even his legs, providing his opponent was not wearing greaves. It can be seen, then, that the stand-up fight of one rank (line abreast) of hoplites against

5

another was not apt to be very lethal. This is confirmed by history which shows that the victorious phalanx suffered few casualties, implying that the heavy losses of the defeated side were inflicted in the pursuit.

In addition to his spear, the hoplite carried a short sword, a good deal shorter than that carried during the heroic period. There were two designs for this sword, one a straight thrusting dagger and the other a cutting weapon not unlike a Gurkha's kukri. Either way these weapons were not important in terms of phalanx warfare.

There are extant some manuals that claim to describe phalanx fighting. They are poor and mostly cover the *sarissa*-armed Macedonian phalanx, however they can occasionally come up with gems of information. Aelian[5] and Asclepiodotus[6] describing the spacing of the files, gives three orders. In Open Order each man took up six feet, three inches (four cubits); in Intermediate Order each man took up three feet, two inches (two cubits); and in Close Order he took up one foot, seven inches (one cubit). Close Order is not practical for soldiers carrying a full sized shield and fighting with sword or spear. If this order had any application at all, it would have been in the Macedonian pikeman era. The Open and Intermediate Orders, however, are of significant interest.

The open order may be taken as the spacing of the files when the phalanx was marching up to within sight of the enemy. The spacing was necessary mostly because of the pure difficulty of manoeuvring a large body of men over fairly rough ground and around obstacles like trees, but also because it was necessary for some basic manoeuvres. A case in point was at the battle of Cunaxa (401 BC) when Persian troops suddenly appeared behind the Greek phalanx and to meet this threat the Greeks conducted a counter-march. This drill involved the leading hoplites in turn, turning about and filing to the rear so that, when they had all done this, the phalanx was facing the other way. This drill could only be carried out in open order.

Having advanced in open order, the hoplites would halt and there would follow discussions among the senior ranks, sacrifices and a harangue from the Commander-in-Chief. Then the front rank would double up to the intermediate order for the advance to contact, this would be done by the second man moving forward to the left of the front man. This advance would be carried out at a steady march, it is true that at Marathon the hoplites charged and hit the Persians at a run, but this was due to the unusual circumstance that the Persians fought mostly by missile action and the hoplites wanted to pass through the beaten zone as quickly as possible

There can be little doubt that the intermediate order was adopted. Asclepiodotus states that the intermediate order was used *'when we are marching the phalanx upon the enemy, the latter* (close order) *when the enemy is marching upon us'*.[7] Thucydides states that as a general observation that advancing phalanxes drift to the right as each hoplite tries *'to find protection for his unarmoured side in the shield of the man next to him on the right, thinking the more closely the shields are locked together, the safer he will be.'*[8] This drift would not have occurred if the troops had stayed in open order because the neighbouring shield would have been too far away to try to hide behind.

It may happen that one phalanx had such a moral ascendancy over the other that after no, or only token, resistance the loser flees as the winning phalanx, fronted by its best men, crashes into it. This would be unusual but did happen. For example, at the Battle of Coronea Xenophon noted that, *'As for the Argives, they did not even wait for Agesilaus and his troops to attack, but fled to mount Helicon'*[9]. This would have been quite understandable since the front rank of the Spartan phalanx was an impressive sight, marching in step and perfectly drilled and there are occasional examples of premature and precipitate retreats from other battles. However phalanx fighting would normally take the form of two front lines, three or four yards apart, fencing with their spears, each man starring in his own private Homeric duel, everyman his own Achilles, as Aeschylus put it *'Man faces man and falls before the spear'*.[10] Doubtlessly some of the heroes were quite reluctant, which will have made the fighting sporadic and kept the casualty rate down. It seems most likely that the shield-touching-shield of the intermediate order would break up as the duelling hoplites needed more room. Behind the front rank the rest of the phalanx was still in open order so that when the file leader was tired or wounded he could move to the rear, and his immediate follower take over the fighting.

It can be seen how important it was to have the men with the best armour in the front rank. They would have the most confidence to start thrusting with their spears. Without that confidence the two phalanxes might just stand a few yards apart and the battle never get started!

Fencing with a spear and carrying a heavy shield would have been very tiring and, after a surprisingly short time [11] each hoplite in turn, like the file leader, even if not wounded, would be falling back to the rear down the left hand side of the file so not to snag the spears of the other hoplites in the file. This was why it was important to have a reliable man as the file closer, he would make sure that the hoplites did not just fade away, routs commonly started at the rear. There can be little doubt that the front man would fall back like this, this *modus operandi* would be the only way of keeping the front ranks reasonably fresh. As an example of this Curtius, describing the plight of some Macedonian light infantry when they were caught in disorder and forced to fight against disciplined hoplites, at the Battle of Issus, wrote, '*But, exhausted as they were, they were continually being met by a fresh adversary*'.[12]

Even so a clash of phalanxes would not be a continuous action, even Spartiates could not stand there hitting their enemies indefinitely. Combat would have proceeded as a series of deadly flurries which, after probably two or three minutes, would die down and the hoplites would back off for a breather and to swap over before starting again. It was in such lulls that Sparta's discipline really counted. Their enemies might pull back a bit in some disorder, but the Spartans would remain perfectly aligned, they would not pursue but, on the word of command, continue their steady march forward. This would often cause their enemies' morale to crumble.

The battle could last some time, then when one side was seen to be weakening it could progress to the next stage, which was known as the *othismos,* the pushing stage. In this stage the front rank, at least, would return to the intermediate order, with their shields touching or overlapping and their spears in the 'V' between them or used overhand. Then they would surge at the enemy hoping to break them. An account of this drill in action is given by Dionysius of Halicarnassus, and refers to the fighting against the Volscians in 493 BC, the Romans can be regarded as hoplites. '*Postumus, being informed of this.... sent the bravest of the youth to his relief. These, doubling their files, charged the enemy; and when the first line failed to sustain their charge, but turned to flight, they pressed forward and found Marcius covered with wounds.*'[13]

As can be seen the round *aspis* was well suited to the *othismos.* The concave design of the shield meant that the hoplite's shoulder would fit in it efficiently for shoulder barging. On the other hand hoplites in the intermediate order were almost in a straitjacket and could not fight as effectively as those in open order, there was only one tactic open to them, to advance. Adopting the *othismos* at exactly the right moment would win a resounding victory, but it was a matter of very fine judgement. The sudden push of the *othismos* was, no doubt, what Polyaenus was referring to when he wrote *'Iphicrates told his men, he would insure them the victory; if mutually animating each other, upon a certain signal he should give, they would advance but a single pace. At the crisis, when victory hung in equal suspense, he gave the signal: the army returned it with acclamations; advanced a pace, and defeated the enemy.'*

The single step concept was so significant that Polyaenus repeated it for Epaminondas: *'In the engagement at Leuctrae, Epaminondas commanded the Thebans, and Cleombrotus the Lacedaemonians. Victory remained long in suspence: when Epaminondas called on his troops, to give him one step more, and he would ensure the victory. They did so: and obtained it.'* [14]

Organisation varied between the Greek states. In general at the lowest level hoplites were organised into *enomotia*. The Spartan version was 32 hoplites strong, so it could form up four, eight or sixteen deep. Four deep was regarded as the minimum depth of an effective fighting line. It may be that other states used this system as the Spartan army enjoyed immense prestige. Higher organisation seems to have been usually on an *ad-hoc* basis according to the views of the generals. However the *enomotai* were usually organised into units called *'lochoi'*. These were based on recruiting areas and do not seem to have had any tactical application. They were 400 to 600 hoplites strong and they are of interest to this study only in that they were of similar size to the Roman cohorts and probably of a natural size for this kind of intermediate unit.

So far this discussion has restricted itself to actions of the hoplite, what Scipio Africanus might have called the 'bludgeon work', and this approach is appropriate when considering the phalanx up to the time of the Peloponnesian War. It was the convention that once the general had deployed his troops and ordered the battle to begin he took his place as a hoplite in the front rank and could no longer control, or even influence, the fighting, so manoeuvre warfare was impossible and it all came down to hard fighting.

Inevitably the most common variation on the simple head on clash of phalanxes would be when one phalanx extended beyond the other so could wrap round its flank. In particular the phalanx's right flank would have been vulnerable in this way because such an attack would come against the hoplites' unshielded side. This might be as much a cause of the drift to the right as was the seeking of the shelter of the neighbour's shield that Thucydides mentioned. The expected result would be the left wing of phalanxes being overwhelmed by flanking attacks and yet this seldom happened. Probably, as the bulk of the phalanx was in open order, there was enough flexibility in it for the fighting front rank to angle back and for each file to put more hoplites in the front rank in intermediate order, thus forcing the attacking front to extend thus making itself vulnerable and so soon reaching its limit.

If, however, one phalanx could significantly out-flank its enemies the effect could be shattering. This was because the out-flankers would still be fighting in files, whereas the out-flanked hoplites were not and would be quickly reduced to a mob. To achieve this the out-flankers would require a high degree of competence at drill as a part of their phalanx would have to execute a left turn during the battle. They would also need a great deal of luck as most phalanxes were deployed with their flanks secured either by a natural obstacle or by cavalry. The Spartans, some of whom were professional soldiers, were among the few troops who could achieve an outflanking movement, for example at the River Nemea in 394 BC, but most hoplite armies could not manage this.

Because the hoplites tended to be right-handed the right flank, being the open flank, was the most dangerous post so regarded as the most honourable. The left flank was the second most dangerous as this flank was judged to be in danger of being out-flanked due to the trend for phalanxes to drift to the right. There is no record of any attempt to organise left-handed hoplites which seems to have been a wasted opportunity. It is, though, just possible that the Theban assault *'like the ram of a trireme'* at Mantinea involved left-handed troops on the principle that triremes had both port and starboard sides and left-handed hoplites formed the right flank of the assault.

All this is not to say that there were no clever stratagems or shattering outflanking movements, for there certainly were, but they were limited by the hoplites' lack of tactical skill and were not generally of importance in this era. They probably made little difference to the soldier for whom every attack was a frontal attack and every battle came down to a duel.

To summarise the above, a phalanx battle would break down into three phases: the initial phase, the attrition phase and the breakthrough. The initial phase would see the front rank deployed in the intermediate order hoping to demoralise and shatter the opposing phalanx. In the attrition phase the front rank break up into a series of individual hoplite duels, with the files of the rest of the phalanx, in open order shuffling forward slowly, supplying replacements for the duelling hoplites as they fall back to the rear either wounded or weary. However the breakthrough stage would only be adopted if the enemy was seen to be weakening. The intermediate order was reinstituted for the front rank which advanced even to the point of shoulder barging the enemy.

Hoplites dominated Greek warfare until well after the end of the Peloponnesian War because the hoplite vs hoplite clash was accepted as decisive. There were, however, other enemies, cavalry and light infantry, these were similar, cavalry usually acting as mounted javelineers. Cavalry could be devastating in pursuit of routed hoplites, but while the hoplites retained their formation they had little to fear. For example, in 457 BC, '*Myronides, the Athenian, when about to fight on an open plain against the Thebans, who were very strong in cavalry, warned his troops that, if they stood their ground, there was some hope of safety, but that, if they gave away, destruction was absolutely certain. In this way he encouraged his men and won the victory*'.[15]

Light infantry used missiles: slingshot, javelins, arrows and, if desperate, rocks. In general it will take a long time for a missile action to be successful, but a hoplite vs hoplite clash was quickly over, and the light infantry had little chance to influence it. Hoplites, providing they kept their ranks steady, and their flanks secure, were immune to arrows and other missiles. It is true that the remnant of the Spartiates at Thermopylae were shot down, but that was because they were surrounded and facing a huge numerical superiority. Also some hoplite-based armies were heavily defeated by light infantry in the mountains and plains to the north of Greece, but these events do not seem to have particularly impressed the main Greek city states. Ancient authors usually differentiate between light infantry and peltasts, but this difference was, at least until the end of the Peloponnesian War, not very meaningful. Peltasts were light infantry who carried a small shield called a *pelte*. As such shields were made of wickerwork, or similar, a few weeks' hard campaigning would have destroyed them and peltasts would no longer have been a separate category of soldiers. Archers, however, are often listed separately. Regardless of such considerations there was one incident during the Peloponnesian War that was a triumph for light infantry, or peltasts, and caused immense shock at the time, this was the Battle of Spaectaria.

The Battle of Spaectaria
Early in 425 BC the Athenians landed a small force on the small peninsula of Pylos on the south-western coast of the Peloponnese. The force landed was initially only 200 hoplites, 20 archers and 40 spearmen, supporting these were around 1,000 crewmen off the ships. The Athenians fortified their land front, and soon a Spartan force attacked it. This force made no progress so the Spartans besieged the peninsula and as a part of this operation they landed a force of 420 hoplites, commanded by Epitadas, on Spaectaria, a small island to the south of Pylos. Of the hoplites, 180 were Spartiates and 240 were allies. They were supported by around 200 helots.

The Spartan force at Spaectaria was soon cut off because the Athenian fleet destroyed the Spartan, and the situation of the force looked dire. Spaectaria is two and a half miles long and a little over half a mile wide, it was uninhabited and had one small spring and generally thick vegetation. The Spartans made their camp round the spring in the middle of the island.

The Athenian naval victory resulted in a blockade of Spaectaria which lasted a total of 71 days. This must have had a debilitating effect on the defenders. Due to a fire, which was most likely to have been deliberately started, the vegetation was burned off and the Spartan situation was easy for the Athenians to access, and they decided to capture the island.

Their commanders were Demosthenes and Cleon, the former usually being given the military credit. They assembled a force of 800 to 1,200 hoplites, 400 to 600 archers, and 800 to 1,200 Thracian peltasts. Once again there were many naval crewmen available, and the most useful function of these men may have been to supply the fighting men with water.

The Athenian force landed at night at several points and easily overcame the watchmen. The peltasts were organised into groups of 200 men and were sent to occupy the high ground around the Spartan camp, the hoplites formed up towards the south of the island on a narrow front running from coast to coast. The front was 100 yards wide and eight to twelve men deep.

The Spartans formed up only around four men deep but due to their well-known superiority in hoplite fighting could probably have handled the Athenian phalanx, unfortunately trying to do so would have exposed their backs to the Athenian light troops. The standard Spartan response to light troops was for the front ranks to make a sudden charge, but in this case the light troops could retreat behind, or through, the Athenian phalanx, and the Spartan hoplites would have come, singly or in disarray, up against the serried ranks of fresh Athenian hoplites. Alternatively the light troops could just run away until they could suddenly turn on individual pursuers and harass them to death. The Spartans were becoming helpless and their helots, because of the Athenian light troops, would not have been able to bring them any water. After much futile skirmishing the Spartans retreated to the north end of the island where there was an old prehistoric fort. Here they presented a solid front to the Athenians. By late morning the action had come down to a stand-off which lasted until some archers worked their way round to the Spartan rear. This was enough for the Spartan commander to accept an offer of surrender.

The result of this battle sent shock waves through Greece. One hundred and twenty Spartiates and 172 allies surrendered. A few years earlier a roughly similar force preferred death to surrender, and many must have wondered of the age of hoplite supremacy might have been passing. It was not, but there were several aspects of the battle that would have degraded the Spartan hoplites' performance and would have been pondered on.

Poor leadership. Not only was Epitadas dead but his second-on-command was badly wounded, believed dead, hence putting the onus of command on someone not expecting it.

Exhaustion. The battle took place in the height of Summer, it lasted around six hours and in its early stages it involved lots of running around as the hoplites tried vainly to engage the peltasts. Further, the Spartans were weakened by 71 days of siege conditions.

Dehydration. This might have been the really critical factor. The helots could not get the water to the hoplites, and for most of the battle could not even get to the spring. The day was hot and the ash from the recently burned undergrowth would have aggravated their thirst, and dehydration will bring even the strongest man down.

All this may be true, but the Spartan casualties were surprisingly light, only a loss of 60 Spartiates and 67 allies, and this after a force of 420 hoplites held at bay a force of between 2,000 and 3,000 men exclusive of naval auxiliaries, for half a day under very difficult circumstances. It may be that if the Spartan force had included a reasonable light infantry component, it could have won the day, but certainly it would take more than a few archers and other light infantry to put an end to the age of the hoplite.

The Post-War Phalanx
The Peloponnesian War changed Greek warfare in many ways, most immediately by increasing the importance of

cavalry and light infantry, and such changes affected the actions of the hoplites. They did so in four ways.

Firstly the major city-states started to enrol regular soldiers. This may have been a result of more specie being available as the Persians took more and more to financing Greek armies and navies. Most of these soldiers were peltasts, but those that were hoplites, being usually well drilled, were used to make up the first two or three ranks of the phalanxes where they would improve the manoeuvrability of the phalanx and its impact in the initial clash. However it seems that citizen hoplites took the view that regular (mercenary) soldiers were less dedicated to the battle than they were, so the mass of the rear ranks, being citizens, would keep the regulars at it.

Secondly the growing numbers of light infantry forced a new drill on the hoplites. On a signal the first rank or two of hoplites would charge out to drive the skirmishers away. It is difficult to imagine that this tactic was very effective and it must have been exhausting but, as the hoplites carried no missile weapons, there was little choice if the phalanx had been caught without its own cavalry and light infantry support.

Thirdly, the Theban army, used to operating in more open country than most other Greek armies, started to increase the depth of its phalanx. At the Battles of Delium (424 BC) and Coronea (394 BC) the Theban phalanx formed up 25 deep. The purpose of such a formation is difficult to understand, however as will be seen in Appendix One, a basic unit of the Macedonian phalanx was a 16x16 square and it may be that the Thebans were using a 25x25 square. Battles, which were now involving contingents from several cities, were requiring more manoeuvre and this new formation may have been a method of providing this. The Thebans may have manoeuvred in these 25x25 bricks, but may have broken them down into smaller units to fight in, possible two 12-man deep units, the odd rank consisting of the leader and his command group. The 625 man brick may have evolved from the *lochoi*, and was similar in size to that of a Roman cohort, which was the largest unit capable of being commanded by the voice of one man. The Thebans had a regular cadre to make this system work, and a regular regiment, the Sacred Band, to provide a cutting edge. The purpose of a deep formation in the attack will be considered below in an account of the Battle of Leuctra.

It is interesting to observe that during the nineteenth century some trials were carried out by the French army to investigate the use of deep columns in the assault, the general idea being that even if the front rank wanted to halt, the succeeding ranks would drive it forward. The result was: '*Experiments made have shown that beyond the sixteenth the impulsion of the ranks in rear has no effect on the front, it is completely taken up by the fifteen ranks already massed behind the first*'.[16] So plainly the deep Theban columns were not expected to blast their way through their opposition by weight of numbers.

Finally light infantry and cavalry made routs much more dangerous for the retreating hoplites. If one phalanx had broken and was pursued only by the victorious hoplites the rout would cause few casualties as the fleeing men could always run faster than their pursuers. Heavy casualties could only be caused if the defeated troops were caught at a choke point, such as a city gate. However this changed when the pursuers were light infantry or cavalry who could ride down or surround the retreating troops. It was in this context that Alcibiades praised Socrates's resolute behaviour during the '*disorderly retreat from Delium*'.[17] It can be presumed that this increased danger played its part in making hoplite service less popular.

The Battle of Leuctra

The Spartans emerged from the Peloponnesian War not only as the victors, but also acknowledged as by far the finest phalanx fighters in the world. However, only a few years later a Spartan army was defeated in a set-piece phalanx battle by the Thebans. The political importance of the outcome of the Battle of Leuctra has been well understood, but the tactics of the phalanxes less so.

In the post-war period Sparta had become progressively unpopular and Thebes had gained in power, this resulted in confrontation and then, in 371 BC, in battle. The basic form of the battle is well known. The Spartans took, as usual, the right wing with various allies, willing and unwilling, in the centre and left. The Spartans and their allies were arrayed twelve deep. The Thebans, under Epaminondas, posted their Theban phalanx, their best troops, on the left opposite the Spartans. The Theban allies were ordered to mark the Spartan allies but not to risk an engagement unless it was forced on them. Epaminondas knew that if he could defeat the Spartans, their army would disintegrate.

The Spartans could hardly have been ignorant of the Theban plan, but they would have been quietly confident. No other phalanx had prevailed against the Spartan, but this one was different. There are two well known points. One is that the Theban assault was to be led by the 300 strong 'Sacred Band', consisting of big, well regarded soldiers. The other is they were leading a phalanx no less than 50 men deep. The Spartans, presumably following their standard tactics, were anticipating making a right flanking attack.

The two sides marched against each other and the first part of the action was the Theban cavalry chasing off the Spartan. After that the sources are so vague that it is really a matter of deducing how it all could have worked to produce the result it did.

Unfortunately the numbers involved are particularly vague. Plutarch writes that the Spartan army included a total of 10,000 foot and 1,000 horse.[18] If 2,000 foot were light infantry and half the remainder were allies then the Spartans had 4,000 hoplites on the battlefield. They formed up twelve deep, giving them a frontage of roughly 333 files. To face this the Thebans must have deployed a front line of an absolute minimum of 250 files. The Theban army had only 6,000 men.[19] Epaminondas had six Boeotarchs with him, and each would normally bring with him 100 cavalry and 1,000 hoplites[20] so the greater part of the 6,000 can be assumed to be hoplites, but the fraction that were Theban is not known. Perhaps it is best to assume that the numbers of Spartan and Theban hoplites were roughly similar. The battle would be decided by these forces.

The Thebans, coming on in their huge column, '*at least fifty shields deep*'[21] were led by their Sacred Band which was in a wedge formation. This information is supplied by Aelian who described this formation as being triangular, its point, almost literally its spearhead, being a rank of three hoplites, followed by a rank of five, then seven, and so on. The commander would take post as the centre hoplite in the front rank, and the hoplites would be in the Intermediate Order.[22]

It is possible that the Thebans had been using the wedge formation for a number of years. At Tegyra, in 375 BC, Pelopidas commanded the Sacred Band which '*he drew up in a close body; hoping that, wherever they charged, they would break through the enemy, though superior in numbers*'. This assault was very successful. '*The shock began in the quarter where the generals fought in person on both sides, and was very violent and furious. The Spartan commanders, who attacked Pelopidas, were among the first that were slain, and all that were near them being either killed or put to flight, the whole army was so terrified, that they opened a lane for the Thebans, through which they might have passed safely, and continued their route if they had pleased. But Pelopidas, disdaining to make his escape so, charged those who yet stood their ground, and made such havoc among them, that they fled in great confusion.'*[23] That this assault caused chaos and heavy casualties is an indication that it was a wedge assault. The clash of the linear fronts of two phalanxes would not initially result in heavy casualties, but the impact of the point of a wedge, probably at the double, would cause chaos and prevent the orderly filing to the rear of wounded and weary hoplites, making their deaths more likely. Earlier than this, in 394 BC at Coronea, a Theban force forced its way through a Spartan phalanx, a fact which implies a wedge assault.

The wedge and column, in action at the Battle of Mantinea (362 BC) was described by Xenophon: '*Epaminondas led his army forward prow on, as it were, like the ram of a trireme, believing that if he could strike and break through at any point, he would destroy the whole enemy army*'[24], a striking image of a deep column headed by a wedge and hurled at the enemy front. At Leuctra the wedge, 300 men, would have consisted of 42 files. The column following the Sacred Band would have been considerably wider, to take some of the pressure off it and the vague figures involved seem to indicate that the Sacred Band would be followed by a column 100 men wide and 50 deep. However a solid block of 5,000 men would be difficult to control and incapable of any significant manoeuvre such as this battle was going to require. In view of this, and the 25x25 'bricks' the Thebans had been using in recent battles, a deployment can be proposed that fits exactly the little that is known of this battle.(*Sketch 1*) The 25x25 brick may have evolved into the 16x16 *speira*, as will be seen in Appendix One. If the Thebans had been using the smaller unit, each side of the army would have been made up of three, but the same general principles would apply.

Following the wedge of the Sacred Band the hoplites were deployed in four 'bricks', two on each side with a significant gap between the two sides. Also there may have been an eight-deep line, 200 files wide, between the two leading bricks to back up the Sacred Band and prevent any infiltration between these bricks. This, allowing for the Sacred Band to consist of 300 men, gives a total of 4,420 Theban heavy infantry, a reasonable number given the vagueness of the sources.

With this deployment Epaminondas could have commanded on horseback between the bricks. A Greek general would normally fight in the front rank, but the most important front line post was occupied by Pelopidas who commanded the Sacred Band. Also this battle would require a far greater degree of control than the usual phalanx clash of the period, and on horseback Epaminondas would be able to see the fighting. Thebes was strong in cavalry, and he could have had some horsemen with him to act as dispatch riders for communicating with the cavalry and allies. All this, of course, is speculation.

Both the Thebans and Spartans had deployed cavalry in front of their phalanxes. This was unusual and was probably done to screen from sight the infantry deployment: the Thebans would want their wedge assault to come as a surprise, and the Spartans would want their out-flanking manoeuvre to also be a surprise. The battle started with the Theban cavalry charging and driving off the Spartan. It seems that some Spartan horsemen crashed into their phalanx causing some disorder and this was quickly followed up by the Sacred Band.

The Sacred Band was not big enough to have made up the vanguard of the entire phalanx, but it was big enough for a specific mission. It was aimed, as at Tegyra, at the Spartan commander who was easily visible in the front rank surrounded by other officers and an elite guard. The assault was a success, the Spartan king and several of his officers were killed, but other hoplites would have fought back and the Sacred Band would have been wiped out if the Theban phalanx had not advanced so that the survivors of the Band could file back through the eight deep ranks.

The Spartans would, following the initial surprise, start to lap round the Theban left wing, and probably also their right. The Thebans would be expecting this and, on an order from Epaminondas the bricks would swing round and deploy to meet the Spartans, probably even out-flanking them and achieving a local numerical superiority. The precise method by which the bricks deployed is impossible to know, but it seems most likely that they broke down into twelve deep sub-units.

At this stage of the battle the Spartans knew they were in trouble. Their front line was struggling, though, presumably, holding its own. Their outflanking manoeuvre, which had been successful before, was plainly failing and just when they needed decisive leadership their king, Cleombrotus was dead. Their allies showed no interest in coming to their aid and they were attacked in the rear by the Theban cavalry and, presumably, light infantry which prevented their helots bring up much needed water. The Spartans did not break, but as the slogging match ground on thirst would have begun to weaken them so when, after a long struggle Epaminodas called for '*one more step*', the Spartans accepted defeat and made a fighting retreat to their camp where they finally grounded their arms in an orderly fashion.

Epaminondas could give his order because, being mounted, he could observe events across the Theban-Spartan front. Also he was not in the front line, like a traditional Greek general, where, like the Spartan commander, he could have died.

The Spartans had lost around a quarter of their strength, but far worse than that they had lost their grip on their allies and, as Epaminondas predicted, their army fell apart.

There is a certain irony in that the tactical withdrawal from Leuctra was probably the Spartans' finest display of battlefield discipline, yet it occurred in the closing phase of the battle that destroyed the Spartan supremacy.

To some extent Leuctra was the apogee of hoplite warfare, which is why this account has been included in this study, but it also showed its limitations. In the years prior to Leuctra the Thebans had significantly improved the phalanx by deploying it in manoeuvrable units and introducing the wedge assault, but, as the battle showed, the course of hoplite battles was still pre-ordained by the initial disposition of the troops, significant battleground manoeuvre was not possible. Furthermore good troops were still almost impossible to break. The Spartan front had been severely disrupted, their planned out-flanking manoeuvre had failed and they were cut off from their water carriers, but still they maintained their formation and were ready to fight again the next day. However the coming years were to see major changes.

Light Infantry
By the period of the Peloponnesian War the Roman army was following its own development path which was different to that of the Greek armies and changes to the hoplite phalanx were of little interest to the Romans. However the last major change listed was relevant to them in that it involved the development of a new type of soldier that would change infantry warfare. Unfortunately ancient writers do not cover this type well and even its title falls foul of semantics, being anglicised as 'peltasts', and

translated as 'targeteers'. Both expressions are based on the small shields and, as 'peltasts' has been used for missile troops, 'targeteers' will be used in this study. The creation of this type of soldier was usually credited to Iphicrates, the famous Athenian leader of mercenary troops. They were light infantry armed and trained to fight against hoplites. As Cornelius Nepos put it: '*he changed the Foot Arms: When, before he was General, they made use of very great Shields, short Spears, and little Swords; he, on the contrary, made the* Pelta *instead of the* Parma, *from which the Foot were afterwards called* Peltastae, *that they might be nimbler for Motion and Engaging. He doubled the Length of the Spear, and made the Swords longer. The same Man changed the Kind of their Coats of mail and gave them Linen ones instead of Iron and Brazen ones; by which Act he rendered the Soldiers more light; for the Weight of their Coats being lessened, he provided what would equally secure the Body, and was light*'. These words are largely repeated by Diodorus Siculus.[25] It is generally agreed that Iphicrates actually increased the length of the spears by only a half, this made it twelve feet long which, according to Aelian, is the minimum length for a *sarissa*.

Modern historians no longer take the view that all these changes were carried out by one man, but rather that they were the result of tactical evolution. They were, though, of great importance.

The question of when the longer spear was adopted is the subject of academic argument. Nepos and Diodorus indicate that it was in the period 377-373 BC while Iphicrates was employed by the Persians to take part in the invasion of Egypt. However, as will be shown in Appendix One, these dates are a little late and it is known that the pike was of much greater antiquity, particularly in Thrace and other areas where light infantry were recruited. The important question to be asked is one of when the pike was first deployed on the battlefield in a planned and controlled way. This would seem to be, in the Greek context, at Lechaeum, in 390 BC.

The Battle of Lechaeum

The main aspects of the battle are well known, and show similarities with Spaectaria. During the Corinthian War between Sparta and an alliance including Corinth, the Spartans placed a garrison at Lechaeum, the port of Corinth. No doubt the Corinthians did not like this, but there was little they could do about it. The road from Lechaeum to the Peloponnese ran just outside the northern wall of Corinth. On the day of the battle a Spartan unit of around 600 hoplites and probably 60 cavalry marched westwards along this road, escorting some allies.

They were watched from the city wall by the Athenian Callias, who was commanding a unit of hoplites roughly equivalent to the Spartan unit, and Iphicrates, who was commanding from 1,200 to 4,000 mercenary peltasts (missile troops). They knew that the Spartans would soon return and decided to attack them

Their plan was simple, as such plans had to be. Callias took his hoplites and formed them up to the west of Corinth on some broken ground three to four hundred yards south of the road. Iphicrates with his peltasts went in front of them, the idea was that, as at Spaectaria, the peltasts would attack the Spartan hoplites, and if necessary fall back behind the Athenian phalanx. The major problem would be the Spartan cavalry.

In the early afternoon the Spartan hoplites returned, accompanied by a crowd of helots but not the cavalry which had been left to escort the allies a little further. The battle started in the predictable way, the peltasts ran close to the Spartans, threw their javelins and slung their shot. The front rank of the Spartans charged, the peltasts ran back and harassed the individual Spartans several of whom were killed. The Spartans may have repeated this charge but if so with similar unfortunate results. This action was on and around the road, about 3,000 yards south of the coast.

The Spartans were obviously getting nowhere. Their helots were either fully employed carrying casualties back to Lechaeum or had been driven away by Iphicrates' men so the hoplites were probably feeling thirsty. However the return of the cavalry gave them fresh hope and the charge was repeated. Normally cavalry would trump peltasts and easily drive them from the field. This case was different and the horsemen just stayed with the hoplites and their effect was negligible. The charge failed again. The implication is that the Spartan commander was killed and they retreated slowly northwards to a small rise close to the coast.

The surviving Spartans took up a defensive position on the rise, and for a short time held out, tired and thirsty, but three things broke them. One was that the commander at Lechaeum sent some boats along the coast to evacuate the hoplites, this naturally tempted some of them to desert. Secondly the Athenian hoplites moved forward seemingly to attack, while the Spartans were less than ready to receive them. Finally the peltasts surrounded the Spartans, raining missiles on them from every angle.

The result was that they broke, some running for the boats, some to Lechaeum along the coast.

All this is well known but there is a question never considered. Why was Iphicrates confident that his light infantry could resist the Spartan cavalry. He must have been confident otherwise he would not have risked a battle because if he assumed, as all precedent indicated, that the cavalry would drive his men off, then the best he could hope for was to lightly harass the Spartans before losing some of his men, then having a stand-off hiding behind the Athenian hoplites, though they might have been able to provide a little fire support over the hoplites' heads. The only answer can be that a small percentage of his men were armed with pikes and able to defend against cavalry. Pikemen might also have been of some use against hoplites but only very limited, probably by jabbing at wounded ones, as the pike made them less mobile than hoplites.

The implication of Iphicrates' decision to accept battle is that some of his light infantry consisted of pikemen, but if this number was small it will have been missed by Greek historians but may well not have been missed by the Romans. Lechaeum was fought in the same year that the Gauls sacked Rome, so it can be assumed that military considerations would have been foremost in Roman minds and they would have been observing any tactical developments very closely.

Comments

The sketch given here of phalanx warfare describes the situation up to the Macedonian conquest of Greece. There are some general points that stand emphasising. One is the slightly artificial nature of this style of warfare. Campaigns were short and decisions were sought before supplies ran out. The decisions were supplied by the clashes of the hoplite phalanxes, and they were accepted by the cities involved because the voters were the hoplites and they naturally wished to dominate warfare and the state. Commenting adversely on the Greeks, Herodotus makes a senior Persian say to Darius shortly before to expedition to Marathon, '*When they declare war on each other, they go off together to the smoothest and levellest bit of ground they can find, and have their battle on it.*'[26] He fully understood the concept of the mass duel and the limited nature of Greek generalship, but if the cities had not accepted the battlefield decisions they would have been opening the door to the employment of a wider range of soldier, poor (financially) light infantry, and this would have forced an extension of the franchise, to the detriment of the hoplite-providing class. The result was that there was no attempt to escalate the war by a recourse to guerrilla warfare or any kind of *guerre a outrance*. A sensible policy that following generations have often chosen to ignore. However the result of this policy was that the hoplite was limited in the forms of warfare he could undertake.

Secondly is the fact that the experience of phalanx battle was not that bad from the point of view of the hoplite. It would involve a minute or two of fencing with his spear, followed by a break of 10 to 15 minutes. This sequence might be repeated once or twice. Then, providing he was on the winning side, he would make up some money by stripping the dead, then go home to the plaudits of a grateful population. The fact that the hoplite experience was not that bad is shown by the way that Greek democracies would vote for war time after time. In these democracies it was common, as mentioned above, for only the hoplite-providing class to be entitled to vote. So if warfare was horrific the self-interest of the voters would have kept states at peace. The same principle would hold for oligarchies which, if not counting votes, would be receptive to public opinion. All of this may make hoplite fighting seem fun, but the penalties for failure were severe. The obvious one was death, but, as Socrates pointed out, '*many are captured alive, and once captured either spend the rest of their lives, perhaps, in the bitterest servitude, or, after being subjected to the most cruel duress and paying in some cases a ransom greater than the sum of their possessions, live out their lives in want and misery*'.[27]

Some authors reject the idea of the hoplite filing to the rear after doing his bit, and according to their model the purpose of the rear ranks was solely to push the leading ranks during the *othismos*.

There are four reasons why this view may be regarded as incorrect. One is that the leading ranks would know that there was no escape, the file would wear away, like a welding rod, and they were just waiting their turn to fall, groaning or screaming, or silently, to the ground. Worse, the rear ranks seeing this would not advance to share this fate. There is a limit to what can be demanded from a soldier, particularly a part-time soldier.

Secondly, according to this model, hoplites numbers five, six and seven would be extremely unlikely to do any fighting. So why have hoplites? They could easily be replaced by labourers, who could push just as well, and to use the hoplites to extend the line. Yet ancient sources make it certain that the entire phalanx consisted of hoplites so they must have been expected to fight, consequently the model must be wrong.

Thirdly, if the front ranks were to advance on the basis of being pushed, then because each file would advance at a different rate depending on the resistance it met, the formation must break up, making the individual hoplites vulnerable. The extra casualties may well halt the advance.

Fourthly, such pushing would be disastrous. These words are being written in Sheffield where, in 1989, 96 football fans were suffocated by being crushed in a crowd. A further 766 were hurt. The effect on the front ranks of a phalanx of the rear ranks pushing may well have been worse.

Remarkably there is no real reason to believe that *othismos* meant pushing by the rear ranks. W Kendrick Pritchett, in his definitive book[28], lists only nine cases of the use of the word in a military context: two by Herodotus, four by Thucydides and three by Xenophon. Not one of these cases appears to mean pushing by the rear ranks, and there is no indication that any other ancient army tried to use *othismos*.

The description of the tactics used at Leuctra has really shown the hoplite phalanx at the limit of its development before it was swept away by the Macedonian *sarissa* at Chaeronea in 338 BC. By that time Roman military evolution had long parted company with the Greek. The Battle of Allia, in 390 BC, had set in train an evolution that would produce an army different and superior to those of the Greeks, but it is interesting to note how the wedge, so important at Leuctra, became the standard Roman assault formation.

Notes
1.   Aeschylus, *The Persians* line 240, in *Prometheus Bound and Other Plays*, Penguin Classics, p129
2.   Homer, *The Iliad*, II.359. Penguin Classics, p49
3.   Xenophon, *Conversations of Socrates*, 3.1, Penguin Classics, p137
4.   Xenophon, *The Persian Expedition*, VI.5, Penguin Classics, p238
5.   Aelian, *The Tactics of Aelian*, 11, Pen and Sword, p35
6.   Asclepiodotus, *Aeneas Tacticus, Asclepiodotus, Onasander*, IV.1, Loeb, p267
7.   Asclepiodotus, *Aeneas Tacticus, Asclepiodotus, Onasander*, IV.3, Loeb, p269
8.   Thucydides, *The Peloponnesian War*, V.70, Penguin Classics, p351
9.   Xenophon, *A History of my Times*, IV.3, Penguin Classics, p154
10. Aeschylus, *Seven against Thebes* line 347, in *Prometheus Bound and Other Plays*, Penguin Classics, p98
11. In the modern British army the soldier may be called on to do milling (aggressive boxing) for one or two minutes. This writer can guarantee that the longer period is literally totally exhausting.

12. Curtius, *The History of Alexander*, III.II.6, Penguin Classics, p42

13. Dionysius of Halicarnassus, *Roman Antiquities,* VI.93.2, Loeb Vol IV, p133

14. Polyaenus, *Stratagems of War*, III.IX.27 and II.III.4, Ares Publishers, p108 and 66

15. Frontinus, *Stratagems*, IV.vii.21, Loeb, p317

16. Colonel A du Picq, *Battle Studies*, Stackpole Books, 1946, p143

17. Plato, *The Symposium*, Penguin Classics, p111

18. *Plutarch's Lives, Pelopidas*, Translated by the Revs J & W Langhorne. No date, p210

19. Diodorus Siculus, *The Library of History*, XV.52, Loeb Vol VI, p97

20. Nancy H Demand, *Thebes in the Fifth Century*, RKP, 1982, p17

21. Xenophon, *A History of my Times*, VI.4, Penguin Classics, p272

22. Aelian, *The Tactics of Aelian*, 47, Pen and Sword, p121

23. *Plutarch's Lives, Pelopidas*, Translated by the Revs J & W Langhorne. No date, p209

24. Xenophon, *A History of my Times*, VII.5, Penguin Classics, p345

25. *Cornelius Nepos's Lives of the Excellent Commanders*, XI.I, London, 1771, p109 and Diodorus Siculus, *The Library of History*, XV.44, Loeb Vol VII, p71.

26. Herodotus, *The Histories*, VII.9, Penguin Classics, p417

27. Xenophon, *Conversations of Socrates*, 3.12, Penguin Classics, p171

28. W Kendrick Pritchett, *The Greek State at War, Part IV*, University of California Press, 1985

Chapter 2: The Republican Period

From Earliest Times to Pyrrhus

Early Roman history is shrouded in myth but there are certain known facts that explain its early military development. The city was founded as a small settlement on easily defended hills close to a crossing of the Tiber. The settlement's small population would have been made up of tradesmen, merchants and similar, but the greater part of the Romans population was made up of semi-nomadic tribes that centred on the settlement, and the most important voices heard in Rome were those of the proud and arrogant tribal chieftains. Warfare, in this early period, was of the kind relevant to tribesmen, that is, raiding. However over the years the population grew and became more settled, and a political system emerged which slowly, through a process based the *domi* vs *militiae* divide which was basic to Roman thinking, broke the power of the tribes and turned the tribesmen into citizens.

It also created a military system. Initially, as the city became more important than the tribes, and fighting over security, territory and trade became more important than raiding, the early military history of Rome became similar to that of the major Greek cities, and it can be assumed that the Roman army passed through its heroic stage, as did the Greek armies, and evolved into a phalanx. However it stands repeating that this is but an assumption.

The nature of the Roman phalanx was influenced by two aspects of Roman history, these being the *Comitia Centuria*, and the Servian Reforms.

The *Comitia Centuria* was the political assembly of the

Roman people in which they were marshalled in their appropriate centuries on the basis of class, or worldly goods. It may well have been adopted to break down earlier factions based on tribe or race. The *Comitia Centuria* was fully functioning by mid-fifth century and was the basis of army recruiting which was done anew each Spring, the army being disbanded in the Autumn.

The *Comitia Centuria* demonstrated how totally militarised Roman society was, but remarkably because of the *domi* vs *militiae* divide the *Comitia Centuria* assemblies, being of a military nature, had to be held outside the city boundaries. The exact form that the centuriate organisation took is open to some debate but there can be little doubt that, in its early days, it was the basis of the organisation of the field army.

The second aspect of Roman society affecting the army was what are commonly called the 'Servian Reforms' though modern historians do not take seriously the implication of the expression. These reforms provided the basis of the centuriate organisation on the basis of property owned against weapons the owner would supply. The property assessment against the arms and armour requirement are given as a table in Note 1, here it is enough to note that Class 1 required the full hoplite array, and Classes 2 to 4 required an oblong shield, a spear and progressively less armour.

From a political point of view it was important that the wealthiest class, Class 1, provided 80 centuries. This gave this class the greatest number of votes, hence political power. However, as hoplites made up less and less of the army, and the army ceased to reflect the *Comitia Centuria,* so the system of recruiting changed to being based on tribes.

In Greek armies, as shown in the previous chapter, the files of the phalanx were made up of the friends, relatives and retainers of the file leader. This was deliberately not so with the files of the Roman legions, and this was the result of the recruiting process which may have been instituted as a means of breaking down the network of family loyalties of the Regal period, with its warlords and war bands.[2] The process was controlled by the tribunes, in it the recruits were selected in small batches of as many men as there were legions being recruited, from each tribe in turn. There were from 21 to 35 tribes. One of the recruits of each batch was sent to each of the legions, in the early years there were two legions, one for each consul. No doubt this was a lengthy process. Naturally there are many difficulties with this process but, regardless of how it is adjusted for details, the result would be the same, the files consisted of strangers, which might have reduced any Patrician-Plebeian antagonism, and their arms and armour became progressively light from front to rear. The Roman knew that if the files consisted of friends and relatives then the best regarded would be the file leaders, and their becoming casualties would have a very demoralising effect on the rest of the file. The system developed by the Romans produced much more resilient files, suitable for the hard and stubborn Roman way of warfare. The alternative to this cumbersome process was potentially private armies of rich families and their retainers. The last significant case of such an army was that of the Fabian clan which, in 479 BC, undertook to maintain the fight against the Etruscans of Veii. Unfortunately this force was wiped out.

After the legionaries had been enrolled the centurions were selected by the tribunes. In theory they would select the best soldiers as opposed to those with family connections, further reducing the powers of the rich families.

There were also significant differences between the Roman and Greek approaches to warfare. Whereas the

Greeks tended to accept the result of the hoplite battle the Romans did not, and their wars consisted not only of battles but also of skirmishes, raids, sieges and ravaging of crops. Inevitably the Roman army had to have a broad range of capabilities, with hoplites for formal set-piece battle and a range of light infantry for the more mobile operations.

Tracing the development of the early Roman army is not easy, and it is apposite to quote Hans Delbruck, the greatest of the military historians of the period: '*If we wished to begin the history of the Roman military system and experience on the same bases that we used for that of the Greeks, we would have to start with the Second Punic War. For it is not until this period that we have accounts that give us a truly reliable and clear picture of the course of a battle and the special character of the Roman methods of combat*'.[3]

Bearing in mind Delbruck's caution, it is the essential thesis of this chapter the organisation of the Roman army evolved from the hoplite phalanx initially in a way similar to that of the Greeks, but this changed dramatically. Consequently the first requirement is to look at the Greek evolution.

As has been shown in the previous chapter, during the Peloponnesian War Greek armies were little more than phalanxes of citizen hoplites, but by its end there was a trend for armies to include significant numbers of light infantry and cavalry. The light infantry component is the most significant for this study. It seems that most light infantrymen were desperately poor mercenaries recruited from the wilder areas north of Greece. They were often badly armed, undisciplined crowds and very vulnerable to cavalry. To provide some defence against cavalry a small fraction of them, probably those less skilled at fighting with missiles, were armed with long spears. In action groups of these spearmen, who became known as 'targeteers', would follow the missile troops to provide a refuge for them if they were attacked by cavalry. When the light infantry was skirmishing directly in front of the hoplite phalanx, these spearmen would form up on the phalanx's flanks. There is no record of them ever being introduced into a phalanx, the difference in armament just would not have worked.

Aelian says '*The peltasts* (ie targeteers) *wear the style of armour known as "argilos", which is similar to Macedonian armour only lighter. This type of soldier carries a small shield, and his spear is much shorter than the Macedonian pike. As such, his armour is in between that of the "heavy infantry" and that of the "light infantry" and this has often caused the peltasts to be confused with the "light infantry".*'[4] The light infantry had been defined as unarmoured missile troops.

Asclepiodotus, having described heavy infantry armed with the long Macedonian *sarissa*, and light infantry as missile troops, writes: '*The corps of targeteers stands in a sense between these two, for the targe is a kind of small, light shield, and their spears are much shorter than those of the hoplites.*'[5]

The characteristics of targeteers were a long spear, small shield and little or no armour and consequently they had a problem in that, if their own skirmishers were driven off, they were vulnerable to missile action which they could not answer therefore a second new type of soldier evolved.

This type of soldier, the '*thureophoroi*' or '*thyreaphoroi*', is, like targeteers, not well covered by ancient authors. Their name means, literally, 'door carriers', a title which they were given because of their tall thin shields, the *thyreos*, which are sometimes regarded as being of Celtic origin. The Roman versions of these were the 'oblong shields' of the Servian Reforms. These soldiers fought primarily with javelins and here will be given the rather cumbersome title of 'shield-and-javelin men'. This troop type evolved to provide close support for the targeteers against missile attack. For this role, naturally, they needed javelins, but because they had to stay with the fighting line they were not as mobile as the attacking skirmishers and so needed large shields, they also needed convincing swords because due to their large shields they could not handle the long spears of the targeteers.

It is a hint of the comparative unimportance of shield-and-javelin men to the Greeks that Polybius, who is usually accurate on military details, gives two different names for them: '*scutati*' and '*light troops armed with breastplate and shield*'.[6]

In Greek and Macedonian armies the shield-and-javelin men were not very important because the phalangites became more armoured and light infantry skirmishers became more organised and controlled, reducing the need for close support missile troops. It seems that under Alexander the Great the shield-and-javelin men evolved into the hypaspists, the finest infantry in his army. The evolution of the Greek and Macedonian infantry into the *sarissa* phalanx is of no immediate relevance to the Roman army and will be considered in Appendix One.

Unfortunately, as Hans Delbruck wrote, the period between Servius Tullius and the Punic Wars is, from the point of view of military organisation, remarkably badly recorded and surviving sources are frequently inaccurate and anachronistic, and yet this period was of critical importance for the creation of the Imperial Roman Army.

It is a reasonable assumption that, after the Servian reforms, that is after around 500 BC, the Roman heavy infantry formed for battle about a core of hoplites with a large number of targeteers on their flanks, and covered with shield-and-javelin men. In front of the heavy infantry would have been a swarm of missile troops.

Throughout the next hundred years the hoplites would have become a progressively small part of the army. The shield-and-javelin men became the front line and were referred to as '*hastati*'. The word '*hasta*', which is usually translated as 'spear' originally meant 'javelin'.[7] The hoplites might have made up the middle line, the '*principes*', which expression can be taken to mean the most important men in the army, as the hoplites originally were. The rear line, which being the third line was named the '*triarii*', was a reserve of targeteers, ready to reinforce either flank as required.

This decline of the Roman hoplite is confirmed by Dionysius of Halicarnassus who wrote: '*It was bound to happen, as might have been expected, that hoplites burdened with helmets, breastplates and shields and advancing against hilly positions by long trails that were not even used by people but were mere goat-paths through woods and crags, would keep no order and, even before the enemy came in sight, would be weakened in body by thirst and fatigue.*

Those who fight in close combat with cavalry spears grasped by the middle with both hands and who usually saved the day in battles are called principes *by the Romans.* '[8]

In this quote Dionysius seems to be defining the *principes* as targeteers. His comment about them holding their spears with both hands shows that they were not hoplites who, because of their shields, could not do this. Unfortunately it is not possible to date exactly the period that Dionysius made this comment about, but it was around the time of the Pyrrhus wars.

Livy writes that the round shields of the hoplites were abandoned when pay was introduced. This was during the siege of Veii (405 to 396 BC) and it would have resulted in a sharp reduction of the importance of hoplites with their expensive shield and other equipment as more citizens could now afford the simpler targeteers' or shield-and-javelin men's kit, and the army increased in size. Further, Veii was only ten miles away from Rome, so wars against it could be dominated by the slow-moving hoplite phalanx, but after the defeat of Veii wars became more wide ranging and over hilly and broken country where fighting with javelins was the norm. The Samnites were regarded as expert javelin men so shield-and-javelin men, with their oblong shields which gave better protection against missiles, became more important, and they were backed up by the spears of the targeteers.

Conversely Polyaenus, echoing Plutarch, gives Camillus the credit for adopting the long spear of the targeteers, probably as a reaction to Allia defeat: *'Camillus was on this occasion a fifth time created dictator; and took the command of the army. Against the broad swords of the Gauls, with which they aimed their blows at the enemy's head, he made his men wear light helmets; by which the swords were soon blunted, and broken: and the Roman target, which was of wood, not being proof against the stroke, he directed them to border it round with a thin plate of brass. He also taught then the use of the long spear; with which they engaged in close fight, and receiving the blow of the sword on their target, made their thrust with the spear: while the Gallic steel, being soft and ill-tempered, the edge of the sword was by means of the brass plate soon turned; and the weapon became unserviceable. By this advantage in the arms, the Romans obtained a cheap and easy victory; many of the Gauls were cut to pieces, and the rest saved themselves by flight'.*[9]

There are certain, very tentative, conclusions that can be

drawn about the early Roman army. The first is the great importance of cavalry, although this may be exaggerated by the meagre surviving sources. Secondly, as the legions were enrolled at the start of each year there was little, if any, time available for training, hence procedures and organisations had to be simple. Thirdly, as recruiting was done via the *Comitia Centuria*, is may be assumed that the soldiers were organised in centuries which, like the *Comitia Centuria*, were grouped in pairs as maniples. These maniples were of one type, either hoplite, targeteer, shield-and-javelin men or skirmishers. Perhaps it was initially thought that the hoplites, with their better armour, should provide the front rank, as was usually done in Greece, but evolved into a battle formation of three rows (*ordines*) of maniples, the first two being composed of shield-and-javelin men, the third of targeteers.

This system may well have taken a long time to develop, not only because of the poor level of training, but because of low priority. There seems to have been few pitched battles, whereas the lightly armoured, hence fast moving, spear-and-javelin men were often involved in raids and other irregular operations, as the Dionysius quotation suggests, so their battlefield tactics would have seemed unimportant. Despite all difficulties, in particular the disbanding of the army at the end of each campaigning season, the continuous warfare that the Romans were involved in did result in the creation of a cadre of experienced centurions. Some of these men were very impressive. Here Dionysius reports a speech by Lucius Siccius Dentatus:

'If I, plebeians, should choose to relate my exploits one by one, a day's time would not suffice me; hence I shall give a mere summary, in the fewest words I can. This is the fortieth year that I have been making campaigns for my country, and the thirtieth that I have continued to hold some military command, sometimes over a cohort and sometimes over a whole legion, beginning with the

consulship of Gaius Aquilius and Titus Siccius, to whom the senate committed the conduct of the war against the Volscians. I was then twenty-seven years of age and in rank I was still under a centurion. When a severe battle occurred and a rout, the commander of the cohort had fallen, and the standards were in the hands of the enemy, I alone, exposing myself in behalf of all, recovered the standards for the cohort, repulsing the enemy, and was clearly the one who saved the centurions from incurring everlasting disgrace – which would have rendered the rest of their lives more bitter than death – as both they themselves acknowledged, by crowning me with a golden crown, and Siccius the consul bore witness, by appointing me commander of the cohort. And in another battle that we had, in which it happened that the primipilus *of the legion was thrown to the ground and the eagle fell into the enemy's hands, I fought in the same manner in defence of the whole legion, recovering the eagle and saved the* primipilus. *In return for the assistance I then gave him he wished to resign his command of the legion in my favour and to give me the eagle; but I refused both, being unwilling to deprive the man whose life I had saved of the honours he enjoyed and of the satisfaction resulting from them. The consul was pleased with my behaviour and gave me the post of* primipilus *in the first legion, which had lost its commander in the battle.*

In a word during the forty years I have continued to serve I have fought about one hundred and twenty battles and received forty-five wounds, all in front and not one behind; twelve of these I happened to receive in one day, when Herdonius the Sabine seized the citadel and the Capitol. As to rewards for valour, I have brought out of those contests fourteen civic crowns, bestowed upon me by those I have saved in battle, three mural crowns for having been the first to mount the enemy's walls and hold them, and eight others for my exploits on the battlefield, with which I was honoured by the generals; and, in addition to these, eighty-three gold collars, one hundred and sixty gold bracelets, eighteen spears, twenty-five splendid decorations. '[10] The text at this point becomes corrupt. Dionysius is reporting a speech made around 453 BC. His mention of cohorts is an example of anachronism, the legions were not organised in cohorts till much later. Even so the speech must have seemed credible to Romans and it does illustrate the existence of a highly experienced cadre of professional soldiers which would provide the framework of a legion, to be fleshed out by the annual levies.

During this period, in 390 BC, shortly after the siege of Veii and the presumed disappearance of the Roman hoplites, occurred one of the greatest military defeats of Roman history, the battle of the Allia. Unfortunately little is known of the tactics used in the battle, or of the formations involved, and the only real account is Livy's which is of very little value. A large army was hastily recruited to meet an approaching army of Gauls. The army consisted of the four consular legions, which Dionysius wrote were '*of picked troops well trained in the wars, and also, from among the other citizens, those who led indoor or easy lives and had had less to do with wars, these being more numerous than the other sort.*'[11] This comment might show a vestige of the old contempt of the tribesman for the city-bred tradesman. The army had marched only 11 miles when it encountered the Gauls where the river Allia joins the Tiber.

The Romans were badly out-numbered, and formed up as a thin line, which was presumably the *hastati*, stretched as far as possible to try to prevent its being outflanked. A substantial reserve, probably the *principes*, was posted on some high ground behind the right flank. According to Livy[12] the Gaulish commander, seeing this, concluded that the Romans reserve was an outflanking force, decided not to make a frontal assault but to charge with most of his men round the Roman right and engage the reserve force. This he did to such an effect that the Roman front line troops totally panicked and ran away as soon as they heard the Gallic war cry to their flank and rear. The reserves held out a little longer and made a reasonable retreat to Rome.

Titus Livius (59 BC to 17 AD), known as Livy, commenced writing his History of Rome at the age of thirty, he died before completing it. One of the main sources he used was the History of Polybius who is generally regarded as the better historian. Even so the accounts Livy provides are more detailed than those of Polybius if, probably, less accurate.

If any deduction can be made from Livy's account, it must be that the *hastati*, once deployed, could not swing round to face a flank. Perhaps they found not having the *principes* deployed in a line behind them unsettling. However an attempt may be made to explain the sudden Roman collapse. The bulk of the army now consisted of shield-and-javelin men whose experience of warfare was against similarly armed men and whose preferred method of fighting was to stay out of physical contact with the enemy, but to throw javelins at him. Perhaps this tactic did not work against the Gauls who approached war with barbarian fury, rushing at their foes and seizing the large and difficult to control Roman shields, prising them away from their owners, exposing them to Gaulish spears. Also it is possible that the Roman shields, being large had to be thin to make them light enough to use, but being thin they were easily penetrated or smashed by the Gauls' spears and clubs. It is often written that, as a result of this battle, major changes were made in the legion's organisation. Although this is very likely there is no direct evidence to support this.

According to Livy, at around 340 BC when the Samnite wars commenced, the Roman legion formed up with a front line of fifteen maniples of *hastati* and a second line of the same number of maniples of *principes*. These two lines were termed the *antepilani* which would seem to indicate that the *hastati* and *principes* were similar, both composed of shield-and-javelin men. The term *pilani* is now taken to mean troops formed up in columns as opposed to lines, but it is at least possible that, as the Latin for hair is *pilus*, the *pilani*, standing with their long spears vertical, reminded the soldiers of their crew cuts, or hairs on a pig. The *pilani* consisted of *'fifteen companies, each one of which was divided into three sections, the first section of each being named the pilus. A company consisted of three sections or vexilla, and a single vexillum comprised sixty soldiers, two centurions and one vexillarius or standard-bearer, so that altogether there were 186 men. The first standard led the triarii, veteran soldiers of proven courage, the second the rorarii, younger and less experienced men, the third the accensi, who were the least reliable group and so relegated to the rearmost line.'*[13] Though what was expected of these last two contingents is not very clear.

The maniples of the *antepilani* formed up with gaps between them. The first line would open the battle, and if it was not successful the *hastati* maniples withdrew through the gaps between the *principes* maniples which would then continue the fight. It can be assumed that the maniples formed up with one century behind the other, and the rear century deployed to fill the gap between the front century and the next maniple. Also it can be assumed that on the battlefield the maniples of the *principes* formed up covering the gaps between the maniples of the *hastati.*

During the battle, forming up behind the *antepilani*, the *'triarii knelt under their standards, with their left legs stretched forward and shields resting against their shoulders, holding their spears fixed in the ground and pointing forwards so that the line seemed to bristle with a protective palisade.'*[14] If the *antepilani* were defeated they fell back between the columns of the *triarii* who then deployed in line. Livy wrote that they then fell upon the enemy. This they may have done but it is easier to believe that they maintained a dogged defence.

It can be seen from the above that, after the great increase in the army's size following the introduction of pay, the bulk of the troops, the *hastati* and *principes*, were shield-and-javelin men and the third rank, which is what *'triarii'* means, were targeteers. The reason why they usually knelt down was to get better protection from their small shields, and, for those that had them, greaves. Despite their battlefield role, the most important function of the *triarii* was defending the army's camp to provide a refuge for the army in the case of a defeat.

The tactics of the shield-and-javelin men depended, predictably, mostly on missile action, as was shown by Livy's description of a battle of 310BC. *'The Etruscans...... charged their enemy sword in hand. By contrast the Romans started to hurl first their javelins, then the rocks, which the place itself provided in plenty, with the result that those of the Etruscans who were not wounded were thrown into disorder when these came raining down on their shields and helmets. It was difficult for them to move up to fight at closer quarters, and they lacked missiles for a battle at long range; so they stood exposed to the attack without any adequate protection until some of them began to move back and the line wavered unsteadily. Then the Roman first and second lines raised another cheer, and charged them with drawn swords. The Etruscans could not withstand this assault.'*[15]

Each Roman, as he stood the front man in his file, would have thrown his javelins then fallen back to the rear of his file. If he came into action a second, or third, time he would have been reliant on throwing stones, presumably with a small sling which he could use overarm without breaking up the formation. This would have been at alarmingly close range. As the enemy weakened he might charge with cold steel, but it is at least possible that the *triarii* would be called forward for the climactic charge.

This has been the description of the Roman army through the period of the Samnite Wars (343 to 290 BC) and up to the wars against Pyrrhus (280 to 275 BC). How the army functioned on the battlefield will now be briefly considered.

The Battle of Sentinum

By the time of the Third Samnite War Rome was by far the strongest single state in Italy, and the war took the general form of the rising of a combination of conquered states. The main combatants opposing Rome were Samnium and Etruria. The war started in 298 BC, in its third year the Etruscans were weakening in resolve so the Samnites sent an army north to reinforce them and keep them in the war. The arrival of the Samnites reignited the war and all participants strained every nerve to increase the size of their armies. However it was the next year that saw the great battle.

Rome had some allies in the Etruria and Umbria regions, one being the city of Camerinum. Early in the year, apparently in response to a Samnite threat to this city a legion with the usual allied contingent was sent ahead across the Appenines to reinforce it. This legion was attacked and severely battered by the Samnite army before the main Roman army caught up. Once it did so the Samnites with their allies fell back 50 miles to Sentinum where they set up their camps and awaited the Romans.

The Samnites had three groups of allies: Gauls, Etruscans

and Umbrians. The last two were similar in outlook and seem to have had little enthusiasm for the fight. The Gauls were present in a predatory capacity and probably not to be relied upon. The Samnite general, Gellius Egnatius, organised the Samnites and Gauls into one camp and the Etruscans and Umbrians into another. His general plan was for his Samnites and Gauls to fight to Romans frontally, and the Etruscans and Umbrians to skirt round the Romans and capture their camp.

The Roman army consisted of four legions, two for each of the two consuls, Fabius Rullianus and Decius Mus, so three legions were now approaching to reinforce the one that had already seen action. The Etruscans and Umbrians seem to have abandoned the Samnites and Gauls as a Roman army was moving against Etruria. Certainly they are not mentioned again in Livy's account of the battle. This was one result of the great Roman superiority of numbers.

The consuls' armies seem to have shared one camp, four or five miles away from the Samnites. Having entrenched, the Romans harassed the Samnites with cavalry and light infantry for two days. On the third the Samnites came out onto the plain in front of their camp to offer battle. The site of the battle is generally accepted as a plain to the north of the town. A small river, the modern name of which is the Sanguerone, runs through this plain.

The Samnites were placed on the left, the Gauls on the right. The cavalry was on the flanks, the Gallic cavalry contingent being particularly large. It is likely that the Samnites and Gauls were separated by the river.

The Romans advanced with Rullianus's first and third legions on the right opposite the Samnites; Decius with the fifth and sixth legions was on the left, facing the Gauls. There was a detachment of 1,000 allied cavalry which seem to have been on the right, this would have left a weak Roman cavalry detachment on the left facing the Gallic horsemen. Four legions should approximate to 16,800 infantrymen and 1,200 horsemen. In general the allies could be expected to provide an equivalent number of infantrymen, but the part they played in the battle has been lost. The Roman army at Sentinum can be estimated at between 35,000 and 40,000 strong. As the battle was hard-fought, the Samnite and confederation troops must have been roughly in the same strength but the Gauls had some chariots that seem to have come as a surprise to the Romans.

As the troops were being marshalled into battle array, a deer and wolf ran between the armies. The Romans, at least, found this to be a good omen. The Gauls, ever practical, killed the deer.

The basic tactic that Rullianus wanted to follow was to stand on the defensive through the early part of the battle, allowing the enemy to tire, then to counter-attack. He took the view that '*both Samnites and Gauls were fierce fighters at the start of an attack but only needed to be withstood, for if the struggle dragged on the spirits of the Samnites would gradually flag, while the physique of the Gauls was quite incapable of standing up to heat and strenuous effort and would soon weaken, so that though they were more than men in the early stages of a battle, they ended up by being less than women.*'[16] Unfortunately Rullianus failed to convince Decius of the wisdom of this plan, and as the two armies approached each other he, Decius, sent his infantry forward, then led his cavalry in a charge.

Livy wrote that the cavalry charged twice. This indicates a high degree of discipline and control in that the cavalry must have rallied after the first charge and quickly reformed its ranks for the second charge. Unfortunately the second charge led to a disaster. The Romans drove the Gallic cavalry back but the Gauls had stationed their chariot troops behind the cavalry and these scattered the Romans. Presumably the chariots could form up and advance next to each other without gaps, so the Roman horses were forced to veer off, crashing into each other and making it impossible for the riders to resist the Gauls' weapons. The Gallic cavalry recovered and the Romans were chased back, some horsemen crashing into the leading *hastati* centuries, disordering them. The advancing Gallic infantry saw this and drove the Roman infantry back. Decius failed to halt the cavalry and the infantry fight seems to have reached a natural pause, probably occasioned by the *triarii* holding firm. During this pause Decius decided to sacrifice himself, no doubt to compensate for his rashness.

He had obviously planned ahead for such an act, one of his forebears had done the same, and he kept a senior priest on hand to perform the pre-sacrifice rituals. These rituals were quite lengthy and included a change of clothes, so the fighting must have ground almost to a halt. Then Decius rode into the Gallic masses and was killed. This act of self-sacrifice put new heart into the Romans who now counter-attacked. The Gauls fell back a little then formed a shield wall and held out.

On the right the Roman plan was working well. The Samnites are usually believed to have fought primarily with javelins. By deploying the rear centuries of the maniples the Romans could have presented a shield wall of their own to the Samnites who would have made no impression on it. After the discouragement of the Samnites there may well have been a pause as there was on the left. Then Rullianus sent his cavalry forward, probing towards the Samnites' open flank. Nothing is known of the actions of the Samnite cavalry. Seeing that the Samnites were easily pushed back Rullianus brought up his reserves and put in a full strength attack.

It is a pity that Livy does not say who these reserves were. Most likely they were his *principes* and *triarii*, but they could have been allies.

The attack was a success and the Samnites broke to be chased and massacred by the cavalry, however the Gauls were still holding out. Two officers took some of the *triarii* from Rullianus' legions across to the left to reinforce the shaken Roman troops, and the Romans began to batter the Gallic *testudo* with javelins and spears. Initially this had little effect, but slowly the Gauls weakened. Also Rullianus was now aware of the situation on the left. He recalled 500 allied horse and sent them round to the rear of the Gauls, a move that would have involved crossing the river. He sent the *principes* of the third legion to follow them. The combined assault was too much for the Gauls who were slaughtered.

Rullianus then took charge of the pursuit of the Samnites. They had formed a line of battle in front of their entrenched camp, but could not withstand the Roman assault. The Samnite commander, Gellius Egnatius, was killed here and his men scattered. Around 8,000 sought refuge in the camp and surrendered there.

The battle cost Rullianus' troops 1,700 fatalities, but Decius' men lost 7,000. This is a suspiciously high total for a victorious army. The Samnites and Gauls lost 25,000. Naturally the accuracy of Livy's figures may be argued, but they do serve to illustrate how hard the fighting was. It is at least possible that Rullianus' plan to exhaust the Samnites and Gauls by standing on the defensive shows that the Romans already had a working system of battlefield reliefs to rotate soldiers into, and out of, the fighting line (as will be described in the next chapter) beyond anything their enemies, in this battle and probably all of Italy, could manage.

Unfortunately Livy's account of the battle gives little information as to how the individual soldiers fought, however his description is consistent with the bulk of the Roman army being shield-and-javelin men. It also showed the importance of the Roman cavalry.

The Punic Wars

The army that fought Pyrrhus was basically that of bands of shield-and-javelin men backed up by some targeteers, but this started to change as Rome's horizons widened and she had access to better quality weapons, in particular, swords. Shield-and-javelin men originally had the task of defending against the enemy's skirmishers, but this was to change as they were to become more like swordsmen.

The sword became standardised as the model known as the 'Spanish Sword' (*Gladius Hispaniensis*). The oldest so far identified is dated approximately 175 BC, it is 30 inches long including the tang, the blade is straight with two cutting edges and a point. As this sword became more common so it became as important as the javelin to the Roman soldier, but despite the best efforts of archaeology it is difficult to see how it differed significantly from the previous model. It may be that the difference was in the quality of the iron used in its manufacture. As a result of the Punic Wars there was a dramatic increase in the demand for weapons and to meet this demand the Romans, who were increasing their hold on Spain, may have started importing quality iron from there. It would have been most economic to have imported blooms and to have beaten them into swords themselves, the state taking over large-scale weapons manufacture. The Romans, then, would have used the word 'Spanish' as a comment on the quality of the blades.

The sword was, when not in use, carried in a scabbard leaving the right hand free so the soldier could still manage his other weapon, the javelin. Initially it was the light javelin carried by the *velites*, and each shield-and-javelin man would have carried at least two or three, but it soon changed into the much heavier, armour piercing, version called the *pilum*. This was the same word as the Latin for 'pestle' and may give the impression of the concept of it pounding through enemy armour, an impression reinforced by Plutarch's description of the *pilum* as 'ponderous'. Describing the Roman army of the Second Punic War, Polybius says that the legionaries carried two javelins, an aspect of the evolution away from being shield-and-javelin men. There was one light javelin and a heavy one, no doubt the engage the enemy at different ranges. It is difficult to see how this system could have worked. Perhaps the front rank men could have used their light javelins, but as second, and subsequent, rank men came into action and were in contact with the enemy they would have found the light javelins pointless. It may be thought that they could have thrown their javelins over the heads of the ranks in front, but this would have been difficult with the soldiers being stationary in their ranks and scarcely able to see their targets. It is just possible that the javelins were passed forward for the front rank men to throw before the hand-to-hand clash, but this seems very unlikely.

Javelins, in one guise or another, have existed from the start of time, but the development of the *pilum*, a specialised javelin, indicated a change in the fighting method of the legionary. The *pilum* is first mentioned in literary sources by Polybius in his account of the battle of Panormus in 250 BC. He says that javelins and *pila* were thrown, indicating that there was a fundamental difference between them, however as archaeology shows there were both heavy and light versions of *pila* so it is not obvious what the fundamental difference could have been. The earliest *pila* found have been dated at 225 to 200 BC. The essence of the *pilum* was that, due to its weight, it was a short-range weapon, and the legionaries would soon have ceased to use light javelins.

It seems that adopting the *pilum* reduced the missile capacity of the *antepilani*, who will now no longer be described as shield-and-javelin men. To compensate for this, shortly after the Battle of Cannae twenty *velites* were attached to each *antepilani* century. This seems to have worked quite well.[17] The evolution of the legionary saw the accent switch to hand-to-hand fighting, the result was that he became less mobile but more successful at the hard toe-to-toe fighting that would become his hallmark.

There can be little doubt that, considering the huge numbers of soldiers mobilised during the Punic Wars, the weaponry was produced in state-controlled factories. This should indicate that the weapon design was carefully thought out and there was a degree of uniformity which would simplify training and improve battlefield performance.

These changes in armament and the general process of rationalisation resulted in what is often termed 'the Polybian Legion'. Polybius had had plenty of military experience in Greece and had spoken to veterans of the wars he described, so it is not surprising that the Polybian organisation is regarded as almost a gold standard, however it must be recognised that it was really only a point on a perpetually changing matrix.

According to Polybius the legion formed up in three lines of heavy infantry, the *Triplex Acies*, these being the well-known *hastati*, *principes* and *triarii*. The Latin expression *Aes Triplex* (triple brass) meaning an impenetrable defence no doubt originated on the battlefield with these three lines of infantry. They were preceded by the skirmishers, the *velites*. The *velites* were the youngest, most agile and poorest of the soldiers. They carried a sword and a round shield, three feet in diameter, and wore a helmet. They carried a number of javelins described as having a thin shaft three feet long and a head about nine inches long but beaten so thin that it would bend on contact with its target so as to be of little use to throw back. The *velites* were not included in the basic establishment of the legion, and their organisation is obscure. Attempts were made to change this, as the next section will show.

The next age group, the *hastati*, were armed and armoured for hand-to-hand fighting. They carried the *scutum* and the Spanish sword. They carried the two javelins, and, if they could afford it, some armour. The *hastati* made up ten maniples and formed the front rank of the legion.

The *principes* were men in what Polybius called the '*prime of life*'. Apart from age they were the same as the *hastati*, however as they were older perhaps their arms and armour were better.

The *triarii* were armed with '*long thrusting spears*' being the final evolution of targeteers, and formed the last line of defence. There were 600 *triarii*, 1,200 of both the *hastati* and *principes*, and 1,000 *velites*. If the legion were larger than 4,000 the extra manpower would be spread among all classes of soldier except for the *triarii* who, presumably, being older and steadier men should not have their quality diluted. Or perhaps it was difficult to extemporize their long spears.

As previously, on the battlefield the maniples formed up in what is usually called a *quincunx* formation. The expression comes from the number five on a dice. Each maniple would cover the gap between the maniples in the line in front of it. This formation was adopted to allow the *hastati* and *principes* to relieve each other in the fighting line. That it was the normal formation was stated by Polybius when, in his description of the battle of Zama, he commented how unusual Scipio's formation was when he stationed the maniples behind each other.[18]

Once the legion had been fully manned the three classes, *hastati*, *principes* and *triarii*, elected twenty centurions, so each class divided up into ten maniples each of two centuries and each having two centurions, the *prior* and *posterior* centurions. The prior centurions attended the military council making them more than the equivalent of modern NCOs. When the maniple was in column, one century behind the other, the *prior* centurion was in command. The centurions selected subordinate officers called *optiones* and standard bearers, *signiferi*. There is some doubt as to if the maniple had one *signifer* or two, one for each century. The only source of information about the standards themselves is in Ovid's *Fasti*. He says: *'Their standards were of hay, but there was as deep a reverence as the eagles now possess.*

'They carried these suspended in bundles (manipulos) *on a long pole and it is for this reason that the soldier is called a* manipularis.'

From this it is reasonable to posit that the standards were unique corn dollies as they only had to last a few months, the maniples and legions being reconstituted each year. Similarly with the number of *signiferi*, one year operating with one per maniple could have been tried; other years two.

The Polybian legion can be regarded as functioning by the end of the First Punic War, and this is confirmed by Polybius's account of the Battle of Telamon, this battle took place in 225 BC, a few years after the end of the First Punic War when fighting broke out with the Gaul in Northern Italy.

'But when the javelineers advanced, as is their usage, from the ranks of the Roman legions and began to hurl their javelins in well-aimed volleys, the Celts in the rear ranks indeed were well protected by their trousers and cloaks, but it fell out far otherwise than they had expected with the naked men in front, and they found themselves in a very difficult and helpless predicament. For the Gaulish shield does not cover the whole body; so that their nakedness was a disadvantage, and the bigger they were the better chance had the missiles of going home. At length, unable to drive off the javelineers owing to the distance and the hail of javelins, and reduced to the utmost distress and perplexity, some of them, in their impotent rage, rushed wildly on the enemy and sacrificed their lives, while others, retreating step by step on the ranks of their comrades, threw them into disorder by their display of faint-heartedness. Thus was the spirit of the Gaesatae broken down by the javelineers; but the main body of the Insubres, Boii, and Taurisci, once the javelineers had withdrawn into the ranks and the Roman maniples attacked them, met the enemy and kept up a stubborn hand-to-hand combat. For, though being almost cut to pieces, they held their ground, equal to their foes in courage, and inferior only, as a force and individually, in their arms. The Roman shields, it should be added, were far more serviceable for defence and their swords for attack, the Gaulish sword being only good for a cut and not for a thrust. But finally, attacked from higher ground and on their flank by the Roman cavalry, which rode down the hill and charged them vigorously, the Celtic infantry were cut to pieces where they stood, their cavalry taking to flight.'[19]

During the Punic Wars the Soldiers' Oath *(ius iurandum)* became official, being administered by the tribunes. In it the soldiers swore *'Never to leave the field in order to save their own skins, nor to abandon their place in the line for any purpose other than to recover or fetch a weapon, to strike an enemy or to save a friend.'* [20] Before this there had been two oaths, the oath of allegiance *(sacramentum)* which was compulsory and administered by the tribunes when the soldiers were first enlisted, and a voluntary oath, which was the basis of the *ius iurandum*, sworn informally between friends. Later oaths tended to become more complex and centred on loyalty initially to the general, then later to the Emperor, and *'to seek a weapon, smite an enemy, or save a citizen'* was often repeated as a formula.

Seeing all these things, the inevitable question arises that if the Roman army was so competent, why did it suffer so badly during the Second Punic War. The answer is, at least partly, because of the genius of Hannibal. To consider this a brief account of the battle of Cannae will be given.

The Battle of Cannae

Throughout its long history Rome suffered three major battlefield defeats: Allia, Cannae and Adrianople. Of these three, Cannae was the worst and also the most difficult to understand. A large Roman army, now armed with the Spanish sword and organised according to the efficient Polybian model, was massacred by a weaker, multi-racial, polyglot army held together only by the hope of plunder and the leadership of Hannibal.

By Summer 216 BC Hannibal and his army had been plundering Italy for two years. Following the disastrous battles of Ticinus, Trebia and Trasimene the Romans, recognising the quality of the Carthaginian army, had declined battle but restricted themselves to harassing the Carthaginians, making foraging difficult for them and keeping them on the move. Such a policy, sensible in military terms, was unpopular politically and it was decided to recruit a huge army and settle the matter.

In the morning of 2nd August the Roman army confronted the Carthaginian army on the right, southern, side of the River Aufidius, which then flowed roughly North-east, though its course has changed significantly since. The Roman army consisted, according to Polybius, of a total of 80,000 infantry and 6,000 cavalry. Half of the infantry and around a third of the cavalry were Romans, the rest were allies.

If there were 40,000 Roman infantry this number will have been provided by eight legions of 5,000 men per legion. This number includes the *velites*. Around 10,000 men were posted in the two camps. Each of the Roman legions had 600 *triarii*, and if the allies had the same number making 9,600 *triarii* then it is at least possible that these men, plus sick, wounded, cooks and bottle-washers would have provided the guards for the two Roman camps. Keeping the *triarii* off the battlefield could have been a major contributing factor to the disaster.

The large size of the Roman army was the result of doubling the number of legions enlisted. It may well be that this had resulted in a sudden reduction in the quality of the legions as the number of veteran centurions in each legion was halved.

The Roman army formed up fairly conventionally with the Roman cavalry on the right wing, between the infantry and the river, and the allied cavalry on the left. It is not known how the Roman and allied legions were placed though it may be expected that the Romans were on the right. There seems to have been little difference between Roman and Allied troops. It is known that the infantry was formed up in very deep columns of maniples. There were two possible reasons why this was done. One was that it was a reasonable defence against elephants and it could have been that Hannibal was rumoured to have some. Another reason might be that such a deep formation was an imitation of the 50 man deep phalanx the Thebans were believed to have used successfully at Leuctra, but unfortunately the Romans did not have the level of training to make this formation work and probably did not understand the special circumstances of that battle. Staking everything on the offensive would have provided the reason why the *triarii* were not thought necessary on the battlefield and were used for camp security.

A significant disadvantage of such a deep formation was that there would have been groups of *velites* sandwiched, somehow, among the maniples. The alternative to this would have been to deploy all the army's *velites* as a single unit, but such an organisation is not mentioned. The *velites*, of course, could not function properly in a close formation, and would tend to hinder those who could. Livy wrote that the *velites* were attached to the centuries only after Cannae, so it may be that this deployment at Cannae was experimental and drills for their use had not been properly worked out.

Hannibal had 40,000 infantry and 10,000 cavalry. The infantry broke down into, very roughly, 10,000 good quality African troops, and 30,000 Spanish and Gaulish troops, including skirmishers. The African troops were equipped with Roman arms and armour salvaged from the defeats they had inflicted on the Romans, and they were organised almost as two legions, which may have caused some Roman soldiers some consternation on the battlefield.

Hannibal, also in a conventional manner, posted his cavalry on his wings, opposite the Roman and allied cavalry, and he put one legion of Africans on each flank of his infantry. He may have hidden them behind the horsemen. Xenophon mentions a standard stratagem concerning infantry: *'It is possible to conceal them effectively, not only between the lines, but in rear also of the troopers – the mounted soldier towering high above his followers on foot'.*[21] The actions and progress of the cavalry battle are not of direct relevance to this study which restricts itself to the infantry fight, suffice it to say that the Roman cavalry was defeated and the survivors driven off. The poorer quality Carthaginian troops, in particular the Gauls, were posted in the centre of their line and as the fighting commenced they were pushed forward, probably goaded by the Roman skirmishers. Their line was fairly thin and when the Roman infantry advanced the centre of the Carthaginian line was driven back.

The Roman infantry surged forward, it was a hot day and the atmosphere soon became thick with dust, that together with the unfamiliar formation resulted in a fatal tactical sluggishness. The African troops on the Carthaginian flanks stood firm, this resulted in the Roman troops becoming funnelled into too small a space to deploy, soon the Africans wheeled round to attack the Roman flanks, driving them inwards, compounding their problem. Then the Carthaginian cavalry, having defeated the Roman cavalry and sent some Numidian light horse to pursue them, started attacking the rear of the Roman infantry. Had the *triarii* been posted at the rear of the legions they would, with their spears, easily held the cavalry off. Also, there may have been a case of what the Romans would call *fides Punica*, when 500 of Hannibal's soldiers surrendered. They threw down their shields, spears and swords and were escorted to the rear, then drew their hidden daggers and assailed the Roman rear ranks. It must be judged that it is unlikely that this actually happened and it is more likely that the story was made up as a part justification for the Roman defeat.[22]

The Roman army was then surrounded. As it could no longer advance the Spanish and Gaulish infantry continued to attack its front. The Africans attacked the flanks and edged towards the Roman rear where the Carthaginian cavalry was attacking. The result was a near total massacre.

The ancient view is well expressed by Plutarch:

'In this battle Hannibal gave great proofs of generalship. In the first place, he took advantage of the ground, to post his men with their backs to the wind, which was then very violent and scorching, and drove from the dry plains, over the heads of the Carthaginians, clouds of sand and dust into the eyes and nostrils of the Romans, so that they were obliged to turn away their faces and break their ranks. In the next place, his troops were drawn up in superior art. He placed the flower of them in the wings, and those upon whom he had less dependence in the main corps, which was considerably more advanced than the wings. Then he commanded those in the wings, that when the enemy had charged and vigorously pushed that advanced body, which he knew would give way, and open a passage for them to the very centre, and when the Romans by this means should be far enough engaged within the two wings, they should both on the right and left take them in the flank, and endeavour to surround them. This was the principle cause of the great carnage that followed. For the enemy pressing upon Hannibal's front which gave ground, the form of his army was changed into a half-moon; and the officers of the select troops caused the two points of the wings to join behind the Romans. Thus they were exposed to the attacks of the Carthaginians on all sides; an incredible slaughter followed; nor did any escape but the few that retreated before the main body was enclosed.' [23]

Plutarch's account of the battle is typical in that he regards the surrounding of the Roman infantry as the decisive factor, and there can be no doubt that it was very important and a result of the genius of Hannibal. However neither Plutarch, nor anyone else, considers how this resulted in the destruction of the Roman troops. The Spanish and Gauls in front of the legions seem to have caused minimal problems, and the cavalry attacking the rear should have been easily held off so long as the Roman ranks remained unbroken, the real destruction was carried out by the African troops making up the equivalent of two legions. Put simply the question becomes '*how did two legions destroy sixteen?*' assuming eight Roman legions and the same number of allied ones.

The answer to this question lies in the formation the troops were fighting in. A maniple consisted of two centuries and formed up one behind another for manoeuvre. For fighting, the rear, *posterior,* century would deploy to the left of the leading, *prior*, century. The strength of the maniples at Cannae is not known for certain, it was usually 120 during this period, but here the legions were greatly overstrength so, as a reasonable approximation, the figures given for the imperial army in Chapter Three will be used.

Normally maniples formed up as columns ten legionaries wide and sixteen deep. This was a convenient unit to manoeuvre, most importantly it could turn to either side quite easily. However it is known that the commanding general decided to alter this, according to Polybius '*the maniples were grouped more closely than in their normal formation, so that the depth of each was several times greater than its width.*'[24] Most likely, because it would have been the easiest order to give, the frontage of the maniples was halved to five and the depth increased to 32, or 40 if the *velites* are included, and the maniples were closed up to each other thus making it impossible to deploy the *posterior* centuries. Also, because each maniple now took up twice its usual depth, there would have been that much less space between the *hastati* and the *principes*.

As the Romans advanced, not only were the maniples forced closer together but, due to the 'concertina effect' that afflicts all marching columns, the maniples of the *principes* would have become contiguous with those of the *hastati*. Then they were attacked from the left and right flanks by the Africans who were correctly organised in files.

The Romans could, of course, turn individually to face the Africans, but they could not turn as files, also it would have been very difficult to create files as the centurions were no longer posted where they would be expected to be, the dust was hampering visibility, the Africans looked just like Romans, and most Romans were surrounded if not by strangers, at least by soldiers they were not used to working with. Files work best as fighting formations if all the soldiers comprising it are known to each other. Consequently, as the fighting developed, the Africans could remain reasonably fresh, fighting for a minute or so then filing to the rear. Conversely the fighting Romans were stuck in the front rank, there was not space for the wearied or wounded soldier to pull back and the man behind him was not willing to take his place. After two or three minutes of hand-to-hand fighting the Roman would have been unable to defend himself. These problems were made worse by the presence of the *velites* within the ranks, men not trained or equipped for hand-to-hand fighting. As Livy put it, it was '*butchery rather than battle.*'[25]

The problem of exhaustion was worsened for the Romans because, as they were surrounded, no water could be brought up for them, whereas the Carthaginians had access to the river and their muleteers and servants could supply their fighting men with plenty.

It is possible that, due to the huge losses of swords and shields at Lake Trasimene and the other battles, some Romans were armed as targeteers with spears and light shields. Because a spearman requires more space than a swordsman to function efficiently he would have been in a worse plight, attacked by Africans with the modern Roman arms he lacked.

Because of the size of the Roman infantry force, the thick dust and the unfamiliar formations the infantry commander did not realise how desperate the situation was until too late. The Romans held out for a while '*but as their outer ranks were continually cut down and the survivors were forced to pull back and huddle together, they were finally all killed where they stood'.*[26] Finally the Romans would have grouped round their standards in the formation knows as the 'orb'. This formation was regarded as an act of desperation, as Livy put it, writing about an earlier war: '*forming a circle for their final hopeless stand*'.[27]

The Battle of Cannae illustrated the importance of fighting in file, and the disastrous consequences of this order being disrupted.

The Marian Reforms

The army the fought Hannibal was a short service militia, embodied for each year as required. It consisted usually of four legions but might be much greater. The legions were internally divided on the bases of age group and class, so the soldiers' loyalty would be primarily directed to his century or maniple, and secondly to Rome. Compared to these two, the legion was a short term and rather artificial organisation which would not have invoked any strong feelings. However the conflict of interests between the different classes of maniples would have ensured that the legion as a whole would have remained faithful to the republic. This system of recruiting and legionary organisation, though sufficient for wars in Italy, was not appropriate for long lasting wars overseas.

As soon as this became apparent a number of changes to

the military system were applied. This happened over a remarkably short time and these changes were to alter the basic nature of the legion. The changes were started during the war against Jugurtha in Africa and were concluded during the war against the Germans at the Battle of Vercellae a period running from 107 to 101 BC.

Taken as a whole these changes are often referred to as the Marian reforms, although Gaius Marius was not responsible for all of them. He was certainly a very good general, as the following section of this chapter will show, so doubtlessly many changes were attributed to him that originated with others or were the results of natural evolution, but however the changes occurred the result was the Roman legion that is the subject of the second part of this study.

Modern authors usually list five main aspects of the Marian reforms:
  Extending recruiting for the legions to the poor.
  The replacement of the manipular organisation of the legion by cohorts.
  The institution of the eagle as a legionary standard.
  The reorganisation of military transportation.
  Changes to the *pilum*.

After the conclusion of the Punic wars Rome became an imperial power and was involved in a war in Africa against the local ruler, Jugurtha. In 107 BC Marius returned to Rome where he achieved consular rank. He then needed to recruit an army to take back to Africa. Long running wars in distant places tend not to be popular and perhaps Marius was expecting a lack of co-operation if he tried to levy troops in the conventional way. However, the use of slave labour on large estates had driven many agricultural workers off the land, there was now a large pool of urban poor available for enlistment, such men would previously have been debarred from legionary service due to failing to meet the property assessment, but he enlisted them in large numbers though initially volunteers formed only a small part of the army. These men, not having farms, would not be clamouring to go home to work on them as soon as the campaigning was over. A soldier's pay was not generous but better than what they had had, and there was always the chance of plunder. As Plutarch described it:

'He was elected with great applause, and immediately began his levies; in which he observed neither law nor custom; for he enlisted many needy persons, and even slaves. The generals that were before him, had not admitted such as these, but entrusted only persons of property with arms as with other honours, considering that property as a pledge to the public for their behaviour.'[28] Plutarch was prejudiced against Marius, and he is the only author to write that he recruited slaves.

The number of years the soldiers enlisted for is vague, it may just have been for hostilities only, but they soon started to display the characteristics of mercenaries, in giving their prime loyalty to their general and not looking forward to peace. Marius was not the first to enlist volunteers, Scipio did in 134 BC, but Marius made it the regular practice.[29] By Caesar's time the system had become standardised. A legion was recruited *en bloc*, served for sixteen years, then was discharged *en bloc*. This was wasteful as it would take two or three years before the legion was well enough trained to be trustworthy. Then, towards the end of its enlistment, attrition would have reduced it to but a shadow of its former self. This system could not be rigorously applied during the civil wars and, after Actium when the legions were established as permanent formations, was replaced by a system based on individual volunteers, sometimes conscripts, recruited by a recruiting officer and forwarded to their legion in batches.

The state had been providing clothing for at least the poorest soldiers since Caius Gracchus passed a law to that effect in 123 BC, which may indicate the enlistment then of poor volunteers. It is not known to what extent the state provided weaponry for the pre-Marian army, but certainly once Marius's recruiting policy had been adopted the state had to provide all weapons and armour. This provided a greater degree of uniformity within the legion than had been the case previously.

The replacement of maniples by cohorts as the main tactical units was an on-going evolution. There can be little doubt that the process started with *ad-hoc* groupings of a maniple each of the *hastati*, *principes* and *triarii*, these groupings may, or may not, have included *velites*. The disparate nature of the maniples involved would have reduced the effectiveness of such *ad-hoc* units. After the change to recruiting these differences faded away and the cohorts began to gel. Probably the *velites* were drafted into the new cohorts as they are no longer mentioned after the recruiting change. That the cohort was a product of evolution is hinted at by there being no definite cohort commander, presumably the senior centurion took on the job.

It is likely that as the legions were now permanent organisations and no longer disbanded each year, the temporary 'corn dolly' type maniple *signa* were replaced by something longer lasting.

The creation of the cohorts meant that the distinctions between the *ordines* of the *hastati*, *principes* and *triarii* became obsolete, as did command at this level and the symbols attached to it. As Pliny the Elder wrote:
'*Caius Marius in his second consulship ordained that the Roman legions should only have the Eagle for their standard. For before that time the Eagle marched foremost, with four others: Wolves, Minotaurs, Horses and Boars; each one in its proper order. Not many years past the Eagle alone began to be advanced in the battle and the*

rest were left behind in the camp. But Marius rejected them altogether. And since this it is observed that scarcely is there a camp of a legion wintered at any time without having a pair of Eagles'.[30] From now on the legionaries followed the Eagle. The *ordines* for the four standards either included the *velites* or the legionary cavalry, probably the former as these soldiers sometimes wore wolf skins to distinguish themselves. The use of standards for the *ordines* may show that this was a natural command level, a concept that will be considered in the next chapter. It is noticeable that before Marius, Roman authors are as likely to give military strength in cohorts as in legions, but after Marius it is usually in legions.

Marius, like all great generals, fully realised the importance of mobility, as would anyone who had fought in the Jugurthine War in the wide open spaces of North Africa. Before Marius the army relied on a large baggage train although it seems that steps had been taken to slim this down. Marius made each soldier carry nearly everything he needed, however some things were too heavy. The soldiers were organised into eight man *contubernia*, and each *contubernium* had a pack animal to carry its tent and other equipment, most importantly its grindstone – rations were issued as grain, the soldiers had to grind them into flour. Now the army could go anywhere a soldier and a mule could, and get there reasonably quickly. The reform of military transportation evoked the well known expression 'Marius's mules', this was a pun: *miles*, soldier – *mulus*, mule. There are two different accounts of the origin of this expression, one by Frontinus:

'For the purpose of limiting the number of pack animals, by which the march of the army was especially hampered, Gaius Marius had his soldiers fasten their utensils and food up in bundles and hang these on forked poles, to make the burden easy and to facilitate rest; whence the expression "Marius's mules"'[31]

The other was by Plutarch:

'*He trained his soldiers to labour while on the road, accustoming them to long and tedious marches, and compelling every man to carry his own baggage, and provide his own victuals. So that afterwards laborious people, who executed readily and without murmuring whatever they were ordered, were called Marius's Mules. Some, indeed, give another reason for this proverbial saying. They say, that when Scipio besieged Numantia, he chose to inspect, not only the arms and horses, but the very mules and wagons, that all might be in readiness and good order; on which occasion Marius brought forth his horse in fine condition, and his mule too in better case, and stronger and gentler than those of others. The general, much pleased with Marius's beasts, often made mention of them; and hence those who by way of raillery praised a drudging and patient man, called him Marius's Mule.*' [32]

That is what Plutarch wrote, but it is at least possible that the jibe was a civilian one derived from observation of the lower intellectual quality of Marius's soldiers and was symptomatic of worsening civil/military relations.

The standardisation of the eight man *contubernium* with its pack animal influenced the formation adopted on the battlefield in that the files were now eight men deep.

The cohorts now consisted of men who were nothing outside the army. They all similarly equipped, and were united by hard work and self interest within their *contubernia*. They were together a long time linking them by shared experience and giving them plenty of time to learn the drills. Their loyalty centred primarily on the legion and the army commander.

The first cohorts contained a degree of missile power, they had probably included some *velites*, and each of the *hastati* and *principes* carried two javelins. Now there were no *velites*, they just ceased to be mentioned, and the soldiers carried only one heavy javelin, the short range *pilum*. Missile action was now to be provided by *auxilia* cohorts. The cohorts were now essentially those making up the legions of the classic age of the Roman army, and the soldiers were now properly equipped for the brutal hand-to-hand fighting required to conquer the Gauls.

There is one further change which Plutarch claimed was made by Marius:

'It is reported that on this occasion he contrived a new form for the javelin. Till then they used to fasten the shaft to the iron head with two iron pins. But Marius now letting one of them remain as it was, had the other taken out, and a weak wooden peg put in its place. By this contrivance he intended, that when the javelin struck in the enemy's shield, it should not stand right out; but that, the wooden peg breaking, and the iron pin bending, the shaft of the weapon should be dragged upon the ground, while the point stuck fast in the shield.'[33]

It is difficult to know what to make of this. In the very unlikely event of the wooden rivet snapping at just the right moment as the *pilum* drove into an enemy shield, the shaft of the *pilum* might hang down instead of jutting forward, but it would hardly inconvenience the enemy soldier more. It must be judged most likely that Plutarch made a mistake with this passage. The *pilum*, by its very nature, tended to bend on contact and will be discussed later in this study.

There is no record that Marius made any changes to the citizen cavalry, but it is noticeable that after his time it quickly declined in importance. The cavalry was manned by wealthy volunteers who may well have been unenthusiastic about the new trend of professional warfare, all year round and in less civilised parts of the world.

At the same time as the Marian Reforms were taking effect a most significant change was initiated by the consul Publius Rutilius Rufus, in 105 BC:

'Practice in the use of weapons was given to the soldiers by the consul P. Rutilius, the colleague of C. Mallius. Doing what no general before him had done, he summoned weapons instructors from the gladiatorial school of C. Aurelius Scaurus and he trained the legionaries in a more flexible method of giving and avoiding blows. Blending skill with courage and courage with skill, he made skill more effective by combining it with courage and courage more courageous by the use of knowledge.[34] This far-sighted measure may very well have initiated the change in shape of the legionary's shield to rectangular and introduced regular sword practice which made the Roman soldier so effective. The measure was probably made necessary by the recruiting of soldiers who were too poor to have had their own weapons so would have had no prior experience of handling them.

There was an aspect of the soldier's life that would have affected his capacity on the battlefield but which has been largely ignored by historians both ancient and modern, and that is the soldiers' slaves or servants. These men were distinct from the great mass of camp followers which, inconvenient though it may have been for the general conducting a mobile campaign, was essential to the functioning, particularly feeding, of a Roman army. An illustration of how the mass of camp followers could become more than just a nuisance was given by Tacitus in his account of the Year of Four Emperors:

'Vitellius was moving ponderously towards Rome. Day by day more despicable and lazy, he made a point of stopping at every pleasant town and country seat. In his train followed 60,000 armed men, dissolute and undisciplined. Even larger was the number of soldier's servants, and the camp-followers were remarkable even

among slaves for their overbearing manners.' [35] This quote should be read with Tacitus's anti-Vitellius bias in mind, even so it is not surprising that Vitellius' reign did not last long.

The slaves or servants considered here would have belonged, or been employed by, one or more soldiers of a *contubernium.* Up until the time when Marius enlisted paupers the Roman soldier always had some money behind him, and he may have been able to bring a slave with him to the annual levy. This changed with Marius, so it is no coincidence that he compelled *'every man to carry his own baggage, and provide his own victuals'.* However, it is known from gravestones that many centurions had one or two servants. This was not surprising as a centurion's pay was significantly more than that of a legionary, there seems to be no direct evidence but it may have been on a sliding scale and around fifteen times greater, with a possibility of 'perks'. However, that many more than centurions owned slaves is hinted at by Appian when he reports the casualties in the early fighting at Philippi. *'It is conjectured that the number of dead on Cassius' side was about 8,000, including slave shield-bearers, and double that number on Octavian's side.'*[36]

The presence of a slave/servant, later a muleteer, in each *contubernium,* which was the same scale they were allowed on in the Macedonian army,[37] should have significantly improved its marching capacity and general efficiency, particularly by such expedients as carrying the kit of sick soldiers. Unfortunately there is no information available on this topic. Muleteers will be considered at greater length in the next chapter.

The change to long service enlistment had one unfortunate result in that there was no longer the large number of ex-servicemen in the countryside. Previously every farmhand and labourer had experience as a legionary and at short notice could be a militarly effective, but now the countryside was depopulated, at least of free men, and those left had no military experience. One result of this was that, in 73 to 71 BC, Spartacus and his followers could march, almost unhindered through Italy.

Caius Marius and his Campaign against the Teutones

Towards the end of the second century BC two major tribes, the Cimbri and the Teutones, began their migrations, and, having destroyed several Roman armies, defeated a consular army under the Consul Manlius and Proconsul Caepio at Arausio (Orange). Fortunately they did not follow this success up and were to spend over two years marauding around Spain and Gaul. Even so the prospect for Italy was alarming so Marius was elected Consul, again, and early in 106 BC sailed with his troops to the Rhone estuary where he reinforced his army with the beaten armies of Gaul and commenced a heavy training schedule. During this training regime Marius had his troops dig a canal joining the Rhone above Arles to the sea, a work known as the *Fossae Mariannae*, a name preserved in that of the village of Foz. It was during this energetic period that the 'Marius's Mules' expression became popular.

In 103 BC the two tribes decided, at last, to attack Italy, but by different routes. The Teutones were to march close to the Mediterranean shore, the Cimbri *via* the Tyrol. The following account of Marius's campaign relies heavily on Plutarch.

Marius fortified a camp on high ground close to Arles, and refused battle which the Teutones were noisily offering. The Teutones assaulted the camp three times but failed to make any real impression and gave up deciding instead to ignore the Romans and proceed to Italy. Their column, which included their families, took six days to pass, some of them shouting to the Romans to ask *'whether they had any commands for their wives, for they should be shortly with them.'* Such witticisms would have been wasted unless the Teutones could shout in Latin.

Once the procession had passed, Marius broke camp and followed. The episode had given the Roman soldiers the chance to have a good look at the enemy and lose any fear that earlier German successes might have inspired.

Finally the Teutones arrived at the well known watering place of Aquae Sextiae (Aix in Provence) where a small town with public baths and all the luxuries of the day, had grown up, a fashionable place for the rich to visit for the medicinal properties of the waters. Having plundered the town, which offered no resistance, of all the valuables it contained, especially wine and provisions, the barbarians had crossed the little river Coenus (Arc) with their wagons and baggage. They established themselves in two camps, the Ambrones in one close to the banks of the rivulet, and not far from the walls of the town; the Teutones in another, more remote, and closer to the mountains. The Ambrones were a major sub-group of the Teutones and seem to have regarded themselves as better than the rest. Marius followed the Teutones, as was his wont, at once seized and occupied a strong hill between the town and the enemy's camps, commanding the whole valley. Favourable as was the position in many respects, it had this defect that it entirely lacked water, which was only to be had from the stream close to the quarters of the Ambrones.

This may have been a part of Marius's plan. He had now resolved to fight a battle, and desired to bring on the conflict apparently by accident, and ensure that his soldiers knew they were fighting out of necessity. When the men grumbled and complained of thirst, Marius laughed at them, and pointing at the river, told them there was water enough, but it must be bought by blood. They then clamoured for instant battle, but Marius would not agree and insisted that they set to fortifying the camp instead.

At this time the barbarians, already gorged with food and wine, and languid after their recent baths, were lying here and there in groups, revelling in the warmth and overcome with previously unknown luxury, some were wallowing in the sparkling and tepid waters. As the legionaries started work on the palisade and *vallum*, some of the slaves and camp followers rushed down to the stream to procure water, carrying besides their water vessels, axes and cleavers, and some of them javelins and swords, and coming suddenly on the barbarians basking half asleep in the sun, put them to the sword without mercy. The cries of these unfortunates alerted the Teutones, especially the Ambrones, who, thirty thousand strong, had had the greater share in the defeat and butchery of the Romans under Manlius and Caepio. These, though they had eaten too much and drunk too much wine, advanced in good order, clashing their arms and shouting in unison their own national name, '*Ambrones! Ambrones*!' to encourage one another and hopefully terrify the enemy with their name.

Then Marius restrained his men no longer. Some cohorts of the Ligurian auxiliaries were the first men in the plain, and these, though ignorant of the fact, and now wholly integrated with the people among whom they dwelt in the plains of the Po, were descendants of an Ambron or Umbrian tribe, which had been banished there centuries before by the Etruscans, and had lost all recollection of their origin except the national name and war-cry, '*Ambrones*!' When these heard the clamour of the barbarians, whether astounded or in defiance, they too set up the same chant, and with both parties shouting at the top of their voices in savage rivalry, and each endeavouring to outdo the other, and the neighbouring mountains redoubling the din, the valley of the Coenus was filled with the uproar before the adversaries had even come to blows. The passage of the river, it would seem, shook and disordered the formation of the Ambrones, who dashed into it recklessly at the sight of the cohorts, and before they could reform their order, the Ligurians were upon them, with a fierce charge sword in hand. The legions quickly came to the support of the Ligurians, and pouring down from the upper ground attacked the Ambrones and forced them back into the channel, where they were slaughtered until the rivulet was heaped with carcasses. Attempting to improve his victory as much as possible, Marius quickly crossed the river and drove the enemy, with tremendous slaughter, to their encampment which was fortified by a square of ponderous wagons. There, however, the pursuit was arrested by the desperation of the women, who rushed out armed with axes and broad swords, cleaving down, in their blind rage, equally the pursuers and the pursued, fighting even more fiercely than their husbands, snatching at the large Roman shields and dieing heroically.

As no further progress could be made, when night fell, the consul drew off his legions, recrossed the river and took post, as before, upon the hill from which he had descended, but which he had been prevented from fortifying by the encounter. That night was one of unmingled horror for there remained myriads of unconquered barbarians, and many of them were bewailing their losses and their dead, not with weeping and groans, like human beings, but with appalling howls and bellowing like wild beasts. A gloomy superstitious horror brooded over the gory plain, and the Romans, though victorious, were awe stricken and Marius himself was ill at ease, knowing his camp was unfortified and expecting at every hour an onslaught from the barbarians. But they did not come either on that night or on the following day, but occupied the time in preparing their arms and making dispositions for battle. This gave the

Romans a day to fortify their camp.

After it was dark on the second night after the battle, Marius detached one of his staff, Claudius Marcellus, with three thousand soldiers (a vexillation) and a motley collection of grooms and camp followers who were to make a noise and give the impression of being cavalry, to gain the rear of the Teutones by a wide detour, and place himself in ambush close behind their lines, which were drawn up immediately in front of the first spurs of the mountains, covered with hanging woods and full of deep ravines, heavily shaded with thickets of oak. The remainder of his forces, having ordered them to breakfast, and arm themselves before dawn, he marched out of his entrenchments, as soon as it was light, and arranged them on the brow of the hill, while he launched his cavalry into the plain, to harass the camp of the Teutones.

Enraged at this sight, and seeing the legionaries arrayed in front of the camp palisades, the Teutones, thirsting for vengeance, armed in haste, and rushed out first to attack the horse, which retired, skirmishing before them in troops and squadrons, faster and faster as they neared their comrades, until they had thrown the enemy into disorder consequent on a rash and ill conducted pursuit. Then wheeling to the left and right they gained the flanks of their own army and drew up in perfect order just as the hordes came roaring and bellowing and clashing their huge broad swords up to the hill up which they swarmed more like ravenous wolves than men and soldiers.

Marius commanded his men not to charge but to stand firm and receive them with the tremendous volley of their ponderous *pila*, hurled from above with double violence, and then to meet them steadily, in serried order with linked shields, as they came staggering up the slippery ascent breathless and with no sure foothold, on the points of their two-edged Spanish swords. He was the first to enforce his precepts by his own example for he was inferior to none in the army in personal vigour and athletic hardihood of body, while in fierce courage he surpassed the boldest. On this day he showed himself not only an admirable leader, but a soldier unrivalled in the use of his own weapons, his orders were obeyed, and his example followed, with perfect success. After a long and deadly conflict, in which the whole front ranks fought hand-to-hand in a series of mortal single combats, foot by foot the Teutones were forced back, though fighting like incarnate fiends, every blow and thrust falling upon them from above until they were thrust down in increasing disorder to the level ground as the bottom of the hill. With the repulse of the barbarians, the Romans advanced, descending from the ridge which they had so stubbornly maintained, in a single ordered line.

The Teutones naturally became more and more disorganised by their descent from the broken ground into the valley of the Coenus, and their confusion was increased by the charges of the Latin horse from the flanks, and the steady forward pressure of the unbroken legions. They fought from early morning until long past noon, and Marius himself avowed that he did not see their backs until at last they were borne backwards across the river nearly to their own encampment, then with the stern, short blast of the Roman trumpets, and the wild Roman cheer, Claudius Marcellus with three thousand soldiers and the camp followers rose from his ambush and charged the Teutones in the rear. That ended the battle, the barbarians broke and dispersed. The greater part of them was slaughtered on the ground by the soldiers; those who escaped the first carnage were hunted down by the natives of the country, and wherever they were overtaken knocked on the head as if they were mad dogs. According to ancient accounts, one hundred thousand men were slain in the action and the subsequent pursuit. The wide plains to the east of Aix were made rancid by the blood and corruption of the unburied carcasses. The name of *Campi Putridi*, still preserved in its modern title of Pourrieres, speaks volumes, and tells more by the untutored eloquence of oral tradition than all the pictured pages of history.

The course of the fighting had shown that for the sustained brutal hand-to-hand fighting necessary to conquer the Gauls, the sword was becoming as important to the Roman soldier as was the *pilum*.

The campaign against the Teutones was over, but not the war, and the next year Marius joined his army with that of Q Lutatius Catulus and destroyed the Cimbri in the Battle of Vercellae. At the end of this battle, Marius stood as the greatest general of the age, but he was a political outsider sometimes referred to as 'The Great Plebeian'. It might be related to prejudice against him the Plutarch relates the following story. '*When Marius was fighting the Cimbri and was being worsted, he saw in a dream that he would conquer if he sacrificed his daughter before the battle; for he had a daughter Calpurnia. Since he placed his fellow-citizens before the ties of nature, he did the deed and won the victory*'.[38]

The Loyalty of the Soldiers

In the period starting with Marius's enlistment of volunteers there was a series of civil wars in which various generals fought each other, most notably Marius vs Sulla; Caesar vs Pompey; and Octavius vs Mark Antony. This was a period lasting 76 years and at its close the principate was established which resulted in a sharp reduction in the number of civil wars, though they still occurred, as in 69 AD. Also, during the civil wars and principate there were many mutinies that are known about and it may well be that many more were not recorded by ancient authors.

During these 76 years Roman politics sometimes

approached mayhem and victory at times went to the side that could secure the loyalty of its soldiers. It may be that this loyalty did not affect the soldiers' behaviour on the battlefield, but it is impossible to be certain, so it will be worth a few lines to consider the factors involved, particularly during this critical period.

Loyalty, in its broadest sense, is based on morality, and during the early Republican period Roman morality was high and maintained in the old fierce self-sacrificial way. An example of this was seen during the war with Pyrrhus when his doctor contacted the Roman consuls offering to poison him. Unfortunately Roman morality changed rapidly during the Punic Wars, as was demonstrated by the vindictiveness they showed to Hannibal, as Livy made him say in his dying speech: *'This day will surely prove how far the moral standards of the Romans have changed. The fathers of these Romans sent a warning to King Pyrrhus, bidding him beware of poison – and he was an enemy in arms, with an army in Italy: these Romans themselves have sent an envoy of consular rank to suggest to Prusias the crime of murdering his guest'*.[39]

After the Punic wars the old Roman high-mindedness had gone, and the general perception was that the accumulation of wealth was more important than service to the Republic. After Marius a progressively large percentage of the soldiers were volunteers, forced into the army by poverty. These men, whose families may very well have lost their farms through financial chicanery, would have seen all this and concluded that their interest lay in self-interest.

As the background of the soldiers changed throughout the Civil War period, so did their motivation. Initially they were occasionally capable of political motivation; Sulla's men, marching on Rome for the first time, may have been genuinely concerned for the Republic. But as the wars dragged on, and the percentage of volunteers increased, so the soldiers became more mercenary.

The individual soldier, volunteer or conscript, on recruitment was allocated to a *contubernium*, which, if fully up to strength, consisted of nine men including the *calo* (muleteer). Each *contubernium* had a tent and a mule, or similar, to carry it. On cold nights, particularly if the tent could not be put up, the mule could be a source of warmth with the soldiers squashed up against it. On campaign the soldiers travelled like gypsies, their prime concern being their comfort. The focus of a soldier's loyalty was to this primary group, the *contubernium* and it was plain to him that the present and future well-being of the *contubernium* depended on their general.

Compared to his commander, Rome could seem a little distant and that for a number of reasons: firstly the soldier was separated from the civilians by the *domi* vs *militiae* divide, so important to Roman political thinking. Secondly that the soldier was usually a countryman, Rome, of course, was a city and country vs town always causes friction, perhaps the soldiers did not like being called 'mules'. Rome offered snug and warm accommodation whereas the soldier on campaign must lie on the cold ground and was, if there was no opportunity to pitch the tent, exposed to wind and weather. Alternatively he might have to shiver through the long cold watches of the night aware of the horrifying punishment awaiting him if he fell asleep. Finally, as citizenship spread through Italy, so the legionary could be racially different from the townsmen of Rome, a place many soldiers would never have seen. His general, on the other hand, was a real person the soldier would have seen and may have heard speak. He sometimes shared the soldier's danger, and sometimes his toil, though perhaps this was done a little artificially. The soldier swore his oath of loyalty to his general – later Emperor – and knew that his general, if he wanted an army, had to have his interest at heart, and if he did not the soldier would mutiny, Roman soldiers were never the over-drilled automata the Potsdam grenadiers are supposed to have been. The plain fact was that there were many times when the general was more able to reward the soldiers than was the Senate. It is not surprising that when Marius found himself criticised by the Senate, he commented that '*the law spoke too softly to be heard amid the din of arms*',[40] and knew that he had the full support of his soldiers who knew that, despite their being Romans citizens, actually political power and money were concentrated in Rome and only their general and their swords would, in the final analysis, guarantee their rights.

This did not change in the empire. The emperor was now the general, and the legions carried his *imago* like a standard to proclaim this, but he still knew that he had to keep the soldier happy. This did not mean that the soldier was well regarded. According to Tacitus, Tiberius's opinion of soldiers was that '*they lacked the old bravery and discipline, since voluntary enlistment attracted penniless vagrants.*'[41] By this time the army had become a caste apart, as Tacitus (again) put it: '*the special glory of the soldier lay in his barracks, for this was his country and his home*'.[42] The result of this was that the good will of the soldiers was now more important to the emperor than that of the civilians who paid for them.

The soldier maintained his place in the world by being in the army, and maintained his place in the army by being an effective fighter. His actions on the battlefield reflected this, by being an effective fighter he was somebody. His tools were his *pilum* and sword, and one thing he dreaded was to have his weapons taken away. Both Caesar and Severus Alexander quelled mutinies by addressing the troops as '*Quirites*' (Citizens), that is, outside the military world, nobodies.[43] However it should be noted that Caesar, at least, met the mutineers' demands. He knew where the power in a civil war lay.

Finally the soldier knew that when he left the army he could not rely on Rome to provide him with any land, and being driven off his farm was probably the reason why he enlisted in first place. As soon as he handed his weapons in to the state armoury he would have lost his place in the world. Experience had shown that Rome could let him down, and he was dependent on his commander to settle him in colonies which would, in their turn, provide a power base for their commander so the soldier could still retain a say in his destiny.

Putting all this together, who can blame the soldiers for trudging through the Rubicon, indifferent to the chaos they might cause in Rome, or for fighting for their general, whoever he was.

Notes

1. Livy, *The Early History of Rome*, I.43, Penguin Classics, p81

Class	Property rating (asses)	Armour	Weapons
1	100,000	Helmet, hoplite shield, greaves, breastplate	Spear, sword
2	75,000	Helmet, oblong shield, greaves	Spear, sword
3	50,000	Helmet, oblong shield	Spear, sword
4	25,000	none	Javelin
5	11,000	none	Sling, stones

2. Polybius, *The Rise of the Roman Empire*, VI.20, Penguin Classics, p319
3. H Delbruck, *Warfare in Antiquity*, Reprinted by University of Nebraska 1975, p255
4. Aelian, *The Tactics of Aelian*, 2, Pen and Sword, p13
5. Asclepiodotus, *Aeneas Tacticus, Asclepiodotus, Onasander*, I.2, Loeb, p249
6. Polybius, *The Histories*, V.53 for '*Scutati*', Loeb, Vol 3, p131. X.29 for '*Light troops armed...*', Vol 4, p173
7. MM Sage, *The Republican Roman Army*, Routledge, 2008, p75

8. Dionysius of Halicarnassus, *Roman Antiquities*, XX.11, Loeb, Vol VII p421
9. Polyaenus, *The Stratagems of War*, VIII,VII,2, Ares Publishers, p310
10. Dionysius of Halicarnassus, *Roman Antiquities*, X.36, Loeb, Vol VI p289-293
11. Dionysius of Halicarnassus, *Roman Antiquities*, XIII.12, Loeb, Vol VII p257
12. Livy, *The Early History of Rome*, V.38, Penguin Classics, p383
13. Livy, *Rome and Italy*, VIII.8, Penguin Classics, p167-168
14. Livy, *Rome and Italy*, VIII.9, Penguin Classics, p168
15. Livy, *Rome and Italy*, IX.35, Penguin Classics, p267
16. Livy, *Rome and Italy*, X.28, Penguin Classics, p327
17. Livy, *The War with Hannibal*, XXVI.4, Penguin Classics, p360
18. Polybius, *The Rise of the Roman Empire*, XV.9, Penguin Classics, p473
19. Polybius, *The Histories*, II.29, Loeb, Vol I, p315-317
20. Livy, *The War with Hannibal*, XXII.37, Penguin Classics, p136
21. Xenophon, *The Cavalry General,*V, CreateSpace Independent Publishing Platform, p29
22. This story is given by three sources: by Appian, who calls the would-be deserters Celtiberians, and by   Frontinus and Livy who call them Numidians:
    Appian, *The Roman History VII.IV.19, (Volume 1: The Foreign Wars),* Digireads, p113
    Frontinus, *Stratagems*, II.v.27, Loeb, p149
    Livy, *The War with Hannibal*, XXII,48, Penguin Classics, p147 and 148
23. *Plutarch's Lives, Fabius Maximus*, Translated by the Revs J & W Langhorne. No date, p135
24. Polybius, *The Rise of the Roman Empire*, III.113, Penguin Classics, p270
25. Livy, *The War with Hannibal*, XXVI,4, Penguin Classics, p360
26. Polybius, *The Rise of the Roman Empire*, III.115, Penguin Classics, p273
27. Livy, *The Early History of Rome*, IV.28, Penguin Classics, p300
28. *Plutarch's Lives, Caius Marius*, Translated by the Revs J

    & W Langhorne. No date, p293

29.   Appian, *The Roman History VI.XIV.84. (Volume 1: The Foreign Wars),* Digireads, p99

30.   Pliny the Elder, *Natural History, book X chapter IV*, from the University of California, Berkeley, site: http://archive.org/stream/plinynaturalhis00plinrich

31.   Frontinus, *Stratagems*, IV,i,7, Loeb, p271

32.   *Plutarch's Lives, Caius Marius*, Translated by the Revs J & W Langhorne. No date, p294

33.   *Plutarch's Lives, Caius Marius*, Translated by the Revs J & W Langhorne. No date, p298

34.   Valerius Maximus, *Memorable Saying and Deeds 2.3.2* as quoted in *The Republican Roman Army, a sourcebook,* Michael Sage, Routledge 2008

35.   Tacitus, *The Histories*, II.87, Penguin Classics, p134

36.   Appian, *The Civil Wars*, IV.112, Penguin Classics, p265

37.   Frontinus, *Stratagems*, IV.i.6, Loeb, p271

38.   Plutarch, *Moralia, Greek and Roman Parallel Stories*, 20, Loeb Vol IV, p287

39.   Livy, *Rome and the Mediterranean*, XXXIX.51, Penguin Classics, p439

40.   *Plutarch's Lives, Caius Marius*, Translated by the Revs J & W Langhorne. No date, p300. This quote may be the origin of the principle '*Silent leges enim inter arma*', found in Cicero's *Pro Milone*, and which was the Roman justification for the imposition of martial law.

41.   Tacitus, *The Annals of Imperial Rome*, IV.5, Penguin Classics, p159

42.   Tacitus, *The Histories*, III.84, Penguin Classics, p198

43.   *Plutarch's Lives, Caesar*, Translated by the Revs J & W Langhorne. No date, p512, and E Gibbon, *The History of the Decline and Fall of the Roman Empire*, chapter VI.

Chapter 3: The Classic Age of the Legion

From Caesar to Trajan

The previous chapters of this study have followed the evolution of legionary fighting from earliest times until this period, roughly 58 BC to 110 AD, which may be called the classic age of the legion and the Roman army in general. There are two aims of this chapter, one is to show that the legion took the form that it did in line with the general strategic situation. It was perfectly designed for that situation, but it was limited in its capabilities and when the situation changed so the legion had to evolve to handle the new strategy. The second aim is to show how the legionary actually fought.

During this period the Roman field army consisted of legions and auxiliaries. Initially the functions of these were different, but towards the end this difference tended to fade away. The auxiliaries were, at least at first, recruited from specific nations so to specialise in the use of their national weapons. The foot were always either light infantry with missile weapons, or spearmen.

The auxiliary infantry was organised in cohorts, similar to those of the legions. The cavalry were in *ala* of a roughly equivalent size. This is a sweeping generalisation, there were some units of double strength and some infantry cohorts were part mounted to allow faster marching. When a Roman army took the field the numbers of legionaries and auxiliaries were roughly similar. The fighting styles of the light infantry auxiliaries and the heavy infantry legionaries were complementary.

It is reasonable to state that the legion fought under a

definite tactical system, and this system was robust enough to function right across the empire, a fact demonstrated by the careers of some centurions who were transferred between legions stationed large distances apart, and also by the similarity of fighting technique shown by legions that fought each other in civil wars.

However any attempt to understand the legionary tactical system must not be distracted by doomed attempts at understanding the command structure of the legion. The Romans were very class and rank conscious, and they had an approach to military appointments which differed from that of a modern army. For example it is not known who commanded a legionary cohort. It is usually assumed that this was done by the senior centurion, but this is only an assumption. The same problem exists for the more junior ranks. Vegetius, assuming a ten man *contubernium*, mentions a *Decanus* as its commander. This rank is sometimes given as *caput contubernii*. Neither of these ranks is known before the fourth century. There were several other ranks of what would now be termed junior NCOs, it is just not known how this worked out.

All this must have affected the way the legion functioned in battle, but it is impossible to tell how. The fact that the Romans thought differently to moderns must be accepted and allowed for.

The Soldier and his Weapons

Field Marshall Montgomery once stated that '*Nothing is more important than the ordinary soldier.*' With his wide military experience he is hardly likely to have been wrong, so this section will start by considering the ordinary soldier.

The legionary was a long service soldier, his length of

service was 16 years in the time of the reign of Augustus, 27 BC to 14 AD, but this had increased to 25 years when the Antonines were in power. After his discharge he joined a reserve force which could be called out (*evocati*) in the case of an emergency. There is no reason to think that he was in any way less intelligent than the modern soldier so he could be expected to be able to respond to a wide range of orders and signals while in action, and carry out a wide range of drills. It must not be forgotten that the legionary could be called on to perform a wide range of non-battlefield tasks, like police or construction work, that would require a reasonable degree of intelligence. The basic unit of which he was a part, the eight man *contubernium*, must have included a leader and a file closer. There is no real evidence for either of these during this period, but it is difficult to see how the *contubernium* could have functioned without them. He lived with his *contubernium* full time and, being in full time contact with the *contubernium* leader, it is impossible to believe that he did not understand the purpose of the drills he learned. This understanding, reaching down to the most junior soldier, explains how the legion could endure the most fearful battering and still continue functioning.

The *contubernium* made up the standard file, the centuries usually fought eight ranks deep although, as will be seen, this could alter. The file leader was naturally the best and most experienced soldier which made it easy for the rest of the *contubernium's* soldiers to follow him where they might have hesitated otherwise.

Also advancement through the ranks made the army a good career when the alternative was the grind of what amounted to subsistence farming, so the average soldier, remembering, as Appian put it '*the toils of farming, the profits of military service*'[1] could be expected to take his soldiering seriously.

The soldier carried two main offensive weapons: a *pilum*, sometimes more than one, and a sword. If he carried two *pila*, on forming up for battle he left one with the file closer as his battle drill required him to use only one at a time. The *pilum* was a heavy throwing weapon, heavier than what would normally be called a javelin, so, to define it, the Latin is used. The adoption of this weapon has been covered in the 'Punic Wars' section of Chapter Two. *Pila* came in a wide variety of shapes and sizes, and if a standard *pilum* is described it must be emphasised that it may not be typical. The *pilum* had a thick and heavy shaft, around a yard long, and the iron head was around two feet long. The point was of an armour-piercing 'bodkin' type, that is, not barbed. Behind the head the shank was thin. The base of the shank was either flattened into a tang or hollowed into a socket. The Praetorian relief, of 51/52 AD, in the Louvre shows *pila* with what look like round weights on the shanks just above their joints with the shafts.

It can be seen that the *pilum* was designed to penetrate the enemy's shield, which would require a small point, but, as the thickness of the shaft would stop the progress of the *pilum* through the shield, the shank had to be long enough to reach the enemy's body before the *pilum* was halted.

There was a useful secondary result of the *pilum's* design. So that the shank could easily pass through the small hole made by the head it had to be thin. In this era weapons were made of soft wrought iron, so it was quite common for the shank of the *pila* to bend on contact. If the *pilum* had missed its target and bent on hitting the ground the fact of its bending would have prevented it being thrown back by the enemy, but this was of minimal importance as *pila* were only thrown at very short range and the enemy would not have had the time to pick it up and return it. However if it stuck in his shield its bending may have made it awkward to pull out.

As Caesar noted during the Helvetian war:

'In the hand-to-hand conflict which followed, the Gauls were sorely handicapped by a curious result of this first volley. In many instances single Roman javelins had cut their way through two or more Helvetian bucklers, locking them together; and as the soft iron heads had bent before the blow, the Gauls could neither wrench them out, nor fight with any freedom with the left hand so impeded. Eventually many of them, after vainly trying to shake their arms clear, had no alternative but to fling away their shields and to fight with the body exposed.[2]

The image of the legionary with his *pilum* is a neat and compelling one but archaeology has found so few *pilum* heads that the impression is given that either this weapon was only issued for a short period, or only to a small percentage of soldiers, or that it was only issued in particular circumstances and at other times the soldiers would be given some light javelins. This would have been appropriate in the east where the enemy was usually light cavalry.

Because of its weight and fragility the *pilum* did not make a useful spear, also because of its weight it could not be thrown very far or fast so would be unlikely to incapacitate its target. Consequently, to be effective, the *pilum* must be quickly followed up by the sword, and it is interesting to note that Vegetius groups the *pilum* with the sword as a hand-to-hand weapon, not as a missile weapon. He refers to close-quarters fighting as '*ad spathos et ad pila*' (to broadswords and javelins).[3] The sword, which known as the 'Spanish' sword, was a short heavy weapon with a straight blade and had changed little since the 175 BC sword. It was designed to be a thrusting weapon but was double-edged and could be used for cutting. Vegetius, praising thrusting over cutting, commented that '*a stab driven two inches in is fatal'*, however it may be that in a melee it was more frequently used for cutting.[4] In fact as a battle wore on the sword would have become progressively blunt and the club-like impact of cutting may soon have been more effective than stabbing. It is easy to imagine that the soldier was taught certain strokes such as cutting at the left leg and hip of his enemy, and stabbing upwards into his stomach, or across the top of his shield aiming at his enemy's head or chest. He would do this while crouching a little, covering himself as much as possible with his shield.

The wounds caused by the Spanish sword could be fearful, and the sight of the bodies of men killed with it could be depressing. That was the effect such a sight had on the troops of Philip V of Macedon after their first significant action against the Romans. *'They had seen wounds caused by spears, arrows, and, rarely, by lances, since they were accustomed to fighting with Greeks and Illyrians; but now they saw bodies dismembered with the 'Spanish' sword, arms cut off with the shoulder attached, or heads severed from bodies, with the necks completely cut through, internal organs exposed, and other horrible wounds, and a general feeling of panic ensued when they discovered the kind of weapons and the kind of men they had to contend with'*.[5]

The defensive weapon, the shield, was characteristic of the legion of this period. It is commonly referred to as the *scutum*, and will be so here, however *'scutum'* is a general term and, correctly, will refer to any shield. The legionary shield was rectangular and curved, and made of something like plywood and leather covered to give it a degree of toughness. It was two foot six inches wide and four feet high, these measurements are given by Polybius when describing the oval shield of the Punic Wars period. As will be seen, the design of the shield is basic to understanding legionary tactics.

The *scutum* was certainly bulky, modern reconstructions being much heavier than the current British army riot shield. As it was carried with the arm straight and vertical, it would have rested against the shoulder and so would form an effective device for shoulder barging the enemy. Being carried this way it would have snagged the soldier's sword scabbard if that were on the left, so the legionary slung his sword on the right, making drawing it a little awkward. The centurions, who did not carry the large shield but sometimes carried a small buckler, slung their swords on their left. It is likely that they were the first soldiers to carry the *spatha*, the longer sword that ultimately replaced the *gladius*. The fact that centurions did not carry the *scutum* explains how so often centurions became involved in individual duels, such fighting would have been near impossible if carrying a *scutum*. Also they are sometimes shown as wearing greaves, not having the long *scuta* to cover their legs. The Roman shield will be considered at greater length in Appendix Two.

The Romans took the loss of a shield, and indeed the loss of any weapon, seriously. Polybius commented:
'those who have lost a shield or a sword or any other weapon on the battlefield often hurl themselves upon the enemy hoping that they will either recover the weapon they have lost, or else escape by death from the inevitable disgrace and the humiliations they would suffer at home.'[6]

The ethos was not lost on Caesar's soldiers, as one event illustrated. *'In Britain, some of the vanguard happened to be entangled in a deep morass, and were there attacked by the enemy, when a private soldier, in the sight of Caesar, threw himself into the midst of the assailants, and, after prodigious exertions of valour, beat off the barbarians, and rescued the men. After which, the soldier, with much difficulty, partly by swimming, partly by wading, passed the morass, but in the passage lost his shield. Caesar, and those about him, astonished at the action, ran to meet him with acclamations of joy; but the soldier, in great distress, threw himself at Caesar's feet, and, with tears in his eyes, begged pardon for the loss of his shield'.*[7]

All this was later enshrined in Roman law. To quote Modestinus from the Corpus Juris Civilis:
'A soldier who, in time of war, loses or disposes of his arms shall suffer death; through indulgence he may be transferred to another branch of the service.'
And Paulus from the same work:
'It is a serious crime for a soldier to dispose of his arms, and this offence is equal to desertion if he disposes of all of them: and also if of a part of them except that a distinction is made: for if he disposes of armour for his legs or his shoulders he shall be punished by flogging; but if it be his breastplate, shield, helmet or sword, he is like a deserter. A recruit is more readily pardoned for this crime, and the blame is attributed largely to the custodian of the arms if he entrusted them to the soldiers at an improper time.'[8]

The finest weapons will not be effective if the soldiers are incapable of using them. The skills required were not great and, although the Roman soldiers were probably more skilful than their various enemies the difference could not have been really decisive. The real edge that the Romans had was that they were skilful longer.

As was mentioned in Chapter One hand-to-hand fighting is very tiring, so the legionaries were trained to withstand this fatigue by heavy construction-type labour and endless fatigues. Their skill-at-arms was maintained by daily practice against the dummy target of a padded post. They would spend time under close supervision belabouring it with heavy drill foils, twice the weight of swords and carrying hurdles twice the weight of the service shields. This drill the Romans called *'armatura'*. As described by

Vegetius: *'Against the post as if against an adversary the recruit trained himself using the foil and hurdle like a sword and shield, so that now he aimed at as it were the head and face, now threatening the flanks, then tried to cut the hamstrings and legs, backed off, came on, sprang, and aimed at the post with every method of attack and art of combat, as though it were an actual opponent. In this training care was taken that the recruit drew himself up to inflict wounds without exposing any part of himself to a blow'*[9] It can appear that attacking a padded post would be better practice at cutting than stabbing, particularly making a quick slashing cut. The shield would have been in the way of more elaborate sword-play, specially its top right-hand corner.

Also maniples would practice against others, the soldiers barging the shields against their opposite numbers and fighting with sticks. There were sometimes exercises for larger formations, but these were as likely to be to impress the audience as to train the soldiers. It is now impossible to tell to what extent the Roman drills could be regarded as the equivalent of modern parade ground drill. The surviving drill manuals were written for the Macedonian phalanx which fought with the *sarissa*, and for them parade drill was important. As will be seen the Romans practiced several battlefield drills, but it was enough for the recruits to be trained *'to keep ranks, follow the standards, and obey commands'*.[10]

Organisation

As has been noted the soldier was a part of an eight-man *contubernium*. In the Acts of the Apostles [11] the 'quaternion' is mentioned and this is given as a unit of four soldiers. As this is the only mention anywhere of such a small unit it can be taken that the expression just meant a group of four soldiers, and not a military unit.

Ten *contubernia* made a century and two centuries made a maniple (*manipulus*) which was really the most important tactical unit, the basic building block of the Roman army. Its importance is shown by the way that it lasted, maniples are mentioned frequently by Ammianus Marcellinus in his account of events during the later Roman Empire.[12] Having two centuries the maniple had two centurions, the *centurio prior* and *centurio posterior*. These two grades would have been, to some extent, the equivalent of modern commissioned officers and warrant officers, although it should be emphasised that Roman ranks do not correspond to equivalent modern military ranks. The *prior* century would form up in front of the *posterior* century and *prior* centurions are sometimes referred to as *primorum ordinum centuriones*. The *prior* centurion would make the tactical decisions. That the *prior* centurions were of a higher social class is shown by the way sometimes one might be sent on a responsible diplomatic mission, and some centurions were promoted to the command of an auxiliary cohort. These tasks were far beyond the *posterior* centurions who had mostly risen from the ranks.

As is well known several centurions are mentioned in the New Testament and portrayed as intelligent and humane men. They would have been *prior* centurions.

That some centurions worked their way up from legionary, and some were directly commissioned into the rank, is shown by Dio Cassius, quoting a speech by Maecenas: *'some knights should be elevated to the Senate even if they have risen no higher than the rank of military tribune in the legions, but not if they have served in the ranks. To include in this category the names of men who have carried loads of firewood and charcoal would be a degradation and a reproach to the senatorial order. But in the case of knights who began their service with the rank of centurion, there should be nothing to prevent the most distinguished of them from rising to a higher order.'*[13] Carrying loads of firewood and charcoal can be taken as an allusion to the toils of the common soldier, (*miles gregarius*). Maecenas was obviously concerned to keep the senate the preserve of the upper class. If a knight were commissioned directly as a centurion this would obviously be as a *prior* centurion, not being put on the same level as an ex-ranker *posterior*.

There are two centurions mentioned by the Younger Pliny who were obviously of the *prior* rank. For one he obtained a post at the cost of 40,000 sesterces, at a time when 100,000 sesterces bought a small farm. It is not known if centurions' appointments were bought and sold as were commissions in the British army until surprisingly late in the 19th Century.

The other case was of a centurion who had an affair with the wife of a military tribune. As tribunes were of the equestrian order and the Romans were very class conscious it is impossible to imagine the lady involved stooping to a liaison with the military equivalent of a foreman of a gang of labourers.[14]

Centurions are mentioned often in Roman literature and in such a variety of roles, such as addressing the senate, carrying out tricky reconnaissance missions, and proscription executions. Tacitus's books are so rife with examples, that the very title of 'centurion' can seem a little suspect.

Consider this passage from Appian: Antonius *'began to enrol his guard and went on adding to it until it numbered 6,000 men. He chose them not from serving rank and file, whom he thought he would easily be able to obtain by other means when he needed them, but entirely from centurions because they had qualities of leadership and were experienced in war and were known to him from service under Caesar.'* [15] Plainly these could not have been 6,000 men who had each commanded 80 soldiers. Perhaps it was an honorific title or Appian was using the expression in terms of something vaguely to do with the *Comitia Centuria*, or to denote a cadre, or class, of professional soldiers, in much the same way as Tacitus uses the expression 'military men' (*viri militares*), and not solely to describe soldiers, or ex-soldiers, who had held a particular rank. Alternatively it might denote the beneficiaries of centuriation, the process of dividing up land into small lots to distribute to discharged soldiers.

In the field the centurions were easy to recognise, they wore helmets with transverse crests and, probably, red cloaks, red being the cheapest dye available in the ancient world. Most centurions were paid very roughly fifteen times as much as legionaries. The *primi ordines*, centurions of the First Cohort, were paid thirty times as much, and the *primus pilus*, sixty times as much. It is not known if there was a difference between the pay of *prior* and *posterior* centurions. Officers junior to centurion were paid significantly more than legionaries, this made soldiering an attractive career for soldiers capable of being promoted.

Ten *contubernia* naturally made up 80 legionaries and since the title of a centurion would indicate that he should command 100 men it is usually assumed that the title was a historic one which had just not changed over the years with minor organisational changes. This may not be the case. He certainly commanded 80 legionaries, but extra to these it may be presumed that each *contubernium* had a *calo* (muleteer) and there was himself, his *optio* (second-in-command), probably a *signifer* (standard bearer) and maybe one or two more under his immediate control, this small command group would also have had its own mule with a *calo*. Further, as the standard bearer had some financial responsibilities, there might have been an extra mule, with *calo*, to carry a strongbox. It would then only take three or four extras to bring the century up to 100. The muleteers could have provided a useful battlefield service, they could have kept the *contubernia* supplied with water. This was an important function, particularly in hot climates, and no-one else seems to have been available to do it. Also they could have escorted, or carried, wounded soldiers back to the medical post, sometimes needing the mules to do this. These muleteers, or *contubernium* servants, may have been useful fighting men. Some may have been soldier's sons or others waiting for a vacancy in the legion, others might have been time-expired men wanting to stay in the framework of a military organisation. Either way they would be willing to put up a fight if necessary, and it has been seen that during Marius's campaign against the Teutones they precipitated a major battle.

The muleteers were not the same as the servants or shield-bearers often mentioned by ancient authors. These servants were owned or engaged privately by military personnel, usually centurions, and are more likely to have remained in the camp, guarding possessions, than to have been present on the battlefield.

The standard bearers were responsible for maintaining the savings accounts of the soldiers, so they must have been educated men. It is at least possible that well-born Romans, awaiting a vacancy as a *prior* centurion, joined a legion as standard bearers to learn their jobs. There is no evidence for this, but it is supported by cases of standard bearers showing officer-type initiative and an example one, Atilius Vergilio, will be given later in this chapter.

Apart from his *optio* and *signifer* the centurion had under him a *tesserarius*. This term derives from *tessera* (watchword) and implies that the holder had special responsibility for communication the watchword to the sentries and hence, probably, security in general. Also, as the watchword was supplied on a wax tablet, the *tesserarius* must have been literate. These three junior officers formed the centurion's *principales* and, presumably, did not form up with the *contubernia* in battle formation. There are secondary questions about them, such as was there a basic difference between the *prior* and *posterior optiones* as there was between the different types of centurion? Was there a simple promotion sequence from legionary up to *optio*, or even *posterior* centurion? It stands repeating that the Romans thought differently to moderns, and trying to project the procedures of a modern army onto the legions will result in misunderstandings.

Promotion for centurions is not easy to follow and it was based on the hierarchy of seniority of the centuries in a cohort. The three maniples were called '*hastatus, princeps*' and '*pilus*', the *pilus* being the most senior. Each maniple had two centuries, for the *pilus* maniple these were '*pilus prior*' and '*pilus posterior*'. The junior centurion of the cohort was *hastatus posterior*, on promotion he would move to *princeps posterior*, unless there were special circumstances he would not advance to a prior appointment. Within the legion the cohorts were graded for seniority and the centurion may have started his career in Cohort X and worked his way up to Cohort II, though this scenario seems a little unlikely as the junior cohort would always have the least experienced centurions and be the least reliable. However it is possible that the junior century, or maniple, was used as a training unit for recruits serving their *tirocinium*. The sequence for Cohort I was slightly different but of no real significance to this study. The senior centurion in this cohort was the *Primus Pilus*, the senior soldier of the legion.

As Roman shields were inscribed not only with their owner's name but also with the centurion's name, it follows that when the centurion was promoted his century moved with him. This would have had the advantage of keeping teams together, but may have caused difficulties when reorganising a cohort after an action causing heavy casualties.

Two centurions commanded a maniple, three maniples made a cohort. The very name indicates that the cohort could be controlled by shouting ('*cohortatio*' is Latin for 'encouragement'), so it can be taken as the largest unit that could be called on for fast manoeuvre on the battlefield. A deployed cohort will have had a normal frontage of 60 legionaries, or 100 yards.

Ten cohorts made a legion. One of these cohorts, the First Cohort, was significantly larger than the others and included all the legion's administrative troops, also this cohort was responsible for camp security and would not normally take the field. Soldiers were transferred into this cohort when approaching 20 years of service in one of the other cohorts as they became less able to cope with the toils of mobile warfare. It is not known if such a man retained his rank and pay, if he had achieved promotion, or if he reverted to legionary (private soldier).

As the First Cohort contained the older men and had special responsibility for camp security it is reasonable to assume that the *triarii* evolved into this cohort.

This left nine manoeuvre cohorts. This number was far too large for the legion's commander to control in battle so it is reasonable to posit that the cohorts were grouped into some sort of intermediate organisation even though there is no direct evidence for this. This organisation would have started as an *ad-hoc* informal grouping and 'gone firm' over time.

As the legion would normally form up for battle in three lines each of three cohorts it would seem reasonable to assume that the cohorts were grouped in threes. Further it is quite possible that units of three cohorts were known as vexillations. Such a unit was too large to be controlled by voice, so a flag (*vexillum*) had to be used, hence the name.

When a part of the legion was sent away from it on detachment that unit was termed a vexillation. The size of such a unit is not specified anywhere, but it was smaller than half a legion, being a detachment, so it had a maximum possible size of four cohorts. Also it was larger than one cohort. So vexillations must have been either two, three or four cohorts strong, and include some troops from cohort number one.

Literary sources do mention, on several occasions, detachments of 2,000 men being sent from legions.[16] From earliest times a thousand was the command of a tribune, in fact it is difficult to believe that there was no etymological connection between the words *mille* (thousand) and *miles* (soldier). So, as a legion had six tribunes, it may be that two thousand (MM) was a simple shorthand for a third of a legion, and could have originated in Roman news bulletins. This figure is quoted often enough to give the impression that it was a standard unit.

The conclusion to this, then, is that cohorts were grouped three to a vexillation giving the commander three large manoeuvre units to control. So, as can be seen the units of a legion increased in size in multiples of three. This would have appealed to the Roman military mind and is reflected in modern armies.

As can be seen, allowing for each century to have a centurion and three *principales*, but not including officers, the nine manoeuvre cohorts had a total establishment of 4,356 soldiers. However the legions were often grossly understrength, something not helped by the system of recruiting and discharging legionaries in batches.

These comments do not obtain in the case of the Praetorian

Guard, which does not seem to have been organised above cohort level.

Standard Drills

The whole purpose of any battlefield organisation is to maximise the effectiveness of the soldier. This is done by getting him in contact with the enemy, by keeping him there while he can fight efficiently, and by making him more lethal when he is there. In order to do this essential military activities are reduced to drills which can be practised, ordered quickly and simply, and carried out with a minimum of thought.

The Romans practiced these drills on the parade ground where they also practiced formations designed to display the might of the army, these were important spectacles, specially during civil wars. It may be conjectured that one of the main functions of the Praetorian Cohorts was to impress the Roman Senate and People this way. The Romans took drills very seriously and this training must have been realistic, as Josephus commented: *'It would not be far from the truth to call their drills bloodless battles, their battles bloody drills'.*[17] Vegetius mentions three formations that the troops were practiced in: the line, of various depth, the 'wedge' and the circle, or 'orb'.[18] This last was to be adopted only as an act of desperation. It involved the sub-units forming around the standards. Ideally this could be forming a circle which could hold out indefinitely, but if any troops retreated then the circumference of the circle, and fighting front, would contract and the soldiers would not have room to fight effectively and the files would not function smoothly, until finally the soldiers were squashed up together and helpless. All of these formations will be mentioned in the following text.

The drills involved form three main groups: those covering battlefield mobility, those providing a continuous front and those concerned with skill-at-arms.

Mobility on the Battlefield

In the late eighteenth century the French army ran a series of trials of systems for drills based on moving in column and fighting in line. This was exactly the same problem faced by the Romans, and they overcame it by moving in maniples and only deploying once the maniples had 'gone firm'. A maniple had a front of ten men and a depth of 16, assuming that it was at full strength. Each soldier took up five foot of front so a maniple had a front of around 17 yards. This was a small enough unit to be led into position by one man and aligned, by him, with the other maniples.

When a legion formed up for battle it usually did so in three lines, the cohorts of the second and third lines covering the gaps between the cohorts of the line in front. This was so that the second line could pass through between the cohorts of the front line, then deploy, replacing it in action. To do this the three maniples of each cohort would have to close in on each other which may seem a little cumbersome compared to passing the maniples through between each other, but it was probably easier to control.

The moment when one vexillation was taking over from the one in front should have been the moment when the formation was most vulnerable, but this was not so. As the relieving vexillation was passing through the retiring one, because the *posterior* centuries were not deployed the enemy was faced with a solid line of maniples 16 men deep, so almost undefeatable. The vexillations may have stood like this for a short time until they were sure that the relieving vexillation could advance a few paces and deploy without too much interference from the enemy.

An advantage of keeping the maniples in column was that it was easier to change direction. The legion could, more easily than troops in other armies, cope with a surprise attack from an unforeseen direction.

In a perfect world the front ranks of the second line vexillation could be within two or three paces of the rear rank of the first, just enough space for the centurion and his *principales*, but the reality was that there had to be a significant space between the vexillations or control could be lost, as may have happened at Cannae.

It could be that his legions being deployed on too shallow a field caused the collapse of Brutus's troops at the Second Battle of Philippi. His army was deployed in the cramped space in front of a line of redoubts joined by a *vallum* and ditch, which meant that he could not conduct a fighting retreat, and if the front line vexillations bowed backwards under the pressure of the fighting, proper spacing could not be maintained. Octavius's and Mark Antony's men could not allow them more space as they would have been backing into a swamp. Brutus's first line vexillations seem to have fought well but finally gave away, but the second, then third, became mixed up, could not be brought into action and ran.(*see Chapter Six*)

Forming a Continuous Front
Naturally it was essential to present the enemy with a front *en muraille*, there must be no gaps for the enemy to pour through and attack the soldiers from the rear. Forming such a front involved deploying from column to line, and this was handled by the Romans in the most simple and effective way. Once the maniples were in position with fronts of ten soldiers, on a signal the *posterior* century would march out to the left, until it reached the next maniple. This was controlled by the *posterior* centurion, pacing out five feet per soldier. If the gap to be filled was over sixteen yards the front of the century was extended by

deploying some of the files as four men deep instead of the standard eight. Conversely if the gap were less than sixteen yards then some files were not deployed and were kept in reserve. As casualties mounted some files could have been reduced to two, but by then the front would usually have been contracted.

That the posterior century would deploy to the left is confirmed by Polybius who states that *'When both centurions are present the senior commands the right half of the maniple and the junior the left'*.[19] The right of the line was always regarded as the most honourable.

If the maniple had to advance with its *posterior* century deployed, then the p*osterior* centurion would be responsible for changing the depth of the files to prevent bunching. Failure to achieve this may have been one of the factors contributing to the Cannae disaster.

The maniple in line would only carry out very limited manoeuvre, a stately march forward, or backward. For rear movement the *posterior* century would draw back behind the *prior*, and the maniple would move in column.

Skill at Arms
The centuries always formed a well-aligned and correctly spaced, usually straight, front. This reduced the vulnerability of individual soldiers to missiles and was necessary for the various drills described here. To use his arms most effectively each soldier needed five feet of space. This was the standard Roman measure of distance, the (double) pace. This might seem a short pace by modern standards, but it had to account for rough and broken country. The need to maintain regular intervals was well understood by Vegetius: *'soldiers should keep their appointed rank in the line, and not mass together or thin out the formation at any point inconveniently. For when densely packed they lose room to fight and impede one*

another, and when too thinly spread and showing the light between them they provide the enemy with an opening to breach.'[20] The Roman pace was twice the width of the legionary's shield, and correct drills for the use of the shield made the legion almost immune to attack by missile weapons like slingshot and arrows.

To achieve this immunity, on an order the front rank man would kneel down behind his shield, the second man would come forward and kneel down by him. Numbers three and four would dress forward and place their shields on top of the first two to produce an eight foot shield wall. They could do this, because of the design of the shields, in one of two ways. Because of the curve of the shields a top layer shield could stand on two of the lower shields or alternatively, the top layer shield could fit inside a lower layer shield, resting on the upper hand grip.

The second alternative given here is also how the tortoise drill worked. In this drill the soldiers held their shield over their heads, each shield lapping under the one in front until it came up against the hand grip. Without that restriction the formation would have been almost impossible to maintain. This defence against missiles involved doubling the front four ranks to produce a two-high shield wall, whereas defence against cavalry would require doubling only the front two ranks, to give a single course of shields. Maintaining such a defence was totally passive and to be successful the legionaries should be supported by cavalry or light troops.

Roman shields were quite thin, to keep their weight down, but bows had not yet achieved Agincourt-like power and arrows seldom penetrated them. However arrows were a genuine threat as shown by the actions of some of Octavian's troops when they occupied a hill and *'brought wicker screens and hides for protection against arrows'*.[21] In an earlier war, during the fighting at

Dyrrachium, in one fort that Pompey's men assaulted, four of Caesar's centurions lost eyes to them while peering, presumably, over their shields, and one centurion's shield was found to have been holed 120 times. After the battle Caesar wrote that 30,000 arrows were picked up in the fort, and every soldier in the garrison had been wounded.[22] To overcome the threat of arrows Roman helmets started to be fitted with peak-like projections usually called 'brow guards'. The arrows would have come at the soldiers in a plunging trajectory so they had only to tilt their heads forward a little for the peaks to protect their faces. Cheek pieces, which were more expensive, came later. The soldiers' feet and legs could be protected by strips of leather wrapped puttee-like round them. As will be seen the power of the Parthian bows at Carrhae came as a shock to the Romans but even though it was believed that rain reduced the effectiveness of these bows.

Naturally doubling the ranks to form the shield wall prohibited the use of the soldiers' weapons, as Lucan observed: *'Pompey's soldiers, closely packed in serried ranks, had joined their shields, boss against boss, to form an unbroken line; they scarce had room, as they stood, to ply their hands and weapons, and their close order made their swords a danger to themselves'.*[23] When to return to the fighting formation would require nice judgement and precise drill.

A tortoise was essentially a passive formation and misusing could be disastrous, as was by Germans fighting Caesar. *'The ardour of our soldiers in the fray cannot be better illustrated than by the fact that, when the barbarians protected themselves by forming a "tortoise" with their shields raised over their heads, the Romans actually leaped on the top of the shields and from there fell upon their throats with their swords'.*[24]

A successful use of the tortoise was described by Plutarch in his life of Mark Antony. The Romans were on the defensive against Parthian attacks, *'Against these attacks the light-armed troops were covered by the legionaries, who placing one knee on the ground, received the arrows on their shields. The rank that was behind covered that which was before in a regular gradation; so that this curious fortification, which defended them from the arrows of the enemy, resembled the roof of a house.'*[25]

It would be interesting to know if there was any attempt to size off the soldiers within a *contubernium*. Obviously the leaders and file closers were not selected for their height, but the tortoise drill would be much more effectively carried out if the soldiers naturally formed up in order of height. The same holds true for forming the shield wall and legionary fighting in general.

A specific instance of the importance of height gradation in a tortoise is given by Ammianus Marcellinus when describing the siege of Cyzicus in 365AD. *'In front men stood on the thwarts with their shields closely interlocked above their heads; behind them were others who stooped a little; and behind these again a third party who bent lower still in descending order, so that the rearmost squatted on their hams and the whole looked like the side of an arched building. The object of this formation, which is used in assaulting walls, is that missiles and stones may glide down the slope which it presents and run off like so much rain'*.[26]

The passive defence provided by the Roman shields against missiles meant that for the enemy to make an impression on a legion he would have to resort to hand-to-hand fighting, and this meant a fight with swords and other personal weapons.

The Romans knew that fighting, particularly with a sword,

despite the *armatura* training, was exhausting, so after a surprisingly short time the first man would fall back to the rear and numbers two to seven would step forward. The last man, the file closer, would stay as the last man, not allowing anyone to leave the ranks unless he had been wounded. The Romans knew that routs start at the rear and Caesar records a case of this happening when his army was caught by surprise and was in a critical state. '*Disheartened by this loss of officers, the rank and file already showed signs of wavering, and there were even cases in the rear of men leaving the ranks in their efforts to avoid the hail of spears.*[27] His prompt action naturally restored the situation.

The file closers may also have had a secondary function of holding spare weapons like *pila,* which could be retrieved, particularly if the cohort was advancing, straightened out and issued to other soldiers. It is possible that they carried a stone or steel to sharpen swords that had been blunted by the fight, Roman swords were essentially wrought iron with a little surface hardening and would blunt easily.

The use of the *pilum* poses something of a question. It is possible that all the troops of a century or maniple threw them in one volley but this seems very unlikely since most would not find a target, particularly as the troops in the rear ranks would not be able to see what and where their targets were. Also the drill would be impossible to control on the battlefield where the centurion's voice would be unlikely to be heard by all his century and trying to control the drill by trumpet would interfere with all the other centuries/maniples in the cohort/vexillation. If this tactic were used, it would be very much a one-shot ploy, much to the encouragement of the surviving enemy. Much more likely is that the man in the front rank would throw his *pilum* at his own discretion when the enemy was really close, then stand ready with his sword, crouching slightly to protect his feet and lower legs with his shield, while the soldier behind him stood with his *pilum* ready to support him, and had a space five feet wide to use to do this most effectively. If the *pilum* could be thrown to penetrate the enemy's shield this would give a significant advantage to the swordsman. As soon as the supporting soldier had thrown his *pilum* the front rank man would dash forward a short distance to stab or slash at the enemy while he was at a disadvantage. After a few seconds he would retire to the rear where the file-closer may have been able to give him another *pilum*. The fast and brutal assault with the sword is described by Dionysius of Halicarnassus, '*the Romans' defence and counter-manoeuvring against the barbarians was steadfast* (or '*well practised*') *and afforded great safety. For while their foes were still raising their swords aloft, they would duck under their arms, holding up their shields, and then, stooping and crouching low, they would render vain and useless the blows of the others, which were aimed too high, while for their own part, holding their swords straight out, they would strike their opponents in the groin, pierce their sides, and drive their blows through their breasts into their vitals. And if they saw any of them keeping these parts of their bodies protected, they would cut the tendons of their knees or ankles and topple them to the ground roaring and biting their shields and uttering cries resembling the howling of wild beasts*'.[28] In this extract Dionysius is recounting fighting with the Gauls around 400 BC, but he was writing during the reign of Augustus and would have been describing contemporary warfare.

The tactics described here are those seemingly shown by a sculptured relief at the fortress at Mainz in which the second soldier is not only standing ready with his *pilum*, so he could not have thrown it in a mass volley, but is also covering the leading man with his shield.[29]

The use of the *pilum* in this manner, as opposed to the mass volley, seems to be supported by Vegetius when, after describing the way that recruits were taught the correct use of the sword by stabbing at a padded post, he comments: *'The recruit who is being trained with the foil at the post is also made to launch spear-shafts of heavier weight than the real javelins will be against the above-mentioned post as though against a man. In this activity the instructor in arms sees to it that he hurl the spear-shaft with great force, and drive the missile with a true aim into or next to the post. For by this exercise the arms gain strength, and skill and experience in throwing javelins is acquired'* [30]

The soldiers could also be given missile support by archers and slingers. The archers were auxiliaries as some of the slingers may have been, but Vegetius states that legionaries were expected to be able to use the sling and excavated examples of lead slingshot, marked with the legion's number, and dated in the first Century BC, show that the legionaries did.

When the troops were in close contact with the enemy, there were only two possible deployments for archers, and hence slingers. One was in groups slightly forward of the fighting line, as was done by the English archers at Agincourt, the other was for the missile troops to stand behind the heavy infantry and shoot over their heads. The first deployment would have been very unlikely in the Roman context as it would have complicated their battlefield drills, so the second deployment can be assumed. Also other light troops posted there could have provided the volleys of javelins often mentioned by ancient authors. However the literary support for this is limited to two passages, the first is from Plutarch's life of Sulla (Sylla). In his description of the Battle of Chaeronea (86 BC) when the Romans met the Pontic phalanx he writes:

'These men, however, owing to the depth and density of their array, and the unnatural courage with which they

held their ground, were only showly repulsed by the Roman men-at-arms; but at last the fiery bolts and the javelins which the Romans in the rear ranks plied unsparingly, threw them into confusion and drove them back.'[31] The courage of the phalangites was described as '*unnatural*' because they were recently freed slaves and desperate men. The '*fiery bolts*' were presumably launched by engines the Romans had brought from the sieges of Athens and the Piraeus.

The second passage is from Josephus:

'*Titus deployed his effective forces opposite the wall on the north and west, in a formation seven deep, infantry drawn up in front, cavalry behind, each in three ranks, with a seventh line in between formed of archers*'.[32] The exact meaning of this quote may be open to discussion, but once again it certainly places the archers behind the heavy infantry.

There is a further fact in favour of this deployment in that the evolution of the legionary helmet up to the end of the classic age of the legion saw progressively large neck guards. This is confirmed by archaeology and the images on Trajan's Column. In the normal run of man-to-man infantry fighting there was no requirement for neck guards, and the only purpose for them would have been as a defence against 'drop-shorts' from the archers, slingers and javelineers to the rear. The same observation may be made about armour for the back, which earlier generations of legionaries would have scorned. The legionaries might have dropped to one knee behind their shields to give the projectiles the greatest clearance possible.

The procedure of deploying missile troops behind the legionary centuries may have evolved over the years until it resulted in the mixed *contubernia*, containing both spearmen and missile men, which are described in Chapter Eight. Unfortunately if and how such an evolution occurred is not mentioned by the sources.

The result of all this was that the enemy soldier had to advance through a barrage of arrows or slingshot, and then face a *pilum*, before crossing swords with the legionary who would be standing ready and waiting for him. The legionary would not run forward to meet his enemy.

Around the turn of the millennium a further weapon was added to the Roman battlefield array. The Romans had used various types of artillery from an early date, but always in a static deployment, that is to say in either the defence or attack of fortifications. It was only with the development of the *carroballista* that battlefield use of artillery became possible.

Some very old *ballista* bolts have been found but it is impossible to tell if they were for *carroballistae*. The oldest ones that can be pinned down as being so were from the Varus battlefield of 9 AD, and this is certain because any static engines would not have been taken that far.

This weapon was really a glorified crossbow set on a pintle mounting on a cart. The general impression of missile weapons in antiquity is of their ineffectiveness: javelins had a short range, arrows did little damage and slingshot were inaccurate. In view of this the *carroballista* became an important weapon. Its range was not great. Although the engines of antiquity could shoot impressive distances, on the battlefield the need was for aimed fire and that presumed a flat trajectory. Because the stock of ammunition (bolts) was limited the crew would probably not have engaged targets at ranges of greater than 200 yards.

Vegetius wrote: '*The legion is accustomed to be victorious not only on account of the number of soldiers but the type of its tools also. Above all, it is equipped with ballista-*

bolts which no cuirass or shield can withstand. For each century customarily has its own carriage-ballista, with mules assigned to draw it and a section, that is, eleven men, to arm and aim it. The larger these machines are the farther and more violently they shoot projectiles. Not only do they defend a camp, but they are also placed on the battlefield behind the line of heavy infantry. Faced with their attack, neither the cavalry cuirassiers not the shield-bearing infantry of the enemy can stand their ground. In one legion there are traditionally 55 carriage-ballistas. There are also ten mangonels, one for each cohort. They are carried around ready-armed on ox-carts, so that should the enemy come to attack the rampart to storm it, the camp can be defended with darts and rocks'.[33]

There are, naturally, difficulties with Vegetius's account. If each century in a manoeuvre cohort had a *carroballista* then there were 54 extra *contubernia* required (ignoring the mangonel crews), almost an extra cohort. This manning requirement could not be met by the 1st Cohort and it is unlikely that men of the required skill could be found by just nominating a *contubernium* in each century. There is, though, no record of an increase in legion manning. Perhaps only as many *carroballistae* were issued as required to support one vexillation, anticipating them staying in action to support the other vexillations as required. This is pure speculation.

The difficulties of manning would have increased as the number of *carroballistae* increased, and finally, in the fourth century AD, special legions of *ballistarii* were formed. How this system would work to provide fire support for the fighting soldiers must remain obscure.

In action the *carroballistae* would follow the maniples and shoot over the soldiers' heads in the way that other missile troops would. With the carts giving the *ballistae* that extra height, and the trajectory of the bolts being comparatively flat, this deployment was much safer for the troops being shot over than would have been the use of other missile troops, and no doubt correspondingly popular.

The drill of having the front rank man, with his sword, backed up by the second rank man with his *pilum* meant that the two must stay close together, that is the front rank man must not run far forward of the fighting line. During the desperate fighting close to the town of Ruspina in North Africa, 46 BC, Caesar ordered his men not to advance more than four feet in front of the line. Although there are several cases in Roman military history of generals and centurions holding back overly aggressive soldiers, this is the only surviving mention of any definite restriction of forward movement, so it has to be taken as standard. The significance of four feet is that it was just less than a Roman pace (five feet).[see note 45 for text] Maintaining this restriction meant that the *pilum* was delivered as short range, and that made it easy to retrieve for re-use. The Soldier's Oath, described in Chapter Two, swearing not '*to abandon their place in the line*' prohibited charging forward just as much as unauthorised retreating. If the Anglo-Saxons that fought at Hastings had taken such an oath, the history of England might have been very different!

As in several different contexts the Romans had an example from their semi-mythological early history which reinforced the four feet rule. During a successful battle against the Aequi, the commander '*Postumius, we are told, did a peculiar thing and altogether unbelievable; for in the battle his own son in his eagerness leaped forward from the station assigned him by his father, and his father, preserving the ancient discipline, had his son executed as one who had left his station*'.[34] Livy also found this event unbelievable, but no doubt it was mentioned repeatedly to the rather less sophisticated soldiers.

Keeping the soldiers within four feet of the front rank would have made it easier to prevent units breaking up when the soldiers wanted to go looting, as happened to units of both Brutus's and Mark Antony's armies in the first Battle of Philippi, and Caesar's at Gergovia. It must not be forgotten how important booty was to the soldier.

As the fighting was dependent on the *pila,* this meant that once they had all been thrown the maniple, or cohort, had done its bit and would expect to be relieved. This is illustrated in the Dead Sea Scrolls: '*And after them, three divisions of foot-soldiers shall advance and shall station themselves between the formations, and the first division shall hurl seven javelins of war towards the enemy formation……All these shall hurl their javelins seven times and shall afterwards return to their positions*'.[35] Although perhaps too much reliance should not be placed on the number seven, which had a sanctity with the Jews and recurs frequently.

The fighting formation of the Roman legion could present a shield-wall resistance to missile weapons, alternatively it could produce a web of swordsmen. If any enemy soldier penetrated the front rank, which was actually not that difficult to do if the attacker were armoured, he would quickly be assailed with swords from several different directions. The disadvantage with this formation is that it had a poor offensive capacity. On the battlefield the soldier's priority is staying alive and, having remained crouched behind his shield for some time, even hours, he will be loath to leave this security. Once the shield wall has been raised, getting the legionaries to attack would have been very difficult. The large shield, which contributed so much to the defensive strength of the legion also hampered fast movement, and charge would be a ponderous affair. A legionary, bursting in among the enemy, having his cumbersome shield to manage and with only his short sword, would be at a disadvantage. The support of the others, from which he gained his strength while on the defensive, would be denied him. This is not to say that the legions never attacked on the battlefield, but it was rare. Vegetius gives the reason: *'Even if they routed the enemy, the heavy armament did not pursue, lest they disturb their own line and battle-order, and the enemy charge back on them while dispersed and overwhelm them when disordered, but the light armament, with slingers, archers, and cavalry, pursued the fleeing foe'*.[36] This was, of course, an application of Caesar's four feet rule.

The Assault

The legion, then, was all but unbeatable in defence, but simple battlefield necessity meant that the legionary had to have some capacity to attack other than the slow tramp forward, and there were two known methods of achieving this. One was the use of *Antisignani*, the other was the use of the 'Wedge'.

The *antisignani* were picked soldiers deployed in light infantry roles. They seem to have been instituted by Julius Caesar to cover the gap left by the *velites* when these were abolished by Marius. Unfortunately Caesar gives no indication how the *antisignani* were organised, were they the front rank of a century, or one *contubernium* of a century, or one century of a cohort? Regardless of this, after Caesar the special use of *antisignani* largely faded away, but although they were not particularly important during the classic age of the legion when the legions were supported by auxiliary light infantry, after it they were to become very important, as will be seen.

The wedge, probably first used by the Thebans at Tegyra, in 375 BC, is listed by Vegetius as being an important formation, unfortunately he gives no details, but it seems reasonable that this formation would be the same as the Theban wedge except that the leading rank would be only two men wide instead of three. This would be because the

Roman commander would not be charging in the front rank. There are many cases cited of legionaries attacking in this formation and there is only one method they could use without breaking up the *contubernium* files. On an order two *contubernia* from the centre of a century would run forward in the attack, the two *contubernia* either side would also advance, but around half a pace behind the leading soldiers. Then the next two *contubernia* would advance, each successive one echeloned back from the leading troops. If the sortie was not a success the wedge could be easily recalled, but if it was a success the enemy would be thrown into confusion and an opportunity given to the auxiliaries. However one of the limitations of Roman weaponry was that it was difficult to launch a *pilum* while running forward, so the wedge went forward with the first rank at least with swords alone, hoping to use physical shock to unbalance the enemy instead of *pila*. The soldiers called the wedge the '*Pig's Head*'.[37] As pigs keep their heads low, this may give the impression of the soldiers storming forward stooping low to cover their legs with their shields.

How all this worked out in practice is related by Tacitus in his account of Boudicca's uprising, he has the Roman commander tell his men: *'Just keep in close order. Throw your javelins, and then carry on: use shield-bosses to fell them, swords to kill them.'* That was the fighting sequence for the soldier: to throw his *pilum* at the enemy, to barge into him with his shield, then to finish him off with a jab of his sword. He continues *'At first the regular troops stood their ground...they launched their javelins accurately at the approaching enemy. Then, in wedge formation, they burst forward. So did the auxiliary infantry. The cavalry, too, with lances extended, demolished all serious resistance. The remaining Britons fled...'*[38]

Pre-battle pep talks like this, if they actually happened which is unlikely, would have been heard by few soldiers and it is possible that any auxiliaries who heard them would not understand them. However it would be only reasonable to assume that the commander would want to do as much as possible to ensure the high morale of his troops. His options were limited, really, to ordering the trumpets to blow and the soldiers to cheer. They would advance *'uttering their war-cry and clashing their swords against their shields as is their custom.'*[39] But even this enthusiasm could be discouraged as too much noise could make the passing of orders difficult.

Apart from these few measures the Romans seem to have taken little trouble to build up the fighting spirit of the common soldiers, expecting legionaries to do the job they were paid to do in a thorough and workman-like way, much as they would lay a road or construct a fort. There was a range of gallantry awards available, but in fact the overwhelming bulk of them went to centurions or above. This range of awards included *torques* for the neck, *armillae* for the arm and *phalerae* for the chest; but the *contubernales* would see none of them.

Also, if the maniple suffered heavy casualties, this would not translate into promotion for the survivors as the centurions and their *principales* took post behind the fighting line, were in least danger, suffered few casualties and created few, if any, vacancies.

The best the *miles gregarius* could hope for, after survival, was a share in any booty taken.

Command and Control

If it were compared to the command structure of a modern army, that of the Roman army must seem bizarre. It was the result of an evolution that started after the last of the kings was expelled from Rome and it evolved in such a way as to ensure that no one man ever became too powerful. Inevitably this resulted in a degree of military inefficiency, but that was a price acceptable to the Romans.

The heads of state were two consuls – initially called *'praetors'*, headmen – they were elected by the senate and served one year. The army consisted of two legions, the origin of the word means 'levy', it too was called up each year and the consuls drew lots to decide which of the legions they commanded.

As can be imagined with such a simple command structure any operation undertaken must be simple and of limited duration. During the fifth century BC a significant improvement was made with the creation of posts for six tribunes per legion. Tribunes had existed before this, the word has the same root as the word 'tribe'. In earliest antiquity there were three tribes and a tribune commanded each tribe's levy of 1,000 men, later the size of the legion and the number of tribunes was doubled. The function of the early tribunes is difficult to define. The tribunes of the republic and empire were young men in their early twenties, the senior one was of the senatorial class and the others were knights. Although it might seem logical that two tribunes should command a three cohort vexillation, that seems not to have been the case. They would not have been welcomed by the senior centurion of the vexillation who might have seen many years of service and may himself have been an equestrian. Also, if tribunes did command at this level they would be mentioned far more often by Roman historians than they are. It must be concluded that, although tribunes might have overseen some routine aspects of legionary administration, in the field the senior tribune temporally commanded the legion and the others functioned as *aides-de-camp* to the army commander.

There can be little doubt that the tribunes and the *prior* centurions provided a class-based leadership of a type not seen in modern armies. It is possible that '*tribunos......et primorum ordinum centuriones*' was a standard latin expression linking officers of these ranks. It was used by Caesar in his Gallic War and by Tacitus in his Annals.[40] In both cases the text described a massacre. As will be shown in Chapter Five, both Ambiorix at Atuatuca and Arminius at Kalkriese knew how to decapitate the leadership of a Roman army. It is, of course, just possible that Tacitus was copying Caesar's expression. Even without Caesar's wording, tribunes and centurions are frequently mentioned together. In these cases it is always *prior* centurions that are meant.

It was basic to Roman thinking that a career in politics meant holding a series of increasingly important posts, each for a year. The Romans did not have a clear-cut distinction between military and civil posts, so every politician passed through the army and had some idea of military realities, even though few might be first class officers. As there were six tribunes per legion and as they were usually all replaced each year, quite soon there was a substantial pool of Roman politicians with military experience available, in theory, to be picked for senior posts or for emergency deployment. However only a small percentage of these politicians would have shown any interest or aptitude for soldiering, these men may well have been given the informal name of '*viri militares*'. These men may have improved their promotion prospects by extending their military experience, and their circle of acquaintances, by serving as volunteers on the personal staff of a governor or general. The high quality of Roman officers is one of the most impressive aspects of Roman military history, and it was the result of consuls and, later, emperors having a large number of *viri militares* to pick them from.

Nothing contrasts the military system of the republic with that of modern armies so much as that there was no such post as legion commander. An army, which may be just one legion, could be commanded by a consul, proconsul, dictator or provincial governor, but the legion was commanded by the six tribunes until around the end of Augustus's reign when there were important changes. Most significantly legates were appointed by the Emperor for each legion. The legates' appointments were for up to four years, they were independent of the *cursus honorum* and were one of the methods the Emperors ensured the loyalty of the army. The legionary second in command was to be the senior tribune, the other five tribunes were not important in the chain of command, but their posting was important to them as it was their first step on their *cursus honorum*. The third in command was the camp prefect, who was a long-service soldier promoted from centurion. He was responsible for the routine functioning of the legion and the upkeep of its camp.

Before, and during, the Punic Wars decisions affecting the legion were taken at the military council which was attended by the *prior* centurions. This worked well enough for the militia-type armies of the time but as the legion became more professional and decisions needed to be made and acted on faster so changes were made. In 168 BC Aemilius Paulus was campaigning against the Macedonians and, under his command, decisions were taken at the highest level and passed on to the *primi pili* by the senior tribunes.[41] This may imply a reduction in the general prestige of centurions. This procedure was maintained, with minimal changes, until the end of the western empire. However taking the orders from the general or legate and forcing them on the legionaries was not easy and required system and communications.

The communicating of orders was always a problem and was considered by Flavius Arrianus, known as Arrian, who has some experience in this field having commander two legions and a large body of auxiliaries when he was governor of Cappadocia. '*The army must get used to receiving commands sharply, some by voice, some by visible signals and some by trumpet. Those revealed in reading happen to be clearer because the revealing is to the whole mind, not just some symbol seen or heard.*

But since many things regarding revealings by voice are blocked out in battles and the noise of equipment, [shouts of] encouragement to each other, the moanings of the wounded, the passing by of the cavalry force and the clatter of their equipment, the horses' neighing and the uproar of the baggage trains going by, one must get the army used even to visible signals.

In addition to these things there will indeed be difficulties which happen such as fog, dust borne aloft, the sun glinting in the face, continuous snowing, furious water from the sky, wooded or hilly locales surging up so that signals so not become visible to the whole phalanx. When hills block out vision, one must make more visible signals. As to obstructions from the air the trumpet is useful and a good thing'.[42]

Arrian was considering general principles, from a legionary's perspective what was important was that each maniple had two centurions, their *principales* and a trumpeter. There is some argument that only the *prior* century had a standard, but this is reasonable as a plethora of standards would not have exactly simplified the situation for the army commander who just wanted to see where the maniples were. It is, just, possible that the *posterior* century had a standard, but it was only displayed after the century had been deployed. There is one indication from Appian's history that hints that there was one standard per maniple. During the fighting in front of Dyrrachium Caesar's men suffered a sharp defeat, to such an extent that one legion's eagle was only saved from capture when its bearer threw it over the ramparts of the

124

camp, implying that that legion was totally routed. Appian says that Caesar's men lost 28 standards[43], which is one per maniple of a legion (excluding its 1st Cohort) plus one for its cavalry detachment. This might, of course, be a coincidence. Caesar in his 'Civil War', to be quoted below, records a loss of 32.

The officers mentioned, and two or three more, with a trumpeter and perhaps what Appian calls a 'crier' for passing orders, did not fight in a *contubernium* but formed a command group which could be expected to have led the maniple until the *posterior* century deployed, then they would have filed to the rear. The standard, *signum*, which would be a simple pole with some identification of the maniple, was used, usually by pointing with it, to pass drill orders to the maniple as a back-up to verbal orders. These verbal orders would not only be shouted by the centurions but would be repeated along the centuries by the front, and rear, rank soldiers so everyone would hear them because noise and the shock of battle were the problems which could prevent orders being passed and acted on. As the Book of Isaiah puts it: '*For every battle of the warrior is with confused noise, and garments rolled in blood*'.[44] Passing orders like this was mentioned by Caesar in his account of the fighting at Ruspina.[45]

An obvious method of passing orders was *via* trumpets, but this could cause problems. Vegetius lists three wind instruments, two of which, the trumpet (*tuba*) and the horn (*cornu*), would have been of importance to the battle line. The horns were used in conjunction with the *signa*, they were sounded to draw attention to the signal being made. The trumpets were sounded to pass a limited range of orders, telling the soldiers '*to fight, stand their ground, pursue or retire*',[46] but their use on the battlefield is problematic, if they were used they would all have to sound the same call at the same time, or they would cause chaos. To what extent the Romans overcame this problem is not known, but the wide range of trumpet and bugle calls that have been used by the British army indicates the potential of this kind of communication.

The trumpet certainly made a loud noise, a fact taken advantage of by Cornelius Gallus who was commanding an army that Mark Antony tried to subvert. When Mark Antony approached to speak to the troops, Gallus had his trumpeters drown him out.[47] This might suggest that the trumpeters were massed at Head Quarters directly under the general, and the horn blowers were attached to the maniples.

With the limited number of orders that could be passed with a *signum*, in all probability it made no real difference to the legionaries if the maniple had one or two of them, except in one context. One of the most important reasons for the 'maniplisation' of the army, a reason forced on it by the battle of Allia, was the necessity of being able to quickly change direction and face to a flank. This would be most easily ordered by a *signifer* standing between the two centuries of the maniple in column and rotating the standard, not just spinning it. The maniple would then, when the horn sounded, rotate around him and the movement would be halted by the centurions when it was facing in the required direction. This important procedure needed only one *signifer* so it seems most likely that there was only one per maniple.

There were few orders that could be passed by the *signifer* as the list below shows:
The maniple to advance or retreat, ordered by inclining the *signum*.
The maniple to halt, ordered by holding the *signum* vertical.
The maniple to deploy, ordered by bobbing the *signum* up and down.
The maniple to turn, ordered by rotating the *signum*.

There is no real record of any of these signals being made, but there is a hint in a Latin set phrase that might just have had its origin in the rotating signal. The expression for 'face about' or 'about turn' is '*conversa signa*' which could be read as 'rotating standards'.[48] Perhaps not too much should be read into this.

There is no record of any of these signals being made, at least at maniple or cohort level. The list is purely supposition, an attempt to illustrate the limitation of this kind of signalling, and shows that for the legionary it was word of mouth, passed along the century, that was important.

However there is a case of a legionary eagle being used to pass an order, this occurred in Lucullus's campaign in Armenia, in 69 BC. During some pre-battle manoeuvres the Roman army was feigning a retreat, then '*they saw the eagle of the foremost legion make a motion to the right by order of Lucullus, and the cohorts proceed in good order to pass the river*'.[49] This one example, put together with '*conversa signa*', is an indication that this list of *signum* signals might have some validity.

The legion's standard, the eagle, borne by the *aquilifer*, was much grander than the *signum*. It was used for ceremonial purposes and, despite the example just given, seldom had any tactical significance other than to denote the location of the commander. However in a crisis both *aquilifer* and *signifer* could be called on to fight in the front rank or to lead an assault, the *signifer*, no doubt, being at the point of a wedge. The most famous case of an *aquilifer* leading occurred at the start of Caesar's first raid on Britain. As he described it, when things were looking tricky '*As the Romans still hesitated, owing chiefly to the great depth of the water, the eagle-bearer of the Tenth legion, with a fervent appeal to the gods that what he was about to do might turn out for the good of the regiment, shouted to his comrades to jump overboard unless they wished to see the eagle in the hands of the enemy. 'I, at any rate,' he exclaimed, 'shall not be found wanting in my duty to my country and general.' With these words, he flung himself out of the ship, and, eagle in hand, made straight for the enemy'.*[50]

The symbolism of the eagle was very potent, it became something of a cult object and the loss if its eagle in battle could result in a legion being disbanded, however all standards became important in the eyes of the legionaries. Appian tells that when Sulla was attacking Rome his *'troops were being driven back, but he seized a standard and risked his life in the front line; this action immediately stayed their rout because of the awe in which they held their general and the dishonour they feared if they lost their standard.'* This story must have been well known, it was repeated many years later by Ammianus Marcellinus.[51] In Appian's account of Caesar's African campaign Caesar was said *'with his own hand to have spun round and dragged to the front a fleeing bearer of one of the eagles, the most important standards'*.[52] A powerful story, repeated by Plutarch but not mentioned by Caesar in his account of this campaign. Perhaps stories of generals seizing standards were more literary devices than objective histories, and there were many recorded.[53]

However such heroics as these did not always run smoothly, even for Caesar. During the fighting at Dyrrachium, seeing some of his troops retreating, *'Caesar ran to meet them, and would have rallied the fugitives, but it was not in his power. He laid hold on the ensign staves to stop them, and some left them in his hands, and others threw them upon the ground, insomuch that no less than thirty-two standards were taken. Caesar himself was very near losing his life; for having laid hold of a tall and strong man, to stop him and make him face about, the soldier in his terror and confusion lifted up his sword to strike him; but Caesar's armour-bearer prevented it by a blow which cut off his arm'*.[54]

Being a standard bearer could involve certain risks, as Frontinus commented of a case in the early history of Rome: *'The dictator Servilius Priscus, having given the command to carry the standards of the legions against the hostile Faliscans, ordered the standard-bearer to be executed for hesitating to obey. The rest, cowed by this example, advanced against the foe.'*[55] On the other hand the soldiers had a strong interest in keeping the standard bearers alive. They were the pay sergeants. So, in the case of a sudden disaster and chaos in the field, the 'orb' would naturally form round them as the soldiers rushed to defend their financial security.

The standards did not have to be carried to inspire the troops. At the battle of Pydna an officer seized a standard and threw it into the enemy phalanx to urge on his attacking legionaries. Plutarch's account of this action will be quoted in the next chapter. This kind of action, like generals seizing standards, might just be another trope, and several cases were recorded.[56]

Raising standards could be a signal to start fighting, as Appian wrote about the Second Battle of Philippi, *'then came a piercing shout from the enemy, the standards were raised on both sides, and the charge was violent and harsh'* (an extract more fully quoted in Chapter Six). Unfortunately it is not obvious what use was made of the standards before the fighting.

Lowering the standard, or even dropping it, was a notification of surrender or at least ceasing fighting, as is illustrated by this action at the battle of Praeneste during the Civil War. *'As the left wing began to give way, five cohorts of infantry and two of cavalry, not waiting for the rout to develop, threw away their standards all at the same time and deserted to Sulla.*'[57]

A similar event, but 448 years later, was recorded by Ammianus Marcellinus. During a battle, '*While the issue was still undecided Agilo turned the scale by suddenly changing sides. He was followed by many others who in the very act of brandishing their pikes and swords deserted to the emperor, holding their standards and shields reversed, which is a sure sign of defection*'.[58] Presumably the shields were held back-to-front to show that their owners were not prepared to fight.

Probably the most dramatic use of the standard as a symbol of surrender was the event that ended the Gildonic revolt of 398AD. To quote Gibbon: '*As Mascezel advanced before the front with fair offers of peace and pardon, he encountered one of the foremost standard-bearers of the Africans, and, on his refusal to yield, struck him on the arm with his sword. The arm, and the standard, sunk under the weight of the blow; and the imaginary act of submission was hastily repeated by all the standards of the line. At this signal the disaffected cohorts proclaimed the name of their lawful sovereign; the barbarians, astonished by the defection of their Roman allies, dispersed, according to their custom, in tumultuary flight.*'[59]

There are other signalling system that should be mentioned. In his account of the wars with Pyrrhus, Dionysius of Halicarnassus recounts: '*When the signals for battle were hoisted, the soldiers first chanted their war songs, and then, raising the battle-cry to Enyalius, advanced to the fray, engaged and fought, displaying all their skill in arms.*'[60] However what these signals were, and how they were hoisted must remain obscure, but certainly the concept lasted as '*Caesar hung out the flag as the signal for battle*' before the Battle of Munda in 45

BC.[61] Finally, the white flag worked in Roman times as it does in modern.

A type of standard that had no tactical function but was useful in other ways was the *imago* of the emperor. It was a portrait or bust carried, as were the other standards, on a pole and served to remind the soldiers whose side they were on, an important factor in a civil war. An incident during the Year of Four Emperors illustrated this: '*an ensign belonging to the cohort which formed Galba's escort – Atilius Vergilio, according to the tradition – ripped from his standard the effigy of Galba and dashed it to the ground, a clear indication that all the troops supported Otho.*'[62]

The *imago*, of course, was not always welcomed by Roman subjects, and it was the Roman insistence in carrying one into Jerusalem that played a large part in igniting the great Jewish revolt.

Battle

The previous sections have shown the legion to be all but unbreakable in defence but otherwise limited. Therefore it is necessary to consider its employment in battle, where it was used to provide the defensive base that the auxiliary light infantry and cavalry could attack from. The legion would undertake the hard work of the campaign, clearing the way for roads, and protecting the transport, but most important of all it would fortify the camp. The regular nature of the Roman camp prevented the mixing of units and allowed stragglers to catch up. It gave the soldiers a night's rest, a secure place for their kit and savings, and sent them calmly to battle in the morning. It will be seen in Chapter Five how disasters could occur when the legions could not fight in their preferred way, marching out of a secure camp.

There is no doubt of the Roman preference for *'war, complete with trumpets and military standards'*,[63] and *'a straightforward regular battle, where courage, not craft, would conquer'*[64], and the grand spectacle of a major battle always had a dramatic effect on the losing side.

On the battlefield a legion would have been a magnificent sight, but during the period in question its main function was to provide a solid defensive base for the army and invite attack. While it was deploying it would have been screened by cavalry and skirmishing auxiliaries. The cavalry would have made observation of the legion difficult for the enemy, and the auxiliaries would have kept his troops occupied till the legion was ready. While the auxiliaries were fighting the maniples would have stayed in column, but when the auxiliaries and cavalry were recalled or defeated and came streaming back between the maniples the *posterior* centuries would deploy to prevent the enemy from following the auxiliaries. This, of course, could be done in the time it takes a man to run sixteen yards. It must have been very frustrating for the enemy who had just defeated the auxiliaries and thought they were winning, to be suddenly confronted with the serried ranks of a legion, *'like a wall of iron'*.[65] The retreating auxiliaries and cavalry, would then move to the flanks to stand ready to attack the enemy's flanks and rear. Frontinus gives several examples of this manoeuvre, enough to show that it would have been practised as a drill.

The basic principle of the legions forming the solid core of the army and the auxiliaries doing the fighting was demonstrated during Agricola's Scottish campaign when, as described by Tacitus, the army was formed up for the battle of Mons Graupius, 84 AD. *'The auxiliary infantry, 8,000 in number, formed a strong centre, while 3,000 cavalry were distributed on the flanks. The legions were stationed in front of the camp rampart: victory would be vastly more glorious if it cost no Roman blood, while if the auxiliaries should be repulsed the legions could come to their rescue.'*[66]

The initial period, while the troops were forming up but before the fighting started, would see a good deal of shouting and chanting; slogans would be shouted and weapons thumped against shields. This was partly to keep the shouters' morale up, and partly to intimidate their enemies. Also the watchword for the day would be shouted to impress it on the soldiers' memories. Shouting was not encouraged during the fighting as it would have made passing orders down the ranks difficult, but it could have its place as an aid to identification. As will be seen tactical opportunities were lost amid the thick dust at Philippi, and no doubt other amicide disasters were avoided by units shouting, on order, the word of the day. This could be particularly important in the rare cases of fighting at night.

The disciplined shouting of thousands of men could be very impressive. Over the years this shouting developed into the roaring known as the *barritus*, described by Ammianus *'it begins with a low murmur and gradually increases in volume till it resounds like the sea dashing against a cliff'*.[67] It is not impossible that legionary shouting provided the background for a verse of the New Testament that includes the words: *'What is thy name? And he said, Legion: because many devils were entered into him.'*[68]

If the legion were drawn into serious fighting it would doggedly stick at it, swapping vexillations over to prevent exhaustion. It was this process of feeding fresh troops into the fighting and pulling back the cohorts that had thrown all their *pila* and blunted their swords that was one of the factors that made Roman battles last so much longer than Greek ones, but another was that there was not always that much actual fighting. It is generally agreed that the victorious Roman armies tended to suffer fewer than 5% casualties and, as the losing side suffered most of its casualties in a rout, its casualties during the fighting would have been reasonably similar to those of the winners. With the long engagement time and low level of casualties it follows that there cannot have been much serious sword-play, and the soldiers that were wounded were quickly taken to the rear so their presence would not depress the fighting men. It is easy to forget how gruesome a battlefield could be, in his description of the Battle if Strasbourg Ammianus Marcellinus wrote: '*So a great number lay mortally wounded, praying for the relief of a speedy death. Others, half-dead and hardly able to breathe, sought to catch a last glimpse of the light with their dying eyes. Some had their heads severed by pikes as massive as beams, so that they hung merely by the throat; others, who had slipped in the blood of their comrades on the muddy and treacherous ground, were suffocated under the heap of bodies which tumbled on them, and died without receiving any wound*'.[69]

There certainly would have been terrifying high-casualty clashes, but after a clash, no matter how successful it was for the Romans, the legionaries, like the Spartans, would not pursue but would maintain their alignment. If their enemy knew that the Romans would not pursue it might have made them more inclined to pull back, but it would have done them little good. The legionaries, carrying out a drill movement, might be ordered to drop to one knee behind their shields giving the *carroballistae* and other missile troops their chance, then, on the word of command, or blast of the trumpet, they would stand up and continue their slow and steady advance ready for the next flurry of action. Their enemy might throw rocks, javelins and other missiles and make a lot of noise, shouting war-cries and insults nerving themselves for another clash, but the legionaries would maintain silence and grip their *pila*.

The enemy's morale would, sooner or later, crumble. This process of gaining the ascendancy and driving the enemy back is illustrated in Livy's account of the Battle of Zama. '*The Roman attack gained solidity as the men pressed on into the enemy by their own weight of numbers and that of their arms; on the other side, there were repeated charges with more speed than power behind them. Consequently the Romans immediately broke the enemy's line at the first attack; then they pressed on with their shoulders and shield-bosses, steadily advancing as the foe fell back, and making considerable progress as no one offered resistance*'.[70] This process can be observed in any modern riot where a crowd confronts a line of shield-carrying police.

One case when this process could not be carried through was during the Siege of Jerusalem, in 70 AD. The Romans were starting to feel the strain and, when they prepared for an assault on the Outer Court of the Temple, instead of using complete units they selected the fittest 30 men out of each of a number of centuries. The troops attacked an hour before dawn but did not achieve surprise. The Jewish defenders reacted with admirable speed and spirit and, in a desperate and confused fight in the dark, halted the Romans. As dawn broke a degree of order asserted itself, as described by Josephus: '*The two sides now separated into opposing formations and began to hurl missiles in an orderly engagement. Neither side gave an inch or showed any sign of weariness*'. The impression is of the two sides, only a few yards apart, crouching behind their shields, hurling missiles, including bricks and lumps of stone, at each other. '*At last, after battling from before dawn to nearly midday, they broke off the fight, without either side having really budged the other from the spot where the first blow was struck, and without any decision being reached*'.[71]

This was an undeniable defeat for the Romans. It could be

that just too much was asked of them, but there may be other contributing factors. The soldiers may not have taken their *pila* with them on what was expected to be a night-time operation. Being in what were really *ad-hoc* units they may not have functioned confidently in files. For the same reason, and for lack of space, they would not have been able to rotate their leading units with reserve cohorts in the way that vexillations could swap over in the open field. These factors, added to heat and exhaustion, resulted in the troops in contact with the enemy not being as effective as would usually be expected.

A related, but slightly different, aspect of the Roman battle was the ability of the legion to sustain a fearsome battering but still function. This was illustrated in 7 AD during the Pannonian War when the rebel '*forces which had swarmed out to meet the army which the consulars Aulus Caecina and Silvanus Plautius were bringing up from the provinces across the sea, surrounded five of our legions, together with the troops of our allies and the cavalry of the king...,and inflicted a disaster that came near to being fatal to all. The horsemen of the king were routed, and the cavalry of the allies put to flight, the cohorts turned their backs to the enemy, and the panic extended even to the standards of the legion. But in this crisis the valour of the Roman soldier claimed for itself a greater share of glory than it left to the generals, who, departing far from the policy of their commander, had allowed themselves to come into contact with the enemy before they had learned through their scouts where the enemy was. At this critical moment, when some tribunes of the soldiers had been slain by the enemy, the prefect of the camp and several prefects of cohorts had been cut off, a numbers of centurions had been wounded, and even some of the centurions of the first rank had fallen, the legions, shouting encouragement to each other, fell upon the enemy, and not content with sustaining their onslaught, broke through their line and wrested a victory from a desperate plight.*'[72]

Since Republican times the *standards of the legion*, which included the eagle and *imago*, had been carried in front of the third (ie rear) line. They may have extended a steadying influence on shaken and disordered troops falling back. It is even possible that the cohorts of the third line were instructed not to let retreating troops through. The location of the standards may be an indication that the third vexillation, containing Cohorts 8, 9 and 10, was the least experienced and was only to be committed to the fighting as a last resort.

It may be that the comment about the lack of reconnaissance was made in the light of the Varus Disaster which followed only two years later and was, to some extent, caused by the same thing.

Unfortunately because of the imprecise language used by ancient writers it is generally impossible to quantify how long battles lasted, the Romans would stick at it until the enemy weakened. The Roman assault would steam-roller on, the soldiers hurling their *pila* in turn. With each of the three vexillations taking its turn, there would be a theoretical minimum of twenty-one *pila* thrown for each five feet of front, enough attrition to wear down almost any enemy. Then the Romans would put in 'wedge' assaults to break up the enemy's front. Even then the Romans preferred not to make a general assault as the dressing of the ranks would have been disrupted and control lost. Once the enemy was broken the auxiliaries would take up the pursuit, cheered on by the legionaries. This part of the action was described, again, by Livy: *'When his men grew tired, the consul revived their spirits by putting in reserve cohorts from the second line. A new line was now constituted; fresh troops with unused weapons attacked an exhausted enemy, and first threw them back with a vigorous charge in wedge formation, and then turned them to scattered flight'*.[73]

The question of how the Roman general controlled such a battle is not easy to answer. It would not be difficult to order the wedge assault, but to have the cavalry follow it up at just the right moment would have been much more difficult. The general may well have left such decisions to his subordinate officers. The battlefield options open to the general were to a large degree limited to making his initial dispositions, then signalling the time for certain pre-planned drills and actions to take place. Any decision taken in response to enemy action would have to be left to a subordinate. These planned actions would have been discussed with senior officers before the battle. Then, once the battle had started, the drills would rumble on almost of their own accord. How this worked at the Battle of Pharsalus was described by Caesar: '*Pompey's cavalry thereupon pressed on the more hotly and began to deploy in squadrons and surround our line on its exposed flank. Observing this, Caesar gave the signal to the fourth line which he had formed of single cohorts. They ran forward swiftly to the attack with their standards and charged at Pompey's cavalry with such force that none of them could hold ground. They all turned, and not only gave ground but fled precipitately to the hilltops............At the same time Caesar gave the order to advance to the third line which had done nothing and had stayed in its position up till then. As a result, when fresh and unscathed troops took the place of the weary, while others were attacking from the rear*'.[74] The important point is that Caesar organised his fourth line, and gave its commander his orders, before the battle. He gave a signal for these orders to be carried out by flag during the battle. He could not possibly have organised this special force during the battle. Ordering up the third line was just ordering a well-practiced drill movement, these cohorts had been held back to provide a reserve.

The Second Battle of Cremona, during the campaign of the

Flavians against the Vitellians, in 69 AD, illustrated what could happen if control was lost and the legionaries joined in an enthusiastic pursuit. The Flavian army was camped by Bedriacum, which was 22 miles from Cremona where the Vitellians were. The Flavian advance guard proceded eight miles along the main road, the Postumian Way, and fought a minor battle with the Vitellian cavalry. They pursued the Vitellians for ten miles. By dusk, around 5pm, the Favian legions caught up with the advance guard. They had covered 18 miles since midday. By this time the Vitellian legions had formed up behind their cavalry and the battle lasted all night. At dawn the Vitellians retreated to their camp and the Flavian forces were in a tricky situation: the legionaries were weary having marched 22 miles and fought all night, whereas the Vitellians were either in their camp or in Cremona, eating and resting, soon they would sally out and continue the battle at an advantage. The Flavians were 22 miles away from their camp, and being without their transport, were not able to construct a camp where they were. The situation would have been a worry for the general, but not for the soldiers. Maddened by a desire for booty, they insisted on assaulting the Vitellian camp which, after a hard fight, they occupied and there recovered from their exertions. Three days later they stormed and sacked Cremona, which burned for four days. The battle was a great success for the Flavians, but the risks had been huge.

The fighting, no matter how successful, would produce casualties. The soldiers, naturally, knew this so the efficient functioning of the medical service was vital in maintaining their morale. Also, from the Emperor's point of view, trained soldiers were important and expensive items and had to be cared for and returned to duty as soon as possible, consequently the Romans developed a system that worked very well. Casualties were handled in two stages. What might be termed 'combat medics' (*capsarii*) would set up a field dressing station close behind the rear line of the legion. The casualties would be taken there, if they could not walk, by the muleteers some of which would have their mules with them for that purpose. The medics would carry out any immediately necessary procedures and send back, probably on carts, those that could be expected to live to the hospital which would usually be within the camp. On Trajan's Column the medics are shown in armour, doubtlessly to show that they could fight to defend the wounded if necessary. The Roman army seems to have made a principle of never abandoning its wounded, a concept which was very important to the soldiers. However if, due to a disaster, such as the Battle of Carrhae, this concept could not be maintained the result could be a decisive drop in morale.

The legion really came into its own during a siege, in an assault of this kind the large legionary shield was a necessity. Sieges fall outside the subject being covered in this study, but a campaign based on a siege would show the legion at its best. This was because the legion, being on the strategic offensive, could pick its timing and battleground. It would march towards its objective, erecting marching camps *en route*, the enemy would be forced to attack it but would fail and suffer at the hands of the auxiliaries, finally the legion would undertake the siege.

However legions deploying without their complement of auxiliaries and losing the strategic initiative could find themselves in a vulnerable position, particularly if they could not deploy properly. Chapter Five will give examples of this, but providing that the legions were deployed as appropriate for their training and armament, on the strategic offensive and the tactical defensive, they were almost unbeatable.

Discipline

All armies are coercive organisations designed to force soldiers to obey orders when they are reluctant to. The Roman army was no exception and generals, centurions and other senior ranks were given wide disciplinary powers, also the general corpus of Roman law forced discipline on the soldier. Most Roman laws affecting soldiers covered such subjects as desertion and mutiny and would have been of no interest to the legionary in battle when he would have been a part of a machine with little chance of independent action. However there can be no doubt that laws did help form the general ethos of a legion, and the legionaries were kept in line by the long-term hope of a reasonable standard of living on discharge, and a short-term recognition of the painful and possibly fatal consequences of military discipline.

The disciplinary ethos of the Roman army had passed through two phases before arriving at that for the classic age of the legion. In the early days of the militia army the soldiers knew what they were fighting for and were eager to play their part, obey orders, and get the war over with. After Marius, during the Civil Wars, the soldiers realised, dimly at first, they were important, their voice should be heard, and their interests were not necessarily the same as those of the state. It can be seen that there was a difference between the types of discipline required for these phases. Finally, after he had brought the last civil war to an end, Augustus recreated discipline:

'*He gave the entire Tenth Legion an ignominious discharge because of their insolent behaviour, and when some other legions also demanded their discharge in a similar riotous manner, he disbanded them, withholding the bounty which they would have earned had they continued loyal. If a company* (Cohortes) *broke in battle, Augustus ordered the survivors to draw lots, then executed*

141

every tenth man, and fed the remainder on barley bread instead of the customary wheat ration. Company commanders (Centuriones) *found absent from their posts were sentenced to death, like other ranks* (Manipulares), *and any lesser dereliction of duty earned them one of several degrading punishments – such as being made to stand all day long in front of general headquarters, sometimes wearing tunics without sword-belts, sometimes carrying ten-foot poles, or even sods of turf – as though they had been private soldiers whose task it was to measure out and build the camp ramparts.*

'When the Civil Wars were over, Augustus no longer addressed the troops as 'Comrades' (Commilitones), *but as 'Men'*(Milites); *and had his sons and step-sons follow suit. He thought 'Comrades' too flattering a term: consonant neither with military discipline, nor with peacetime service, nor with the respect due to himself and his family'.*[75]

Some of the Latin terms have been given to illustrate the difficulties of translation. The disbandment of a Tenth Legion is not mentioned elsewhere, however a Tenth Legion was amalgamated with another legion by Octavian in 30 BC to produce the Tenth *Gemina*. This might be the event referred to by Suetonius. The issue of barley instead of wheat would have been very unpopular, the bread produced from it would have been an almost uneatable unleaven crust. However the Roman treasury would have approved, the cost of barley was around a third that of wheat.[76]

As the above quote shows, there were two legal facts that legionaries would bear in mind. One was that if the unit, be it legion, cohort or maniple, failed *en bloc* the survivors could be decimated. In this gruesome punishment each tenth man, selected by lot, was cudgelled to death by the remaining nine. It was often used in the semi-mythological days of the early republic, but would have been difficult to apply in the age of the professional soldier, when the trained legionary was an expensive item. The last known case was Galba's punishment of the partly trained 'Naval' legion in 69 AD, and that case is less than certain.

More certain is Mark Antony's treatment of some troops who had been chased off some siege works during his Parthian campaign of 36 BC. As Plutarch described the occasion: *'Antony, at his return, punished the fugitives by decimation. That is, he divided them into tens; and, in each division, put one to death, on whom the lot happened to fall. Those who escaped had their allowance in barley instead of wheat'.*[77] The issue of barley cannot be taken literally as the Romans were, at that time, desperately short of food of any kind.

Regardless of how often it was carried out the threat of decimation would last at least as long as the Wesern Empire. As late as 408 AD Stilicho used it against some mutineers, so the soldiers involved must have known what to expect.[78]

On a less vicious level, during the Second Punic War the survivors of Cannae, judged as having failed in their duty, were sent to Sicily for the duration. This is the only known example of the Roman use of a punishment posting, but the term could be flexible and during the empire doubtlessly there were many unpopular stations where failing units could find themselves. After the fall of Jerusalem, Titus *'Remembering that while Cestius was in command the Twelfth Legion had given way before the Jews, he banished it from Syria altogether – it had earlier been stationed at Raphanaeae – and sent it away to Melitine, beside the Euphrates between Armenia and Cappadocia'.*[79]

There may be a case for the existence of, if not punishment postings, penal units. There is evidence that some legions owned troupes of gladiators.[80] If this is so then it is possible that, as gladiators were generally held in contempt, refractory soldiers were assigned to such a troupe either for a set period or until their valour and skill-at-arms earned them their return to their maniples. If this was so, it was certainly not a widespread practice, but would have been good for discipline. Alexander the Great certainly had a disciplinary unit, but this was for political criminals

The second legal fact for the legionary to consider was that if he ran away he could find himself condemned to die. The normal Roman procedure was to do this in public, to flog the condemned man then to cut his head off. As Arrius Menander, a contemporary of Septimius Severus, wrote in the Corpus Juris Civilis: '*The first to take flight in battle shall be punished with death in view of the soldiers, by way of example.*'[81]

Military executions, of course, continued long after the end of the Empire, but probably not by the brutal flogging and beheading. This is implied by the case of ten men, who had fled in the face of the enemy during Julian's Persian campaign of 363AD, and may have been the victims of a decimation. Julian seems in general to have been trying to turn the clock back, and Ammianus Marcellinus remarks that these soldiers were '*put to death in conformity with ancient Roman practice*'.[82]

It can be seen that, with legal sanctions against both the unit and the individual, the legionary in the front line must have been in little doubt of the serious consequences of failure.

The Roman disciplinary system can seem brutal, but it should be remembered that in Hellenistic armies, mutineers were apt to be trampled to death by elephants.

Conclusion

As a conclusion to this chapter an attempt will be made to summarize the essential factors that made the legion and the legionary so formidable on the battlefield.

The legion worked so well because the Romans had perfected the essential drills of manoeuvring in column and fighting in line. The individual soldier fought well because:

His task was predictable, so he did not have to worry about the unknown.
His task was reasonable, so he could have faith in his weapons and fighting procedures.
His task was fair, he knew that every man in the legion would play his part.
His task was forced on him, the disciplinary system of the legion would not excuse him the fight.

But all this only obtained while he could fight in file.

Considering the legion at the height of its powers it is not surprising that Vegetius would write: '*It was not by human counsel alone but by divine inspiration as well, in my opinion, that the Romans organized the legions.*'[83]

Notes
1. Appian, *The Civil Wars*, III.42, Penguin Classics, p178
2. *Caesar's Gallic War*, I.20, translated by the Rev FP Long MA, Oxford 1911, p20
3. Vegetius, *Epitome of Military Science*, I.20, translated by NP Milner, Liverpool UP, 2011, p22
4. Vegetius, *Epitome of Military Science*, I.12, translated by NP Milner, Liverpool UP, 2011, p13
5. Livy, *Rome and the Mediterranean*, XXXI.34, Penguin Classics, p54
6. Polybius, *The Rise of the Roman Empire*, VI.37, Penguin Classics, p333

7. *Plutarch's Lives, Caesar*, Translated by the Revs J & W Langhorne. No date, p500
8. Quoted in *Roman Military Law*, CE Brand, University of Texas, 1968, p191
9. Vegetius, *Epitome of Military Science*, I.13, translated by NP Milner, Liverpool UP, 2011, p13
10. Sallust, *Jugurthine War*, 81.1, Penguin Classics, p113
11. The Acts of the Apostles, Chapter 12, Verse 4
12. Ammianus Marcellinus, *The Later Roman Empire*, 17.13, 21.13, 23.5, 26.1, Penguin Classics, p140, 226, 262, 315
13. Dio Cassius, *The Roman History: The Reign of Augustus*, 52.25, Penguin Classics, p108
14. *The Letters of the Younger Pliny*, VI.31, Penguin Classics, p180
15. Appian, *The Civil Wars*, III.5, Penguin Classics, p156
16. Examples:
    Livy, *Rome and the Mediterranean*, XXXIII.7, XXXVI.16, XXXVII.43, XLIV.8, Penguin Classics, p113, 253, 321 and 564
    Tacitus, *The Annals of Imperial Rome*, XIV.34, Penguin Classics, p331
    Tacitus, *The Histories*, II.11, Penguin Classics, p88
    Josephus, *The Jewish War*, Chap 9, Penguin Classics, p159
    Plutarch's Lives, Crassus, Translated by the Revs J & W Langhorne. No date, p383
17. Josephus, *The Jewish War, Excursus III*, Penguin Classics, p378
18. Vegetius, *Epitome of Military Science*, I.26, translated by NP Milner, Liverpool UP, 2011, p26
19. Polybius, *The Rise of the Roman Empire*, VI.24, Penguin Classics, p322
20. Vegetius, *Epitome of Military Science*, I.26, translated by NP Milner, Liverpool UP, 2011, p25
21. Appian *The Civil Wars*, IV.121, Penguin Classics, p269
22. Caesar, *The Civil War*, III.53, Penguin Classics, p133
23. Lucan, *The Civil War*, VII. Line 494, Loeb, p407
24. Florus, *Epitome of Roman History*, I.XLV, Loeb, p205
    Also see *Caesar's Gallic War*, I.52, translated by the Rev FP Long MA, Oxford 1911, p45
25. *Plutarch's Lives, Antony*, Translated by the Revs J & W Langhorne. No date, p646

26. Ammianus Marcellinus, *The Later Roman Empire*, 26.8, Penguin Classics, p328

27. *Caesar's Gallic War*, II.25, translated by the Rev FP Long MA, Oxford 1911, p66

28. *Dionysius of Halicarnassus*, XIV.10, Loeb, Vol VII p275

29. www.livius.org/mo-mt/mogontiacum/mainz_pedestals.html

30. Vegetius, *Epitome of Military Science*, I.14, translated by NP Milner, Liverpool UP, 2011, p15

31. Plutarch, *The Life of Sulla*, 18.6, Loeb, p387

32. Josephus, *The Jewish War*, Chap 17, Penguin Classics, p273

33. Vegetius, *Epitome of Military Science*, II.25, translated by NP Milner, Liverpool UP, 2011, p59

34. Diodorus Siculus, *The Library of History, XII.64*, Loeb, p63.
    Livy, *The Early History of Rome*, IV,30, Penguin Classics, p301

35. *The Complete Dead Sea Scrolls in English, The War Scroll, VI*, translated by Geza Vermes, Penguin Classics, 2011, p171

36. Vegetius, *Epitome of Military Science*, II.17, translated by NP Milner, Liverpool UP, 2011, p50

37. Ammianus Marcellinus, *The Later Roman Empire*, 13.5, Penguin Classics, p137

38. Tacitus, *The Annals of Imperial Rome*, XIV.34, Penguin Classics, p330

39. Polybius, *The Rise of the Roman Empire*, XV.13, Penguin Classics, p476

40. '*Tribunos militum circum se habebat et primorum ordinum centuriones*'. Caesar, *Gallic War*, 5.37. Read in www.penelope.uchicago.edu/Thayer/E/Roman/Texts/
    '*Tribunos ac primorum ordinum centuriones*', Tacitus, *Annals*, 1.61. Read in www.sacred-texts.com/cla/tac/

41. Livy, *Rome and the Mediterranean*, XLIV.33, Penguin Classics, p584

42. Arrian, *Tactical Handbook*, 27, Ares publishers, p76

43. Appian, *The Civil Wars*, II.63, Penguin Classics, p102

44. The Book of the Prophet Isaiah, Chapter 9, verse 5

45. Caesar's text was '*edicit per ordines nequis miles ab signis IIII pedes longius procederet*',
    www.sacred-texts.com. A clear reference to passing

orders along the ranks

46.   Vegetius, *Epitome of Military Science*, II.22, translated by NP Milner, Liverpool UP, 2011, p56

47.   Dio Cassius, *The Roman History: The Reign of Augustus*, 51.9, Penguin Classics, p70

48.   This expression was used by Caesar in his *Gallic War 1.25: 'Romani conversa signa bipertito intulerunt'*, translated as; 'The Romans faced about and advanced to the attack in two divisions'. www.sacred-texts.com

49.   *Plutarch's Lives, Lucullus*, Translated by the Revs J & W Langhorne. No date, p357

50.   *Caesar's Gallic War*, IV.25, translated by the Rev FP Long MA, Oxford 1911, p111

51.   Appian, *The Civil Wars*, I.58, Penguin Classics, p32
Ammianus Marcellinus, *The Later Roman Empire*, 16.12, Penguin Classics, p112

52.   Appian, *The Civil Wars*, II.95, Penguin Classics, p120

53.   Examples of these: Polyaenus,
The Stratagems of War, VIII,IX,2, Ares Publishers, p312
Livy, *The War with Hannibal*, XXVI.5, Penguin Classics, p361
Livy, *Rome and Italy*, VI.8, Penguin Classics, p47
Tacitus, *The Histories*, III.17, Penguin Classics, p155
Frontinus, *Stratagems*, II,viii,4-5, Loeb, p179
Plutarch's Lives, Caesar, Translated by the Revs J & W Langhorne. No date, p513
Plutarch's Lives, Sylla, Translated by the Revs J & W Langhorne. No date, p328
Plutarch's Lives, Marcus Brutus, Translated by the Revs J & W Langhorne. No date, p686
Florus, *Epitome of Roman History*, II.XV, Loeb, p303

54.   *Plutarch's Lives, Caesar*, Translated by the Revs J & W Langhorne. No date, p509

55.   Frontinus, *Stratagems*, II,viii,8, Loeb, p179, also Livy, *The Early History of Rome*, Penguin Classics, p321

56.   Examples of these:
Frontinus, *Stratagems*, II,viii,1-3, Loeb, p177-179
Livy, *The Early History of Rome*, IV.30, Penguin Classics, p301
The trope continues into later military history. At the Battle of Castagnaro, in 1387AD, Sir John Hawkwood is believed to have thrown his baton into the enemy ranks

(Steven Cooper, *Sir John Hawkwood*, Pen & Sword, 2008, p138), and at the Battle of Fribourg, 1644AD, the Duc d'Enghien did similar (W Fitz Patrick, *The Great Conde*, London, 1873, Vol I, p75). Unfortunately history is silent as to if the standards or batons were ever retrieved.

57. Appian, *The Civil Wars*, I.87, Penguin Classics, p47
58. Ammianus Marcellinus, *The Later Roman Empire*, 26.9, Penguin Classics, p330
59. E Gibbon, *The History of the Decline and Fall of the Roman Empire*, chapter XXIX, based on Orosius and Zosimus
60. *Dionysius of Halicarnassus*, XX.1, Loeb, Vol VII p391. Enyalius was a version of Mars
61. Caesar, *The Spanish War*, 28, Penguin Classics, The Civil War, p279
62. Tacitus, *The Histories*, I.41, Penguin Classics, p46
63. Appian, The Civil Wars, I.58, Penguin Classics, p32
64. Livy, *Rome and the Mediterranean*, XXXV.5, Penguin Classics, p199
65. Vegetius, *Epitome of Military Science*, II.17, translated by NP Milner, Liverpool UP, 2011, p50
66. Tacitus, *The Agricola and the Germania*, 35, Penguin Classics, p86
67. Ammianus Marcellinus, *The Later Roman Empire*, 12.42, Penguin Classics, p112
68. The Gospel According to St Luke, Chapter 8, verse 30
69. Ammianus Marcellinus, *The Later Roman Empire*, 12.48, Penguin Classics, p113
70. Livy, *The War with Hannibal*, XXX.34, Penguin Classics, p662
71. Josephus, *The Jewish War,* Chap 20, Penguin Classics, p314
72. Velleius Paterculus, *Compendium of Roman History*, II.cxii,4, Loeb, p283
73. Livy, *Rome and the Mediterranean*, XXXIV.15, Penguin Classics, p156
74. Caesar, *The Civil War*, III.94, Penguin Classics, p153
75. Suetonius, *The Twelve Caesars*, II.24, Penguin Classics, p62, Latin terms from the Loeb translation
76. The Revelation of St John the Divine, Chapter 6, Verse 6
77. *Plutarch's Lives, Antony*, Translated by the Revs J & W

Langhorne. No date, p644

78. Zosimus Historicus, *Nova Historia*, 5.156, no publisher or date

79. Josephus, *The Jewish War,* Chap 22, Penguin Classics, p340

80. T Wiedemann, *Emperors and Gladiators*, Routledge, 1992, p45

81. Quoted in *Roman Military Law,* CE Brand, University of Texas, 1968, p185

82. Ammianus Marcellinus, *The Later Roman Empire*, 24.3, Penguin Classics, p273

83. Vegetius, *Epitome of Military Science*, II.20, translated by NP Milner, Liverpool UP, 2011, p55

Chapter 4: The Legion and its Enemies

Barbarians

The defensive tactics described in the previous chapter were those appropriate for defeating barbarians. This class of enemy was, compared to the Romans, in general poorly armed, and being limited in organisation and discipline was only capable of two modes of action. One was long range harassment with missile weapons, the other was the assault. For the assault they would come on in a disorganised mass and hurl themselves on the legion which, providing only that it could deploy on a reasonable battlefield, would wear the enemy down with better weapons and through the drill of swapping vexillations. The barbarians, being tribal, were led by their chieftains. These had to lead so were the men most likely to be killed and when this happened, their followers would tend to fade away, this was the cause of the barbarians' lack of staying power. When the barbarians were seen to weaken the Romans would put in a short, sharp counter-attack to shatter their confidence. Then, providing the legion was backed up by auxiliary light infantry and cavalry, the victory was won. In other phases of the campaign the legion would be at risk if without a proper force of auxiliaries.

In view of all this, it can be seen what a surprise the Varus disaster was to the Romans.

The Macedonian Phalanx

The great clashes the Romans had with Macedonian-type phalanxes occurred during the republican period before the legion took on its final form, but even so they show the mechanism of the legionaries in the attack. Appendix One describes the formations the phalanx used.

A phalangite, with his long pike (*sarissa*) could fight, as it were, in one direction only and had to be a part of a formed unit. He needed both hands to manage his pike so the only shield he could carry would be a little smaller than that of the hoplite, it was strapped to his left arm. Phalangites, at least the leading ranks, were well armoured and did not fear missiles. These ranks were made up of the best soldiers, the rear ranks of less experienced and badly equipped men. The consequence of this was that, as the leading ranks had done their bit and filed to the rear, so poorly trained and badly armoured phalangites came to the front and the phalanx became progressively vulnerable to missiles. Another consequence was that the rear of the phalanx, and to a degree its flanks, were much more vulnerable than would have been expected.

The phalanx, provided it could retain its order, was a major problem for the legion. The *pila* did not have much effect of the heavily armoured front ranks, and the legionaries could not get close enough to use their swords, as illustrated by Livy in his account of the assault on Atrax during the Second Macedonian War: '*The Macedonians in their close array thrust out in front of them spears of enormous length: while the Romans discharged their javelins to no effect against a formation resembling a* testudo *constructed of close-packed shields. Then the Romans drew their swords, but they could not get to close quarters, nor could they chop off the ends of the spears, and if they did cut or break off any of them, the broken remnant of the spear was itself sharp and combined with the points of the unbroken shafts to make up a kind of palisade*'.[1]

The best hope for the legion was that the phalanx could be

attacked from the rear or flank, but for the troops in contact with the front of the phalanx their chance would only come if, due to obstacles or unevenness of the ground, or uneven resistance along the front causing sub-units to advance at different rates, gaps appeared in the ranks of the phalanx and a wedge assault could immediately drive into it. When that could be done effectively the phalanx was lost. As Plutarch wrote about the Battle of Cynoscephalae when the phalanx's front was starting to break up: *'they could not keep in the close form of a phalanx, nor line their ranks to any great depth, but were forced to fight man to man, in heavy and unwieldy armour. For the Macedonian phalanx is like an animal of enormous strength, while it keeps in one body, and preserves its union of locked shields; but when that is broken, each particular soldier loses of its force, as well because of the form of his armour, as because the strength of each consists rather in his being a part of the whole, than in his single person'.*[2]

The *pila* could defeat the phalanx if its order could be disrupted. At the Battle of Magnesia when the light troops were driven into the phalanx. *'There, as soon as the ranks were disordered and the use of the long spears – the Macedonians call them* sarissae *– was prevented because their comrades were rushing among them, the Roman legions advanced and hurled their spears into the disordered enemy'.*[3] Even so the phalanx was shot at for a considerable time before it retreated.

The legion-phalanx clash is well described by Livy in his well-known account of the Battle of Pydna, 168 BC: *'The strength of the phalanx is irresistible when it is close-packed and bristling with extended spears; but if by attacks at different point you force the troops to swing around their spears, unwieldy as they are by reason of their length and weight, they become entangled in a disorderly mass; and further, the noise of any commotion on the flank or in the rear throws them into confusion, and then the whole formation collapses. That is what happened in this battle, when the phalanx was forced to meet the Romans who were attacking in small groups, with the Macedonian line broken at many points. The Romans kept infiltrating their files at every place where a gap offered. If they had made a frontal attack with their whole line against an orderly phalanx, the Romans would have impaled themselves on the spears and would not have withstood the dense formation.* '[4] The possibility of the pikes becoming *entangled in a disorderly mass* is a comment on how important a high standard of drill was to a phalanx.

It is quite possible that this action was a bit more desperate than Livy's account suggests. Plutarch's account runs: '*The Romans, who engaged the phalanx, being unable to break it, Salius a Pelignian officer, snatched the ensign of his company and threw it among the enemy. Hereupon, the Pelignians, rushing forward to recover it, for the Italians looked upon it as a great crime and disgrace to abandon their standard, a dreadful conflict and slaughter on both sides ensued. The Romans attempting to cut the pikes of the Macedonians asunder with their swords, to beat them back with their shields, or to put them by with their hands, but the Macedonians, holding them steady with both hands, pierced their adversaries through their armour, for neither shield nor corslet was proof against the pike. The Pelignians, and Marrucinians were thrown headlong down, who without any sort of discretion, or rather with a brutal fury, had exposed themselves to wounds, and run upon certain death. The first line thus cut in pieces, those that were behind were forced to give back, and though they did not fly, yet they retreated towards Mount Olocrus. Aemilius seeing this, rent his clothes, as Posidonius tells us. He was reduced almost to despair, to find that part of his men had retired, and that the rest declined the combat with the phalanx which, by reason of the pikes that*

154

defended it on all sides like a rampart, appeared impenetrable and invincible. But as the unevenness of the ground and the large extent of the front would not permit their bucklers to be joined through the whole, he observed several interstices and openings in the Macedonian line; as it happens in great armies, according to the different efforts of the combatants, who in one part press forward, and in another are forced to give back. For this reason, he divided his troops, with all possible expedition, into platoons, which he ordered to throw themselves into the void spaces of the enemy's front; and so, not to engage with the whole at once, but to make many impressions at the same time in different parts. These orders being given by Aemilius to the officers, and by the officers to the soldiers, they immediately made their way between the pikes, wherever there was an opening which was no sooner done, than some took the enemy in flank, where they were quite exposed, while others fetched a compass, and attacked them in the rear; thus was the phalanx soon broken, and its strength, which depended upon one united effort, was no more. When they came to fight man with man, and party with party, the Macedonians had only short swords to strike the long shields of the Romans, that reached from head to foot, and slight bucklers to oppose to the Roman swords, which, by reason of their weight and the force with which they were managed, pierced through all their armour to the bodies; so that they maintained their ground with difficulty, and in the end were entirely routed.[5]

Plutarch's account of Aemilius reorganising his troops during a battle is highly improbable; it is much more likely that Aemilius was claiming credit for what was happening of its own accord. The Romans had taken a great deal of trouble to re-enlist old soldiers who had seen plenty of action in the irregular fighting in Spain and other wars. They would have been used to fighting in small units and would have provided the initiative and leadership. As

155

previously noted, command at sub-century level is not fully understood.

The soldiers in the first part of this narrative, Pelignians, and Marrucinians, were Italian allies. The implication here is that they were serving as light troops.

In later years, when the *carroballistae* were widely issued, these weapons would have proven lethal to a phalanx, but by then the age of the phalanx had passed. There is, though, one early action which is worth considering. A passage from Plutarch's description of the Battle of Chaeronea (86 BC) has already been given (Chapter 3, note 31) to illustrate the location of Roman missile troops. The passage mentions the phalanx being hit by *'fiery bolts and the javelins which the Romans in the rear ranks plied unsparingly'*. The significance of this passage is that shortly before the battle, Sulla's troops had laid siege to and captured, the Piraeus, and destroyed the Athenian ship yards so it can be presumed that they had some siege engines and plenty of bitumen and other flammable materials to produce *'fiery bolts'*. Defining the projectiles as bolts indicates that the engines were of the *ballista* type presumably firing bolts with rags wrapped round them, daubed with bitumen and lit just before the moment of firing. Also the Romans could reasonably predict where the Pontic phalanx would attack, so could move their siege engines into position to counter it. The system seems to have worked well, as Plutarch wrote it *'threw them into confusion and drove them back'*. Unfortunately he gives no indication as to if these engines could be moved during the battle. In view of all this it seems that the Romans did attack a phalanx with *ballistae* in 86 BC but after that it took a surprisingly long time for the *carroballista* system to be developed.

Other Legions

As Rome was the only power to use legions, fighting between legions could only occur during a civil war and civil wars can be unpredictable. The reason for this is that factors concerning the soldiers' sentiments and prejudices can be as important as the usual military virtues such as courage, skill and endurance. It is against this background that legions fought each other, and there were two ways they could go about it.

In one case the opposing cohorts would march up to within a few yards of each other, halt and throw their *pila*, then rather gingerly start fencing. Alternatively the *pilum* phase could be ignored in favour of an instant rough-house.

The first option was demonstrated at the Battle of Pharsalus, 48 BC. There was a definite halt before the fighting. Caesar put what may be called a positive spin on it: '*Our men, on the signal, ran forward with* pila *levelled; but when they observed that Pompey's men were not running to meet them, thanks to the practical experience and training they had had in earlier battles they checked their charge and halted about half-way, so as not to approach worn out. Then after a short interval they renewed the charge, threw their* pila *and, as ordered by Caesar, quickly drew their swords.*'[6] Actually it would have been difficult to throw a *pilum* while advancing at the double, a short halt would have been necessary.

This short halt is more poetically described by Lucan. '*When they had traversed at speed the ground that delayed the fiat of destiny, and were parted only by a little space, each looked to see where his own javelin would light, or whose hand on the other side destiny threatened to use against him. That they might learn what horrors they were about to commit, they saw their fathers' faces over against them and their brothers' weapons close beside them; but they cared not to shift their ground. Nevertheless a numbness froze each bosom and the blood gathered cold at each heart, from the shock to natural affection; and whole companies long held their* pila *in rest with rigid muscles.'*[7]

Clearly the legionaries of Caesar and Pompey did not regard each other as natural enemies, which is not surprising as troops had been transferred between the two commands. But then at that time civil war was still a novelty. This reluctant warfare may be contrasted with the more full-blooded version demonstrated in the Mutina campaign of 43 BC and described by Appian: *'Thus fired by anger and ambition they fell on each other in the belief that this battle was more their own concern than their commanders'. Because of their experience, they raised no battle-cry, which would have terrified neither side, nor did any of them utter a sound as they fought, whether they were winning or losing. Since the marshes and ditches gave them no chance of making outflanking movements or charging, and they were unable to push each other back, they were locked together with their swords as if in a wrestling contest. Every blow found a target, but instead of cries there were only wounds, and men dying, and groans. If a man fell he was immediately carried away and another took his place. They had no need of encouragement or cheering on, because each man's experience made him his own commanding officer. When they were tired, they separated for a few moments to recover as if they were engaged in training exercises, and then grappled with each other again. When the new recruits arrived they were amazed to see this going on with such discipline and silence.'*[8]

This description is similar to a later one given by Tacitus concerning events in 69 AD: *'On the high road, Vitellians and Orthonians fought hand-to-hand, throwing the weight of their bodies and shield-bosses against each other. The usual discharge of javelins was scrapped, and swords and axes used to pierce helmets and armour. Knowing each other, watched by their comrades, they fought the fight that was to settle the whole campaign.'*[9]

Clearly times and sentiments had changed quickly after Caesar's day. One reason for this would have been the increasing size of the empire. This resulted in legions being stationed for many decades large distances from some other legions consequently becoming almost foreign to them. Another reason was the increasingly mercenary nature of the army, the legionaries would fight anyone for money.

However there is another possible interpretation of these events. Perhaps the soldiers, in a spirit of reciprocity, were not really trying to kill each other. Perhaps they were just shoulder barging each other, as they would have done on many a training exercise, and putting on a show for their officers and pay-masters, and gullible civilians. Certainly the silence and lack of *pila* are suspicious, and there were other cases throughout the Civil Wars when operations were hampered by veterans fraternizing. Certainly the non-lethal interpretation was hinted at by Appian when he mentioned '*training exercises*'. Civil wars can be very unpredictable!

Throughout the classic age of the legion, artillery became progressively more important, so it was inevitable that, as legions were defensive organisations, in legion vs legion actions the artillery would come to dominate, to some extent replacing the *pila*, its bolts passing easily through the legionaries' shields. In his description of the Second Battle of Cremona, 69 AD, Tacitus wrote: '*After relieving the Seventh, they drove the enemy back, only to be driven back themselves. The reason for this was that the Vitellians had concentrated their artillery upon the highway so as to command an unobstructed field of fire over the open ground. Their shooting had at first been sporadic, and the shots had struck the vineprops without hurting the enemy. The Sixteenth Legion had an enormous field-piece which hurled massive stones. These were now mowing down the opposing front-line, and would have inflicted extensive havoc but for an act of heroism on the part of two soldiers. They concealed their identity by catching up shields from the fallen, and severed the tackle by which the engine was operated. They were killed immediately and so their names have perished, but that the deed was done is beyond question.*

Neither side had had the advantage until, in the middle of the night, the moon rose, displaying – and deceiving – the combatants. But the light favoured the Flavians, being behind them; on their side the shadows of horses and men were exaggerated, and the enemy fire fell short though the gunlayers imagined that they were on target. But the Vitellians were brilliantly illuminated by the light shining full in their faces, and so without realizing it provided an easy mark for an enemy aiming from what were virtually concealed positions.'[10]

Dio Cassius recounts how fierce the fighting was initially, but also how it slowed overnight. '*Again one soldier would have a private conversation with an opponent: "Comrade, fellow-citizen, what are we doing? Why are we fighting? Come over to my side." "No, indeed! You come to my side." But what is there surprising about this, considering that when the women of the city in the course of the night brought food and drink to give to the soldiers of Vitellius, the latter, after eating and drinking themselves, passed the supplies on to their antagonists? One of them would call out the name of his adversity (for they practically all knew one another and were well acquainted) and would say: "Comrade, take and eat this; I give you, not a sword, but bread".'*[11]

The fighting seems to have been winding down when a

misunderstanding gave both sides the impression that Flavian reinforcements were arriving, and the Vitellians retreated to their camp and Cremona. A few days later soldiers of both armies joined in sacking Cremona.

The incident with the two soldiers showed that the front must have been fluid and not one formed by serried ranks of legionaries. The impression given by Tacitus is that in some phases of the battle the legionaries did little more than from a guard around the artillery and, if so, this would illustrate the high-point of *ballista* tactics.

Because of lack of information generalisations are difficult but it seems that after Trajan, to an extent, the use of *carrobalistae* faded away. This may have been due to training difficulties but, as *ballistae* stayed in service on fortifications, it could be that as the range of personal weapons, like *manuballistae*, improved so the *carroballistae* horses (or mules) became too vulnerable to use on the battlefield.

Cavalry

Cavalry may be divided into two types, light and heavy. In ancient times the great majority of cavalry were light, which is to say, their principal use was in scouting and other non-battlefield roles, on the battlefield they depended mainly on missile weapons.

A legion in battle formation had little to fear from light cavalry, but the sad fact is that if light cavalry could not hurt the legion, the legion could not hurt the cavalry.

On the other hand, if light cavalry could catch the legionaries before they deployed, so without a continuous front, the cavalry could surge round behind the maniples and attack them from flanks and rear, and easily destroy them. The same was true if the cavalry could outflank the legion as happened to the Roman left wing at the battle of Magnesia, in late 190 or early 189 BC.

The standard cavalry tactic was to gallop up close to the infantry, hurl a javelin and wheel away. If this could be done often enough and well enough the infantry should start to show signs of disorganisation. Once the infantry's formation was broken the cavalry would be in among it, lashing out with their swords. Fear of disorder was the basis of Caesar's concern at Ruspina, mentioned earlier, when his men were attacked by Moorish cavalry.

The only formation available to a legion was to double the shields of the front rank only, producing a shield wall the legionaries could see over and over which they could jab at the cavalrymen with their *pila*. Throwing the *pila*, because of their weight and short range would not have been effective enough to compensate for the loss of these important weapons, and jabbing at the horses would not have been that effective due to the heads of the *pila* being so easily bent. It would have been impossible to handle a *pilum* like a real pike because that would require both hands, and the legionaries had to manage their shields. As has been seen, losing a shield was a serious offence in the Roman army.

This tactic of jabbing at the cavalrymen was, presumably, according to Appian, what Caesar meant on the day of the Battle of Pharsalus when he instructed some cohorts to *'thrust their spears directly in the faces of their opponents.'*[12] This tactic at Pharsalus is mentioned twice by Plutarch, by Polyaenus, and by Frontinus who wrote: *'Since in the army of Pompey there was a large force of Roman cavalry, which by its skill in arms wrought havoc among the soldiers of Gaius Caesar, the latter ordered his troops to aim with their swords at the faces and eyes of the enemy. He thus forced the enemy to avert their faces and retire.* '[13] Some of this may be silly, but the germ of the idea is there.

It is of interest that Appian refers to the legionaries' weapons as spears. He wrote in Greek and it is just possible that he actually meant *pila*, but if not then this would hint that there was still a vestige left of the Polybian *triarii* in the legionary organisation. At Pharsalus Caesar took one cohort from the rear rank of each of his legions, this gave him 3,000 of his '*bravest*' men, armed with spears, which would be a fair description of the *triarii*.

As it became common for archers, and other missile troops, to stand behind the legionary maniples, it may be that when the cavalry attacked and the shield wall was raised, archers would run down between the legionary files to shoot over the shields. The most effective light cavalry were the Parthian mounted archers, but even these would have been inferior to foot archers. However, as will be seen in the next chapter, at Carrhae the Romans could not mount an effective defence against mounted archers, so either their army did not contain enough missile troops, or appropriate tactics were not adopted.

It could be that the comparative helplessness of the legion against cavalry and the generally poor state of archery were among the driving forces behind the increase in the number of missile troops, and the development of the legion's artillery component. By 69 AD this component was fully developed, each legion having a nominal 54 *carroballistae*. They were excellent anti-cavalry weapons and it can be assumed that their basic tactic was to trot up behind the deployed centuries, speak to the centurions who would order the legionaries to go down on one knee, giving the 'gunners' a good field of fire over the soldiers' heads. By around this time the Romans were using caltrops to slow down the enemy cavalry. It is quite possible that numbers of caltrops were carried on the *ballista* carts. The first known use of caltrops was in the First Battle of Bedriacum, in 69 AD:

> '*On the first day Otho was victor but on the second Vitelius. For he had during the night strewn the ground with three-pronged irons. And in the morning, after they had drawn up in order of battle, when Vitellius feigned flight Otho pursued after them with this troops. And they reached the place on which the irons were strewn. Then were the horses lamed, and it was impossible either for the horses or for the men to extricate themselves. And the soldiers of Vitellius, who had turned back, slew all who lay there. But Otho saw what had befallen and killed himself*'.[14]

A successful use of caltrops, in 217AD, was recounted by Herodian: '*But when the fighting came to close quarters, the Romans easily defeated the barbarians; for when the swarms of Parthian cavalry and hordes of camel riders were mauling them, the Romans pretended to retreat and then they threw down caltrops and other keen-pointed iron devices. Covered by the sand, these were invisible to the horsemen and the camel riders and were fatal to the animals. The horses, and particularly the tender-footed camels, stepped on these devices and, falling, threw their riders. As long as they are mounted on horses and camels, the barbarians in those regions fight bravely, but if they dismount or are thrown, they are very easily captured; they cannot stand up to hand-to-hand fighting*'.[15]

The disadvantage of caltrops was, of course, that they were static and as will be seen in the next chapter the legion became vulnerable to cavalry when it was on the move.

If caltrops were static then earthworks were even more so, but they could be effective against cavalry. They were, though, seldom used against cavalry on the battlefield because cavalry, to be most effective, will be unpredictable and digging earthworks involved predicting where the cavalry would come. Also they were difficult to use because that can take some time to dig, and during that time the diggers were vulnerable. The soldiers of Sulla found themselves in such a situation at Orchomenos in 85 BC during the wars against Mithridates. The Pontic cavalry caught them at work and they started to panic and run for the safety of the camp, but it was Sulla's finest moment, he *'leaped from his horse, seized one of the ensigns, and pushed through the middle of the fugitives towards the enemy, crying out, "Here, Romans, is the bed of honour I am to die in. Do you, when you are asked where you betrayed your general, remember to say, it was at Orchomenus." These words stopped them in their flight'*[16](Perhaps they sounded better in Latin).

Possible the most successful battlefield application of an anti-cavalry ditch was by the troops of Clodius Albinus at the Battle of Lugdunum in 197 AD during his war with Septimius Severus. Albinus lost the battle, but it started well for him, his *'troops on the right wing, having concealed trenches in front of them and pits covered over with earth on the surface, advanced as far as these pitfalls and hurled their javelins at long range; then, instead of continuing to go forward, they turned back, as if frightened, with the purpose of drawing their foes in pursuit. And this is exactly what happened. ...... Great, indeed, was the loss of life among both these and those who had fallen into the trenches, as horses and men perished in wild confusion.'*[17]

So far this section has considered only light cavalry but, at Carrhae in 53 BC, the Romans met heavy cavalry, armoured horsemen known as cataphracts. They had been met previously, at Tigranocerta in 69 BC, but it seems were hardly noticed.

Cataphracts were described by Ammianus Marcellinus as *'mailed cavalrymen, the so-called Ironclads, wearing masks and equipped with cuirasses and belts of steel; they seemed more like statues polished by the hand of Praxiteles than living men. Their limbs were entirely covered by a garment of thin circular plates fitted to the curves of the body, and so cunningly articulated that it adapted itself to any movement the wearer needed to make'.*[18] Roman cataphracts were known as *clibanarii*, a name which derives from *clibanus*, a baking oven, a comment on the discomfort endured on hot days by these soldiers, however because of their armour, and because many of their horses were also armoured, they were immune to arrows and most javelins.

The offensive weapon of a cataphract was a pike; longer than a spear, it took two hands to handle, its Greek term translated as 'barge-pole'. Cataphracts worked best in combination with mounted archers, their tactic was to trot up to the Romans in a line and jab at them with this pike while they were being subjected to a storm of arrows. They would be effective only if they retained perfect order. If the Roman line held firm then they could send out light infantry to attack the cataphracts who, with their long pikes, could not defend themselves against infantry who were trying to hamstring their horses or knock the riders out of their saddles with clubs, and they became more vulnerable the more tired their overloaded horses were. These light infantry would, in their turn, become vulnerable to Parthian mounted archers so would need to be backed up by foot archers. In 69 BC, in the fighting before Tigranocerta, Lucullus when attacked by cataphracts *'ordered his men not to make any use of their javelins, but to come to close action, and to aim their blows at their enemies' legs and thighs, in which parts alone they were not armed.'*[19] They could not wear leg armour because of the difficulty of riding without stirrups.

As with all cavalry, the Romans could cope with cataphracts providing they could maintain an unbroken front line, and keep their flanks covered.

The cataphracts were the forerunners of the armoured knights that dominated European warfare during the Middle Ages, but they could not develop their full potential because the great *destriers* require had not yet been bred, and stirrups had not been invented, light cavalry could fight without them, heavy cavalry could not.

Notes

1.   Livy, *Rome and the Mediterranean*, XXXII.17, Penguin Classics, p84
2.   *Plutarch's Lives, Titus Quinctius Flaminius*, Translated by the Revs J & W Langhorne. No date, p268
3.   Livy, *Rome and the Mediterranean*, XXXVII.42, Penguin Classics, p320
4.   *Plutarch's Lives, Paulus Aemilius*, Translated by the Revs J & W Langhorne. No date, p194
5.   Livy, *Rome and the Mediterranean*, XLIV.41, Penguin Classics, p594-595
6.   Caesar, *The Civil War*, III.93, Penguin Classics, p152-153
7.   Lucan, *The Civil War*, VII. Line 462, Loeb, p403-405
8.   Appian, *The Civil War*, III.68, Penguin Classics, p192-193
9.   Tacitus, *The Histories*, II.42, Penguin Classics, p106
10.   Tacitus, *The Histories*, III.23, Penguin Classics, p159
11.   Dio Cassius, *Roman History*, LXIV.13, Loeb vol VIII, p241
12.   Appian, *The Civil War*, II.76, Penguin Classics, p109
13.   Frontinus, *Stratagems,* IV,vii,32, Loeb, p323
14.   Josephus, *The Jewish War*. This quote is from the Slavonic text, derived from Josephus's original Aramaic version, and is not widely available. This section was reproduced in Rupert Furneaux, *The Other Side of the Story*, Cassell & Co, 1953, p109
15.   Herodian of Antioch, *History of the Roman Empire*, IV.XV.2, University of California Press, p133.
16.   *Plutarch's Lives, Sylla*, Translated by the Revs J & W Langhorne. No date, p328
17.   Dio Cassius, *Roman History*, LXXVI.6, Loeb vol IX,

p209

18. Ammianus Marcellinus, *The Later Roman Empire*, 16.10.4, Penguin Clasics, p100

19. *Plutarch's Lives, Lucullus*, Translated by the Revs J & W Langhorne. No date, p358

Chapter 5: The Legionary on Campaign

Mobility and Security

The basic fighting technique of the Roman legion has been described, a technique which brought almost unbroken success on the battlefield. This chapter will consider how the legionary was brought to the battlefield, which is to say, Roman Marching, and the problems that had to be overcome.

During the classic age of the legion the Roman army was usually employed aggressively against foreign enemies. A standard campaign would involve the Roman army marching on the enemy's capital city, or something else that he must defend, thus forcing the enemy to attack. In such a situation the legions, being all but unbreakable in defence, could expect victory.

If the enemy was of a low degree of civilisation and had no cities worth attacking, the Romans would try to goad him into fighting by destroying his crops, requisitioning his animals, destroying any buildings and massacring or enslaving his population. This did not guarantee success. In the years before the Varus disaster the Romans campaigned extensively in Germany but actually achieved little.

Naturally when the army was marching through enemy territory the essential requirement was for security and this was achieved by training and by adhering to standard procedures which centred on marching, the baggage train and marching camps.

The Romans took marching seriously. Marching, with full

pack, was a part of basic training and Vegetius says that recruits were sent of training marches of twenty miles three times a month, but that did not involve setting up a camp which could halve the distance marched. An example of such training marches was provided by Galba, who was to become Emperor for a few days in 69 AD. He took over as governor of Greater Germany and sent his troops on manoeuvres. When the Emperor Caligula inspected the troops '*Galba scored a personal success by doubling for twenty miles, shield on shoulder, beside the Emperor's chariot, while continuing to direct manoeuvres*'.[1] Galba was obviously very fit, he might have been carrying his shield for signalling purposes. His soldiers slogged along repeating the doggerel, '*disce miles militare, Galba est, non Gaetulicus*'.[2] ie 'soldier, learn soldiering, Galba has replaced Gaetulicus'.

The soldier in marching order carried upwards of 100lbs, though this figure is an approximation and would vary with the number of days' rations being carried and what tools were carried by the *contubernium* mule. It was mostly made up of weapons and his personal kit. The mule would carry *contubernium* kit, like a grindstone, tent and stakes for the camp rampart. The *contubernium* mules may be termed first line transport. If the march was non-tactical the *contubernium* and its mule would plod along together on the march making a compact group, and the ten *contubernia* of a century would follow their *signum*, carried with the centurion's command group, which would keep them all together. However, as will be seen, if the march was tactical the mules would be separate from the fighting men.

The legion would have a supply train consisting of carts, usually two-wheeled. They would carry extra rations, for men and beasts, tools, senior officers' kit and the wounded. These carts may be termed second line transport, and keeping second line transport down to a minimum was one reason why, during the greater part of the age of the legion, soldiers were not allowed to marry.

The soldier in fighting order carried only the weapons and armour he needed on the battlefield. As can be seen the soldiers could not march and fight at the same time, and this was the basis of the importance of marching camps. These were temporary fortifications in the image of legionary forts and they provided security for unloading the mules and passing the night. Because of their temporary nature very few have survived and this is unfortunate because they were basic to Roman warfare.

At the start of the campaign, when marching out of winter quarters, and subsequently when marching out of a marching camp, the same procedure was followed and was described by Polybius. '*As soon as the first signal is given, the men strike their tents and assemble their baggage, but no soldier may strike or set it up until this has first been done for the tribunes and the consul. At the second signal they load the baggage on to the pack animals, and at the third the leading maniples must advance and set the whole camp in motion*'.[3] A further detail was added by Josephus, after the third signal '*the announcer, standing on the right of the supreme commander, asks three times in their native language whether they are ready for war. They three times shout loudly and with enthusiasm 'Ready', hardly waiting for the question, and filled with a kind of martial fervour raise their right arms as they shout. Then they step off, all marching silently and in good order, as on active service every man keeping his place in the column*'.[4] Perhaps the shouting only took place at the start of the campaign.

Naturally the order of march was important and very different from the non-tactical procession already described. Though there would have been variations, the best description is given, again, by Josephus: '*Vespasian, eager to invade Galilee himself, set out from Ptolemais with his army arranged in the usual Roman marching order. The light-armed auxiliaries and bowmen formed the vanguard, with orders to repel sudden enemy rushes and reconnoitre woods suspected of concealing ambushes. Next came a body of heavy-armed Roman troops, mounted and unmounted. These were followed by ten men from every century carrying, besides their own kit, the instruments for marking out the camp-site. After them came roadmakers to straighten out bends in the highway, level rough surfaces, and cut down obstructive woods, so that the army would not be exhausted by laborious marching. In the rear of these the personal baggage of the commander and his senior officers was concentrated under the protection of a strong cavalry force, behind which rode Vespasian himself with the cream of his horse and foot and a body of spearmen. Next came the legionary cavalry; for each legion has its own troop of 120 horse. These were followed by the mules that carried the Batterers and other mechanical devices. After them came the generals, cohort-commanders, and tribunes, with a bodyguard of picked troops; next the standards enclosing the Eagle which is at the head of every legion, as the king of birds and most fearless of all: this they regard as the symbol of empire and portend of victory, no matter who opposes them. The sacred emblems were followed by the trumpeters, and in their wake came the main body, shoulder to shoulder, six men abreast, accompanied as always by a centurion to maintain the formation. The servants of every legion marched in a body behind the infantry, looking after the soldiers' baggage carried by the mules and other beasts. In the rear of all the legions marched the bulk of the mercenaries, followed by a protective rearguard of light and heavy infantry with a strong body of cavalry.'* [5]

Josephus did not mention that well out in front of the army would be small parties of mounted scouts operating up to a day's march in front of the advance party and returning to the camp at night. These units would be based on legionary cavalry, they would include local language speakers and would be commanded by an officer. Later in the empire, scouts would be organised as independent regular units. The cavalry screen, operating two or three miles in front of the advance party, would be based on auxiliary cavalry. He noted that the legionaries marched in sixes. This was not because of six-man *contubernia*, but because, as he wrote, two men were taken out of each *contubernium*: one, the file leader, was with the advance guard ensuring a proper location for his *contubernium*, and one would have been on pioneer duties.

Naturally not all Roman marches were carried out as well as the one described by Josephus. One of the worst was the march of the Othonian troops prior to the First Battle of Cremona. '*As the cumbrous army set itself in motion, an observer might have been pardoned for thinking that it was setting out for a campaign, not a battle*'. That is, despite the closeness of enemy forces, the troops were in marching order with the transport scattered throughout the column. Inevitably the Vitellians attacked, confidently deployed for battle. '*The Othonians afforded a different spectacle – frightened generals who were unpopular with their men, a confusion of vehicles and camp-followers, and a road which, thanks to the sheer ditches which accompanied it on either side, would have been somewhat narrow even for a column advancing calmly. Some of the Othonian troops were massed round their respective standards, others were looking for them. Everywhere there was a confused hubbub of rushing and shouting men*'.[6] The chaos was the result of sloppy marching in the wrong formation. The outcome of this battle was hardly in doubt.

After a successful march the camp would be constructed. Marking out the camp would have been done under the supervison of officers from the 1st Cohort, and, it must be judged that that cohort would have supplied some transport so that the advance party could march in fighting order. After marking out the site the soldiers would light some fires, partly as a signal to the army as to where the site was, and partly to help the following soldiers in lighting their own cooking fires. The mass of the legionaries, in their marching order, would then arrive.

On arrival at the new site the legionaries would put down their packs and tether their mules in the standard and preordained positions, The *calones* would be left to guard the legionaries' packs and unpack and feed the mule while the soldiers, still carrying their arms and shields, took their tools and stakes from the mules and set to digging a ditch and, with the spoil, raising a rampart. First they would strip the turf, cutting it into sections to use to build up the front face of the rampart and, if possible, the rear face. If the soil was too sandy to provide useable turfs, sandbags could be used. Then, because Roman metallurgy did not run to making useful shovels and spades, they had to break up the ground and collect it by hand in baskets to tip it down behind the turf front face. Panels on Trajan's Column show legionaries constructing camps wearing their armour and with their shields, with their helmets, propped up close by, ready to be snatched up if there were a sudden attack. In permanent camps arms would be kept in the armoury (probably as a precaution against rioting) but in a marching camp the legionaries would keep their arms with them. Along the top of the rampart the legionaries would drive in their stakes, joining them with bars across the top. This, of course, did not provide a very effective obstacle, but it did provide a sentry walk and a location for the troops in the case of a night attack. Also strips of material would be hung over the horizontal bars to prevent any attacker seeing into the camp, and to break the trajectory of incoming missiles, like slingshot. Caltrops may well have been placed particularly in approaches to the camp which could not be seen by sentries on the rampart. Depending on the level of threat, patrols, both infantry and cavalry, would have roamed the surrounding area all night. Roman camps were almost impossible to surprise.

Entrenching a camp was time consuming and hard work, and troops had to be continually practiced in this skill. The difficulties involved were illustrated by three cohorts of the Praetorian Guard, in 69AD, when they marched north to face the Vitellian forces: '*When the Po was sighted and the night drew on, it was decided to entrench camp. The physical labour (a novelty for troops normally stationed in the capitol) effectually broke their spirit*'.[7] The Praetorians would usually function as a gendarmerie and not be required to undertake such work, probably not even having the appropriate tools.

Constructing a marching camp took four to six hours, time which had to be planned for when manoeuvring troops. During his first march on Rome, Sulla used this process to outwit the members of an embassy sent from the City. '*He promised to grant them all they asked; and, as if he intended to encamp there, ordered his officers, as usual, to mark the ground. The ambassadors took their leave with entire confidence in his honour*'.[8] They believed his army would be fully occupied for some hours, but as soon as they left, he set his troops marching to Rome.

Once the defences had been approved, presumably by the acting *praefectis castrorum* going the rounds, the troops not detailed for camp security would carry out their share of communal tasks, like erecting the commander's quarters, digging latrines or digging internal drainage ditches. After that they would put up their own tent and feed themselves. Those that were detailed for camp security would prepare moveable defences for the four gates and man sentry posts.

The second line transport, with a substantial escort, would follow one camp behind, though some carts would have been shuttled forward to keep the first line stores topped up. The two camps would usually have been within visual signalling range of each other, of not a temporary signal station, half-way between them, would have been set up, so any attack on the second line transport could be quickly responded to. Naturally it was difficult, if not impossible, to follow this procedure when the army was carrying out a spoiling raid in enemy territory, as the Teutoburg battle was to show.

The Romans preferred to fight their battles just in front of a camp, so that their soldiers could have a secure night's rest then march out in an orderly fashion to a nearby battlefield where they could fight secure in the knowledge that they had a camp to fall back to if the battle did not go well, and that regardless of the result of the fighting, their kit was secure. If the entire legion was deployed then the defence of the camp was the responsibility of the 1st Cohort, but in the case of an expeditionary force when less than the entire 1st Cohort was deployed, *ad hoc* measures would be employed.

It can, then, be seen that switching smoothly between marching and fighting depended on camp construction, to such an extent that more than one modern commentator has referred to some Roman campaigns as being like 'mobile trench warfare'.[9] When commenting on the importance of marching camps, Vegetius wrote that '*if a camp has been properly constructed, soldiers spend days and nights so secure behind the ramparts – even if the enemy is besieging it – that they seem to carry a walled city with them everywhere*'.[10] This is also a comment on the importance of the legion's transport, particularly the *contubernium* mules. If these, with the digging tools and rampart stakes, were lost, then the legion could be in trouble. More disastrously if, because of a sudden action, the soldier had to abandon his personal kit and the mule was chased off, then although he could fight for the rest of the day, he could not feed himself or assist in setting up the marching camp. Naturally, in the case of an ambush it was difficult to deploy the legionaries away from where they had dropped their kit.

The importance and apparent vulnerability of the baggage train were obvious. For example Caesar has Vercingetorix say: '*We can either kill them or strip them of their baggage – which will be equally effective, since without it they cannot keep the field*'[11], and again: '*If the whole column of infantry halts to come to the rescue, they cannot continue their march; if – which I feel sure is more likely – they abandon the baggage and try to save their own skins, they will be stripped of the supplies without which they cannot live, and disgraced into the bargain*'.[12] However this vulnerability was more apparent than real providing that standard precautions were taken. Even if not, the loss of the second line transport was not fatal providing that the *contubernium* mules were saved with their loads of rations and tools for camp construction. The basic problem, though, remained: a soldier could not march carrying his kit, and be prepared to fight. This problem could only be solved if some of the second line transport carts were available to carry the soldiers' kit so that they could march in fighting order formed up in their maniples. This was done by Corbulo during his Armenian campaign of 58 AD. '*His forces were as ready for fighting as for marching; on the right flank stood the third brigade* (legion), *on the left the sixth, with picked troops of the tenth in the centre. The baggage was brought within the lines. A thousand cavalry protected the rear, with orders to resist hand-to-hand attack but not to follow if the enemy withdrew*'.[13] For the soldiers to be ready for fighting, their kit would have been on the carts which were fully protected by the army. Such a formation as this could only be maintained for a short distance.

Because setting up a marching camp took a long time, when action was not expected, or when a purely administrative move was being made, it was not done and the troops could move significantly faster. The normal procedure was for the second line transport to form a central column and the legionaries, with their mules, to march along on either side. This was particularly easy on properly made Roman roads where the undergrowth on both sides was cleared right back. The troops would bivouac just where they were when the column halted. The stakes would be used to set up a perimeter fence, probably of a 'knife-rest' pattern, just enough to delimit the military area and prevent any untethered animals escaping. The senior officers, no doubt, would accept hospitality at some local aristocrat's villa.

Even in the case of an administrative move, if the local population was in any degree unfriendly or just lawless then an escort must be provided. This was a routine matter and of little interest to Roman writers, but there is an example to be seen in the New Testament. In 58 AD Paul, the future saint, had to be escorted the 100 or so miles from Jerusalem to Caesarea Maritima. There were rumours that a 40-strong gang was out to kill him so the Officer Commanding *'called unto him two centurions, saying, Make ready two hundred soldiers to go to Caesarea, and horsemen threescore and ten, and spearmen two hundred, at the third hour of the night; and provide them beasts, that they may set Paul on'*.[14] This amounts to a small task force comprising a legionary maniple, two cavalry *turmae* and two centuries of javelineers. It may have been for Paul's benefit, but it is easier to believe that it was the standard escort for a regular Jerusalem-Caesarea convoy: the maniple to provide the solid defence, the cavalry to range across the open ground and the javelineers to scour ground so broken it was an obstacle to cavalry.

It is not known how typical this example is but it does illustrate the toils involved in escort duty, and the level of precaution sheds a light of the problems that were going to face Cestius Gallus eight years later and will be discussed later in this chapter.

Disasters

As has been shown, a Roman army could not march and fight at the same time, and the change from marching to fighting was made *via* the construction of a marching camp. The disruption of this drill provided the basis of the disasters considered here.

These examples are not being presented as some sort of general survey of Roman vulnerability, the historic record is too patchy, to say the least, to undertake that. For example it is known that a detachment of the Ninth Legion was wiped out during Boudicca's revolt, but there is no surviving information as to how this happened. Worse there is no information at all about how or where the entire legion was destroyed, or at least disappeared, in around 120 AD. These are two actions that are known to have taken place, but there must have been many more that are totally lost.

Rather these examples illustrate the toil and difficulty in getting the soldiers to the battlefield, the circumstances of the campaign and the problems that might ensue.

Atuatuca

In 54 BC, after returning from his second raid on Britain, Julius Caesar dispersed his army into winter quarters. No doubt dispersing his legions made their supply easier and showed them to the population, which had expected them to be lost in Britain, but it would have been better if each camp had been within a day's march of another. This dispersion turned out to be a disaster.[15]

The most exposed of these camps was Atuatuca, its location is uncertain. One authority places it at the modern city of Tongres,[16] another at Aachen,[17] another at Liege.[18] It was very roughly 50 miles from Cicero's camp at Namur and 80 from Labienus's at Trier. The Fifteenth Legion with a further five unspecified cohorts were posted here. Their commanders were Quintus Titurius Sabinus and Lucius Aurunculeius Cotta, Sabinus being the senior of the two. The legion was only recently recruited and the unspecified cohorts may have been veteran units posted there to stiffen it. This was certainly not a good location. A large part of the local population had recently immigrated from Germany and, being close to Germany, it was still closely linked to German tribes across the Rhine, and the Germans still had plenty of fight left in them. Consequently, when the local chieftain, Ambiorix, decided to drive the Romans out, he found it easy to raise a local army and expected a large German reinforcement.

Ambiorix's troops surrounded the Roman camp cutting it off from all supplies, but an assault was easily held, heavy casualties being inflicted by some Spanish cavalry who, unfortunately, are not mentioned again by Caesar. Ambiorix asked for a parley and Sabinus sent two Roman officers to confer with him. The essence of his message was that a large force of Germans was *en route* to attack the camp, and he offered Sabinus and his army a safe passage to either Namur or Trier. Sabinus decided to take up this offer. This decision was opposed by many of the other officers, but they had to accept Sabinus's authority. Caesar records that some survivors reached Labienus's camp, so it must have been decided to march south-east to Trier. This decision is difficult to understand, not only is

Trier the more distant of the two obvious options, but the route there passed through the hilly and forested Ardennes. The only possible reason for this decision is that the route to Namur, along the Meuse, was badly interdicted by the local tribes. The legionary camp at Namur was unsuccessfully attacked soon after the Atuatuca battle.

Because the country was potentially hostile the soldiers had to march in fighting order, their packs were to be carried on carts. There were not enough carts to carry all the full packs so the soldiers were obliged to abandon some of their personal kit. Loading the carts was a noisy process and took all night.

In the morning the legion marched out, all the baggage carts in a central column and the legionaries marching either side. The legion had only gone about two miles when it was ambushed and trapped in a defile. It is not obvious why the Spanish cavalry was not sent forward to prevent this happening, but it was not and the legion was stuck. The column had straggled, and when it ran into the trap the cohorts were difficult to marshal into a fighting line. Ambiorix's troops struck at both the front and rear of the column, causing maximum confusion. The generals realised that the troops could not hold out in their present formation and ordered them to form an 'orb' at the rear of the column. This naturally meant that the carts, with the soldiers' personal kit, were being abandoned. Many of the soldiers broke ranks to run to the carts to retrieve their belongings. This could well have been a turning point. Before that it might have been possible, with determined leadership, to turn the legion round, march back and re-establish the camp, but once the transport had been abandoned the only plan could have been to hold out till dusk then make a desperate dash for Trier, 80 miles away.

It seems likely that when the legionaries broke ranks the attackers took instant advantage and burst in among them causing more casualties and chaos. Whether this was so or not, the orb was formed. Initially this might have taken the form of a hollow square, with the cohorts still properly ordered.[19] At this stage Sabinus tried to negotiate with Ambiorix but Ambiorix used this as an opportunity to have Sabinus with some tribunes and *prior* centurions murdered. Like Arminius, 63 years later, he knew how to decapitate a legion

The fight lasted most of the day, the Romans being progressively worn down. The attackers would not close with the Romans, but assailed them with javelins and other missile weapons. To try to engage them, individual cohorts charged out but these charges were easily evaded and, by breaking up the defensive formation, exposed the soldiers more to the missiles. Throughout the afternoon the troops were worn down. The *primus pilus*, who must have been fighting in the front rank, was mortally wounded, which shows how desperate the situation was, and finally the troops grouped round their standards but whether they did this as an inchoate crowd or still maintaining their ranks is not recorded. In this formation, which is not a mobile one, they were finally overcome by sheer numbers and massacred.

A small number did succeed in reaching their destination, Labienus's camp, to pass on the news. A small number of other soldiers fought their way back to the camp. The legion's *aquilifer* nearly made it, but just before he was killed he managed to throw the eagle into the camp. The soldiers may have reached the camp they had just left but this was of little advantage to them. They no longer had the stakes for the ramparts, and being few in number they could not man the old ramparts or, with no tools, build new ones. Worse, they had nothing to eat. Consequently, seeing no hope, they committed suicide. This was recounted by Caesar who obtained the information from prisoners.

The Battle of Carrhae

In June 53 BC a Roman army under Marcus Licinius Crassus, probably anticipating a repeat of the successful and profitable campaigning enjoyed by the army of Lucius Licinius Lucullus in Armenia in the previous decade, invaded the Parthian province of Mesopotamia with the intention of annexing it. The campaign was a disaster and halted the Roman *drang nach osten* which had, until then, seemed unstoppable. Although there were later Roman campaigns in Mesopotamia, and for a short while it became a Roman province after being captured by Trajan, Mesopotamia, the modern Iraq with all its oil, has really been debatable ground ever since the Battle of Carrhae which must therefore be numbered as one of the decisive battles of history.

The Roman force consisted of seven legions, although some cohorts may have been detached as garrisons. This was a substantial force but its cavalry and auxiliary infantry components were weak. There were only 4,000 cavalrymen, 1,000 of which were high quality Gallic troops sent by Julius Caesar, the remainder were supplied by allies and do not seem to have made much of a contribution to the fighting and may even have treacherously attacked the Romans. Accounts of the fighting hardly mention light troops, so it can be assumed that the auxiliary infantry component was small.

In 54 BC Crassus and his army had crossed the Euphrates, defeated the local satrap and occupied the area between that river and the Belikh. This area contained a number of Hellenistic cities where garrisons were left. Then Crassus pulled back westwards and over winter fought a minor campaign in Judea. His army would be quite well experienced.

It appears that during the hiatus between Crassus's two Parthian campaigns, Parthian cavalry raided the occupied area, and Roman soldiers that had been caught in the open bore alarming tales about the cavalrymen. '*It is impossible either to escape them when they pursue, or to take them when they fly. They have a new and strange sort of arrows, which are swifter than lightning, and reach their mark before you can see they are discharged; nor are they less fatal in their effects than swift in their course. The offensive arms of their cavalry pierce through everything, and the defensive arms are so well tempered, that nothing can pierce them*'.[20] This sort of rumour would not have improved the morale of Crassus's soldiers. Neither would the rumour, current since Lucullus's day, that the Parthian arrow heads were poisoned.[21]

It may well be that the Parthian cavalry so dominated the countryside that they presented Crassus with a 'scorched earth' and this added to the Romans' supply worries.

In 53 BC Crassus's army again crossed the Euphrates and marched towards the Belikh. Their last encampment before the fighting started must have been close to the city of Carrhae. Next morning as the march started a reconnoitring party returned having had a skirmish and losing several of its number. It reported that they had encountered the Parthians who were advancing and were in high spirits but not great numbers.

Crassus immediately deployed his legions in line, with his cavalry on the flanks. Then he observed that, as his army had just broken up the camp, if any Parthians could out-flank him then his transport would be at risk, so he reorganised the army and enclosed the transport, mostly mules, in a hollow square each side of which was twelve legionary cohorts. These cohorts were supported by squadrons of cavalry, these were most likely to have been the legionary cavalry.

The square comprised of 48 cohorts and the leading front

was extended on both sides by wings of around eight cohorts. The cavalry remained on the wings. This formation accounts for 64 cohorts which, allowing for six to have been left as garrisons, covers the whole seven legions.

The number of transport animals is not easy to assess. Each legion would have around 720 *contubernium* mules, so an outside total could be 1,000 mules per legion, making under 7,000 for the legions (some cohorts had been left behind) but the cavalry and auxiliaries may have increased the total to 8,000. This number, giving a column under ideal circumstances of 160 mules wide and 50 mules long, could easily be contained in the hollow square. Extra space would have been taken up by wheeled transport, or spare mules, which would have been necessary to carry the soldiers' packs so that they could march in fighting order.

The front presented contained 28 cohorts, if these were drawn up in the usual three lines (the wings having two cohorts in the third line) the front would be ten cohorts wide, and deployed with the proper spacing the front would be at least 1,000 yards long, excluding cavalry.

This was the formation in which the Roman army crossed the Belikh to face the Parthians. The river itself was not much of an obstacle but its crossing would have slowed the army down. Each of the thousands of draft animals would have insisted in having a drink, and many would have been carrying water-skins that the muleteers would have topped up. After crossing the river the army would have halted to check its dressing then started forward looking for the enemy. This was not in accord with standard Roman practice which would have been to set up a camp after crossing the river, and secure the transport in it. Naturally it would have been necessary to leave a garrison but it would mean that the army in the field would not have to worry about protecting the transport.

The march was unpleasant for the Romans.They would have been closed up almost to battle formation. The air breathed by the men in the centre would have been heavy with dust, it would have congested their lungs and irritated their eyes and noses. Heatstroke and respiratory problems would have started to take their toll. However Crassus was determined to go straight for the enemy, and he did not have to go far. The Parthians, all mounted, were an impressive sight, and there were more of them than the scouts had reported. Many of their mounted archers had been hidden behind the cataphracts who had hidden their armour, and therefore the type of soldiers they were, with their cloaks. Even so the Parthian army was not large. It was only 10,000 strong, around 1,000 were cataphracts, armoured lancers, the remainder being archers.

In preparation for the coming battle the Parthians began beating drums. This sound was a novelty to the Roman soldiers and had an unnerving effect on them. As Plutarch put it *'the field resounded with a horrid din and dreadful bellowing. For the Parthians do not excite their men to action with cornets and trumpets, but with certain hollow instruments covered with leather, and surrounded with brass bells, which they beat continually. The sound is deep and dismal, something between the howling of wild beasts and the crashing of thunder'... 'the Romans were trembling at the horrid noise'.*[22]

Whether the Romans were trembling or not they did well enough in the first stage of the battle. The Parthians decided to throw in their cataphracts, possible hoping that the Romans would not be prepared to cope with this kind of cavalry. *'At first, the barbarians intended to have charged with their pikes, and opened a way through their foremost ranks; but when they saw the depth of the Roman battalions, the closeness of their order, and the firmness of their standing, they drew back, and, under the appearance of breaking their ranks and dispersing, wheeled about and surrounded the Romans. At that instant Crassus ordered his archers and light infantry to begin the charge. But they had not gone far before they were saluted with a shower of arrows, which came with such force and did so much execution, as drove them back upon the battalions. This was the beginning of disorder and consternation among the heavy-armed, when they beheld the force and strength of the arrows, against which no armour was proof, and whose keenness nothing could resist'.*[23] The cataphracts pulled back to await further events.

The legions, expecting cavalry, could defend themselves quite well. The legionaries would have carried more than one throwing spear, which may have been shorter and lighter than the *pilum*. Some legionaries may have been stationed behind their centuries to act as slingers, and some allied or auxiliary archers were also there ready to surge through between the files to attack the cataphracts. Also there were cavalry handy to attack the Parthians if they became too involved with the Roman infantry.

However Parthian attacks had halted the Romans and it began to appear that there was no end to the Parthian assault. The cause of the problem was seen to be that the Parthians were supported by 1,000 camels carrying supplies of arrows so that the archers had only to ride a short distance to refill their quivers. The Parthian assault showed no signs of finishing. Crassus knew that battles are not won by defensive tactics and sooner of later his troops would be worn down. He had to attack and he had to make his decisions quickly, it would already be mid-afternoon. Unfortunately the hurried decision he made in the heat and the dust of the day resulted in disaster. Crassus sent his son, Publius Crassus, at the head of the Gallic cavalry, supported by a further 300 cavalry, 500 archers and the eight legionary cohorts of the right wing, forward into the assault. It seems most likely that the immediate tactical objective was the Parthian camels. If they could be captured or destroyed the mounted archers must soon run out of ammunition and their attacks stop. Further, the Parthians deciding to fight for these camels would be the best outcome for the Romans because in such a fight the Roman superiority in hand-to-hand fighting would soon win the day.

It is just possible the Crassus's decision was based on his reading of military history and the recurring Roman obsession with emulating Alexander the Great. Crassus had undertaken the unnecessary war primarily to enhance his reputation compared to that of the other triumvirs, Caesar and Pompey; the latter actually styled himself as 'the Great' – *Magnus* – in apparent emulation of Alexander. Crassus had crossed the Euphrates close to where Alexander crossed, and now that he faced a Parthian army he wanted to defeat it by the same manoeuvre by which Alexander defeated Darius's army at Guagamela (in 331 BC). That battle was won when Alexander, in person, led an assault from the right wing at the head of his companion cavalry, closely supported by the hypaspists, while the rest of his army was stationary enduring Persian attacks. The Gallic cavalry was Crassus's best, the legionaries were latter day hypaspists, and he cast his son as the Roman Alexander.

The result was a disaster. The Pathian general had held his cataphracts back for such an occasion. There were 1,000 caraphracts against 1,300 Gauls and other cavalry but the cataphracts were armoured lancers, well equipped for mounted combat, and although the Gauls fought hard they were wiped out. The task force survivors took up a position on a low hill and formed an orb. Their commander wanted the legionaries to sally out against the Parthians but they demurred, showing him how some soldiers had had their feet wounded by arrows and how others had had arrows piercing their shields, pinning their hands to the plywood. This, incidentally, shows that the legionaries were not carrying their shields by handles behind the shield bosses (see Appendix Two). The end was inevitable. Only 500 survived to be made prisoners. Publius Crassus and his senior officers committed suicide.

As the task force had been commanded by his son, the pressure on Crassus can be imagined. Initially he spurred his infantry forward, but this made the troops more vulnerable to the horse-archers' arrows, as the shield wall could not be maintained on the march. Also the disaster had cost Crassus a large portion of his archers, making defence against the Parthians more difficult. The forward march did not last long once the fate of the task force became known and Publius's head had been displayed to the Romans.

The Parthians, having defeated Publius Crassus, then returned to attacking the main Roman army. The Parthians seem to have become progressively more effective at exploiting Roman weaknesses. As a defence against the archers the Romans would double their front rank, but this would make them vulnerable to the cataphracts whose lances could reach the men behind the shields. To defend against the caraphracts, the Romans would open their ranks so that they could throw their javelins, but instantly became vulnerable to the archers. As Dio put it: '*if they decided to lock shields for the purpose of avoiding the arrows by the closeness of their array, the pikemen were upon them with a rush, striking down some, and at least scattering the others; and if they extended their ranks to avoid this, they would be struck with the arrows. Hereupon many died from fright at the very charge of the pikemen, and many perished hemmed in by the horsemen. Others were knocked over by the pikes or were carried off transfixed*'.[24] Obviously Dio did not have a word for 'cataphracts' And used a term he was familiar with.

There can be no doubt that the Parthian archery spread consternation among the Roman ranks. The barbed heads of some of their arrows caused horrifying wounds, the soldiers hit *'rolled about in agonies of pain with the arrows sticking in them, and before they died endeavoured to pull out the barbed points which were entangled within their veins and sinews: an effort that served only to enlarge their wounds and add to their torture'*.[25] Arrows with barbed heads would not be as aerodynamically efficient as those with bodkin-type heads which would be more effective against shields, but as the battle wore on the Romans would have thrown all their javelins and the surviving auxiliaries would have loosed all their arrows, so the Parthians could ride up close to shoot their arrows and the difference became less marked. Modern studies have shown that Hun mounted archers could shoot three arrows in six seconds and Parthians should have been able to do the same. Under this kind of assault the morale of the Romans would have crumbled. Fortunately it was soon dusk and the fighting petered out. The Romans encamped were they were.

The next morning the remains of the Roman army were back at Carrhae, with its organisation shattered and its transport train lost. Having lost its transport it lost its ability to construct marching camps and with that its security. Had it had that ability the army could have proceeded back to the Euphrates united and unstoppable, but as it was it split up into several separate columns which were to suffer heavy casualties.

The critical aspect of the Carrhae campaign is the actions of the army overnight and these are best described as between mutiny and panic.

The camp was constructed, but, according to Plutarch, in a slovenly way. The dead were not buried and the soldiers were reduced to apathy. There is no doubt they realised that they had been defeated. Plutarch says that there were 4,000 seriously wounded legionaries and that figure would imply 1,000 dead. That is out of 56 cohorts, a 20% casualty rate. If the eight cohorts totally lost with Publius Crassus were included it would be a 30% loss across 64 cohorts.

These are high casualty rates though, of course, it is not known how reliable Plutarch was, but they do indicate that the losses among centurions, the backbone of the army, would have been disastrous. The centurions would have spent a disproportionate time in the front line, organising and encouraging, and they carried only small shields, increasing their vulnerability. With a shortage of senior ranks, discipline started to weaken.

Right from the start of the campaign there seems to have been a degree of contention among some of the officers. The opposition to Crassus was led by Cassius, though it is possible that Plutarch was making some sort of point as Cassius, after surviving this campaign, went on to assassinate Caesar. After dusk Cassius and other senior officers, seeing that Crassus was no longer functioning in a command capacity, called the surviving *prior* centurions to a Council of War. It seems that both the army in general and the meeting in general wanted to return to Carrhae but this course of action would involve abandoning the wounded, alternatively the loads of 4,000 mules must be dumped to save the wounded. This might have been possible in daytime with proper supervision, but not in the prevailing circumstances.

The options before the Council were either to go or stay. It is unlikely that the feelings of meeting were unanimous. Two senior officers, Octavius and Petronius, were close enough to Crassus to die with him and would not have agreed with Cassius, and it might be that the meeting broke up before reaching a conclusion. Dio hints at a treacherous attack by erstwhile allies which might have brought discussions to a halt. Plutarch states that a cavalry unit, the first to desert the camp, arrived at Carrhae around midnight.

It may be significant that Plutarch describes all the Roman deployments as by numbers of cohorts, not by legions. This might be a hint that the chain of command was convoluted. Whether this was significant or not, lacking firm leadership the army started to break up, soldiers hearing the orders that they wanted to hear, and ignoring the others. Mule loads were dumped and wounded soldiers mounted in their place, but some were to be pushed off and replaced by others. The wounded who were being abandoned were howling. Cohorts on the march, thinking the enemy were close kept forming up for action, so losing their mules, and everyone rushed to the river for some water. The camp, with its rampart stakes, was abandoned, and most of the mule loads, like water-skins, some of which would have been punctured by arrows, and extra rations, were also left, as the army rushed westwards.

In the morning the Parthians occupied the camp and massacred the wounded. They also killed many stragglers. One Roman formation of four cohorts that had become separated from the main army, finished up on a small hill where they were surrounded and massacred, only 20 men escaping.

The garrison of Carrhae marched out and escorted the survivors of the army back, but they could not stay being short of rations, and made for the Euphrates in small columns. Around 10,000 made it. Crassus was murdered by the Parthians having been forced to parley by the ill discipline of his soldiers.

There can be no doubt that the Parthian archers made a huge impression on the Romans and may have hastened the development of the *carroballista* which substantially increased the legion's firepower. Even so the Roman reaction to the archery threat was unimaginative. Over 400 years later Ammianus Marcellinus was highly impressed by Persian archery, writing '*The curved horns of these weapons which extend on both sides of the stock were so pliable that, when the strings were released after being drawn back by the brute strength of the fingers, they despatched iron-tipped arrows which crashed into the bodies in their path and stuck there with fatal results*', and '*the archers, practised from the very cradle in a skill in which that people especially excels, were bending their flexible bows. Their arms stretched so wide that while the point of the arrow touched their left hand the string brushed their right breast. By highly skilful finger-work the shafts flew with a loud hiss, dealing deadly wounds*'.[26] This seems to show that during the four centuries following Carrhae the Romans failed to adopt the composite bow, an amazing lack of adaptability.

Despite the soldiers' rumours of poisoned arrowheads the difficulties in the supply of thousands of these would have made this impossible. For the same reason the rumour that the Parthian arrows had double heads, one loosely fitted so that it would be left in the wound, must also be discounted.

As important as archery was, perhaps the cataphracts were more important and, after the Roman Empire, armoured lancers would dominate warfare for many centuries. The lack of Roman interest was another amazing lack of adaptability. Also the best defence against cataphracts was the pike phalanx. There were some very minor experiments in this direction, but otherwise the Romans showed no interest.

Carrhae emphasised the limitations of the legion and the necessity of armies including strong cavalry and light infantry components, but it also showed that legionaries in their fighting formation and expecting an attack could hold off cataphracts. This was again illustrated during the fighting in Anatolia after Carrhae when a large number of cataphracts charged, uphill, against legionaries who were expecting them, and as a result suffered heavy casualties.

Naturally in the tense political atmosphere of the time, other leading lights wanted to establish their credentials by avenging Crassus. Julius Caesar planned a campaign against the Parthians, but was murdered before he could leave Rome. He had organised an army of 16 legions and 10,000 cavalry, proportions of cavalry to infantry similar to those deployed by Crassus.[27] Taking into account Caesar's usual slapdash approach to supply, it must be judged that even the great Caesar would have failed.

Some years later, in 36 BC, Mark Antony launched his campaign against the Parthians. It may be that he thought that the sling would defeat the Parthian bow, perhaps the slingers were issued with lead shot. Dio Cassius reports that in at least one action this seemed to work: '*Hence, when he met then a little later, he routed them, for as his slingers were numerous and could shoot farther than the archers, they inflicted severe injury upon all, even upon the men in armour; yet he did not kill any considerable number of the enemy, because the barbarians could ride fast*'.[28]   Despite this the campaign was not a success, though certainly not a failure on the Carrhae scale. Mark Antony was a better general than Crassus and had plenty of light infantry, his legionaries were better drilled and probably had better shields but even so he lost some standards. The Parthians could only be defeated in battle by a cavalry-based army, and the Romans did not achieve this.

As a diplomatic gesture the captured legionary standards of both Crassus and Mark Antony, along with some prisoners, were handed over to Augustus in 21 BC.

Rome's eastern front saw many campaigns and much hardship for the soldiers. Another disaster occurred in 233 AD during Alexander Severus's campaign against the Sassanian Persians. It is mentioned here because of Herodian's description of the defeat of a major formation.

'*The king attacked it unexpectedly with his entire force and trapped the Romans like fish in a net; firing their arrows from all sides at the encircled soldiers, the Persians massacred the whole army. The outnumbered Romans were unable to stem the attack of the Persian horde; they used their shields to protect those parts of their bodies exposed to the Persian arrows. Content merely to protect themselves, they offered no resistance. As a result, all the Romans were driven into one spot, where they made a wall of their shields and fought like an army under siege. Hit and wounded from every side, they held out bravely as long as they could, but in the end all were killed. The Romans suffered a staggering disaster; it is not easy to recall another like it, one in which a great army was destroyed, an army inferior in strength and determination to none of the armies of old.*'[29]

It is difficult to judge how accurate this description is as the emperor mounted a propaganda campaign to convince the Roman Senate and People that the war had been a success, and took the title *Parthicus Maximus*. The fact that the Persians did not follow up their victory but remained quiet for years may indicate that the fighting was not as one-sided as Herodian indicated.

Herodian has described a heavy infantry force, unable to counter lancers and mounted archers, being driven to adopt the 'orb' formation and finally being ground down under the Persian arrow storm. This is, of course, how the last of Leonidas's spartiates died at Thermopylae.

The Varus Disaster

This battle is in modern times usually known as the Battle of the Teutoburg Wald, the expression comes from Tacitus,[30] however it seems that the Romans named it from the Roman commander, Publius Quinctilius Varus. In 9 AD a Roman army consisting of the greater part of three legions was attacked and destroyed in North Germany by an army of tribesmen. This disaster was one of the greatest Roman military defeats of the classic age of the legion, but surprisingly little is known about it. However recent archaeology and a careful reading of the few literary sources allow the four days of battle to be reasonably well understood.

Significantly the most important aspect of the battle, the final mass surrender, is not mentioned in any of the sources. This fact may hint at a deliberate cover-up by the Roman authorities, but it has certainly resulted in a great deal of misunderstanding.

The contemporary Roman view may be illustrated by a quote from Velleius Paterculus's history:

'The details of this terrible calamity, the heaviest that had befallen the Romans on foreign soil since the disaster of Crassus in Parthia, I shall endeavour to set forth, as others have done, in my larger work. Here I can merely lament the disaster as a whole. An army unexcelled in bravery, the first of Roman armies in discipline, in energy, and in experience in the field, through the negligence of its general, the perfidy of the enemy, and the unkindness of fortune was surrounded, nor was as much opportunity as they had wished given to the soldiers either of fighting or of extricating themselves, except against heavy odds; nay, some were even heavily chastised for using the arms and showing the spirit of Romans. Hemmed in by forests and marches and ambuscades, it was exterminated almost to a man by the very enemy whom it had always slaughtered

like cattle, whose life or death had depended solely upon the wrath or the pity of the Romans. The general had more courage to die than to fight, for, following the example of his father and grandfather, he ran himself through with his sword. Of the two prefects of the camp, Lucius Eggius furnished a precedent as noble as that of Ceionius was base, who, after the greater part of the army had perished, proposed its surrender, preferring to die by torture at the hands of the enemy than in battle. Vala Numonius, lieutenant of Varus, who, in the rest of his life, had been an inoffensive and an honourable man, also set a fearful example in that he left the infantry unprotected by the cavalry and in flight tried to reach the Rhine with his squadrons of horse. But fortune avenged his act, for he did not survive those whom he had abandoned, but died in the act of deserting them. The body of Varus, partially burned, was mangled by the enemy in their barbarity; his head was cut off and taken to Maroboduus and was sent by him to Caesar; but in spite of the disaster it was honoured by burial in the tomb of his family.' [31]

The situation at the start of the year was that the Rhine was accepted as the boundary between the Empire and Germany, and was heavily militarised. However there was a steady penetration into Germany along the Lippe which ran to the east a few miles north of the Ruhr valley. There were forts at Haltern (Aliso) and Anreppen.

Previous years had seen heavy fighting in Germany under Nero Claudius Drusus, concluding with his death in 9 BC. The fighting was continued by Tiberius, Augustus's stepson and successor, and by 7 BC the Roman view was that Germany was practically a Roman province. After Tiberius the fighting continued in a desultory way till he returned in 4 AD, staying two years. His troops again campaigned successfully and marched as far as the Elbe. However in the end all the Roman campaigns had done was to march the legions round Germany and leave it much as they found it, despite this it was judged that Germany was cowed militarily, and becoming civilised. The Roman view was that *'The barbarians were adapting themselves to Roman ways, were becoming accustomed to hold markets, and were meeting in peaceful assemblages'.*[32]

This view was grossly over-optimistic, the German tribes were not becoming civilised, at least in Roman terms, but it was as a result of this view that the task of setting up a civilian administration was allocated to Varus, who in 6 or 7 AD was made governor of Germany.

Varus decided to spend the summer of 9 AD in Germany, but where has been a subject of some disagreement. Archaeology has located the decisive action of the campaign at the Kalkrieser Berg, so the location of the summer camp must bear a simple relationship to that of the Berg. Dio says that the Germans lured Varus away from the Rhine. *'Now they did not openly revolt, since they saw that there were many Roman troops near the Rhine and many within their own borders; instead, they received Varus, pretending that they would do all he demanded of them, and thus they drew him far away from the Rhine into the land of the Cherusci, towards the Visurgis* (Weser)'.[33] This would put Varus close to the Weser, the obvious location being the area of Minden which is close to and due east of the Kalkriese Berg, and where there is extensive Roman archaeology.

A site on the Weser would make sense to Varus. The civilian administrative staff could have been taken there by boat. This would have been convenient, but to an extent by insulating these people from the realities of Germany, it may have given them an unrealistic view of the suitability of Germany for inclusion in the Empire.

Velleius Paterculus gave Varus's army as being of *'three*

legions, of as many divisions (alae) *of cavalry, and of six cohorts'*.[34] However these figures require some analysis. A fully manned legion would have a fighting strength of approximately 5,200 men and a ration strength of many more, to include staffs, muleteers and supply staff. The legions can be expected to have been understrength, having been called on to send drafts to Illyricum, and they will have left garrisons in the Rhine and Lippe. In 14 AD Germanicus led an army across the Rhine, it contained 12,000 men from four legions[35] which is 3,000 from each legion, which is a reasonably accurate figure for two vexillations. Assuming the same procedure was followed by Varus, his army included 9,000 legionaries. The figure of three *ala* is open to interpretation. It could refer to three *ala* of auxiliary cavalry, these would have had a nominal strength of 480 each. Or it could refer to the cavalry squadrons of the legions, 120 men each. Or it could refer to the German allies, commanded by Arminius. It is impossible to say which of these options obtains, but the first one must be judged the least likely, three important units could not just disappear leaving no record. The six cohorts were auxiliary infantry. There is no information about these, but Dio Cassius mentions bows so perhaps some were archers. It seems a reasonable conclusion that Varus's army, excluding German allies, consisted of around 12,000 fighting men.

The Romans do not seem at this stage to have had a great regard for the Germans as fighting men. They were mostly poorly armed, around 90 years later Tacitus wrote '*iron is not plentiful; this has been inferred from the sort of weapons they have. Only a few of them use swords or large lances: they carry spears – called* frameae *in their language – with short and narrow blades, but so sharp and easy to handle that they can be used, as required, either at close quarters or in long range fighting'*.[36] However, despite Tacitus, it may be that the standard German weapon was a large club made from the branch of a tree. The Romans knew that they could always beat the Germans in a stand-up fight.

To go to Minden the legions would march east along the Lippe then swing roughly north through the Bielefeld pass, and through 20 miles of hilly and forested countryside to emerge through the Porta Westfalica pass by Minden. The hilly country, bounded on the north by the Wielen ridge running east to west, was Cheruscan territory. It is quite possible that marching the legions through their territory did not endear the Romans to the Cherusci. One of the Cheruscan chieftains was Arminius. He was serving as an officer in the Roman army and was thoroughly familiar with its workings. He had soldiered in the Illyrian revolt and knew that Rome was not invincible. He now commanded the German cavalry in Varus's army. He was also a confidant of Varus and is usually taken to be the driving force behind the German rising.

As the Romans progressed through the Cheruscan territory they left behind a series of small units for escort and general security duties. Dio records that they were requested by the local people, which most likely means Arminius. These detachments are most likely to have been from the auxiliary cohorts.

Early in September 9 AD Varus abandoned the fort by the Weser. No doubt many VIPs, not wanting to trudge all the way back to the Rhine, left by ship, but the army had to march. The logical route would have been back through the Porta Westfalica pass, and south to the Lippe. Had Varus followed this route the disaster would not have occurred and his name would have remained obscure in history, but shortly before the Romans left Minden word came of an uprising by one of the tribes presumably to the north of the Wiehen ridge and well to the west of Minden. It is not too obvious what such an uprising would involve, possibly a massacre of Roman traders, or it might be a reference to a small party of soldiers, possible on road making or surveying duties, being attacked. However it is also possible that the rising was a hoax and did not actually happen. No doubt it did not look very threatening and Varus could assume that the presence of three legions would have served to restore peace.

The long quote of Velleius Paterculus gives the impression that the legions were commanded by their camp prefects. He mentions two with the army, and the third was in a camp on the Lippe where he might have been sent on in advance, that being the presumed route, to organise supplies leaving his legion under the command of its *Primus Pilus*. The camp prefects were third in command of a legion, were promoted from centurion and were responsible for routine functions. The legates and senior tribunes, legionary commanders and second-in-command, would have sailed with the civilian VIPs. If this is so then the three officers who could most influence Varus were missing, as was a vital link in the chain of command.(*see note 45*) These considerations illustrate how the march was expected to be a routine peacetime move.

Remarkably the troops were paid in Minden. Paydays only came three times a year, and cheap wine brought up the river and German beer would have created a festive atmosphere. Perhaps Varus believed that markets were being held and that the Germans were moving onto a cash economy, and as the soldiers had money they would be able to buy food as they passed through Germany. On that basis he may have saved some money by letting his stocks of provisions for men and animals run down.

The route the Romans took was due west, just to the north of the Wiehen Ridge. It would have followed reasonably closely to modern Federal Road 65. The ground is low and flat and would have been generally swampy in 9 AD, but there are frequent modern villages and small towns along this road that would have been built on slightly higher and drier ground that would have been suitable for Roman camps, but initially the Romans did not set up any camps. Because there was every reason to believe that they were in friendly territory Varus's army was not marching tactically. The second line transport was distributed throughout the column, forming a central column with the infantry on either side of the carts. Also the army was accompanied by a large number of non-combatants. These included traders, servants and prostitutes.

Naturally when marching non-tactically the army could move much faster than when it would have had to spend about half each day setting up a camp, but even so it is difficult to imagine that the army covered fifteen miles. Initially the countryside was endlessly broken by ravine-like streams, to the south (left) were the thickly forested hills and to the north were endless swamps. Then heavy rains started. The march, miserable as it was, was peaceful and Arminius with his German auxiliary cavalry, with Varus's permission, left the army supposedly to mobilise other tribes to put down the rising. This would have dramatically reduced the Roman reconnaissance capacity.

The next day the battle began. The Romans were totally wrong-footed, they were not deployed for fighting, they had lost their cavalry screen and were not psychologically ready. Many years later Vegetius reflected on troops in such a situation: *'Those who have made a careful study of the art of war assert that more dangers tend to arise on the march than in battle itself. For in battle everyone is armed, and they see the enemy at close quarters and come mentally prepared for fighting. On the march, the soldier is less armed and less alert; he is thrown into instant confusion by a sudden attack or concealed ambush. Therefore the general should take steps with all caution and prudence to ensure that the army suffer no attack on the march, or may easily repel a raid without loss'.*[37]

Arminius's plan was working perfectly, he had taken command of large numbers of warriors who had collected in the woods, then '*they came upon Varus in the midst of forests by this time almost impenetrable. And there, at the very moment of revealing themselves as enemies instead of subjects, they wrought great and dire havoc.*

The mountains had an uneven surface broken by ravines, and the trees grew close together and very high. Hence the Romans, even before the enemy assailed them, were having a hard time of it felling trees, building roads, and bridging places that required it. They had with them many wagons and many beasts of burden as in time of peace; moreover, not a few women and children and a large retinue of servants were following them – one more reason for their advancing in scattered groups. Meanwhile a violent rain and wind camp up that separated them still further, while the ground, that had become slippery around the roots and logs, made walking very treacherous for them, and the tops of the trees kept breaking off and falling down, causing much confusion. While the Romans were in such difficulties, the barbarians suddenly surrounded them on all sides at once, coming through the densest thickets, as they were acquainted with the paths. At first they hurled their volleys from a distance; then, as no one defended himself and many were wounded, they approached closer to them. For the Romans were not proceeding in any regular order, but were mixed in helter-skelter with the wagons and the unarmed, and so, being unable to form readily anywhere in a body, and being fewer at every point than their assailants, they suffered greatly and could offer no resistance at all.

Accordingly they encamped on the spot, after securing a suitable place, so far as that was possible on a wooded mountain; and afterwards they either burned or abandoned most of their wagons and everything else that was not absolutely necessary to them. '[38]

The day's fighting would have been difficult and tiring for the Romans, but would not have caused many casualties. It did, though, reveal a problem in that there was a shortage of light (auxiliary) troops, particularly of course the desertion of the German cavalry. At the day's close the Roman situation could be seen as unpleasant but not desperate. To some extent the day was critical in that it was the last real chance Varus had of turning back to Minden and taking the southern route along the Lippe. This option was not taken, perhaps the supply situation suddenly looked difficult and the direct route to the Rhine seemed best even though there were supplies at the Lippe forts. Perhaps also Varus believed that once out of the trees and in the open the legions would be able to deploy their unstoppable might and problems would fade away. Further, around now, news was received that some of the security detachments left with local communities in the Cheruscan territory had been massacred, so these auxiliary troops would not be rejoining the main column. This would have ensured that the local people were actively anti-Roman and reinforced the decision not to take the Lippe route. It was necessary to burn or abandon the second line transport as it could not be accommodated in the marching camp. It is probable that most of the stores carried were non-essential, personal belongings of Varus and other senior officers, or relevant to the civilian government. Such draft animals as were suitable were passed on as *contubernium* transport as it was obvious that the legionaries would have to march in fighting order and the mules would have to carry their packs. The *carroballistae* were not, of course, destroyed.

The morning of the second day doubtlessly saw the soldiers wet, dispirited and cold, but the military machine was functioning correctly; they would have eaten, then removed the posts and rails from the camp's ramparts and packed their mules as they had done many times before. Varus must have been confident. Although he had been deserted by the German allies he will have had some scouts out and they would have reported an ambush set up at Kalkriese only a few miles ahead. This looked like an ideal situation for a Roman army. A camp set up behind them, a short march to the enemy, then a stand-up fight in the open. Varus would also have been aware that 20 years previously a Roman army under Drusus was ambushed quite close to his present location at the unidentified site, Arbalo. For short while this army had been in trouble but discipline held and the Romans won the day. Varus must have been confident.

The nature of the challenge facing the Romans would not have been obvious. There was a high prominent hill, the Kalkrieser Berg standing slightly to the north of the Wiehen ridge, and to the north of that was a swamp, the Grosses Moor. The two were separated by only a few hundred yards, and the wet weather was extending the swamp southwards until the dry ground might have been as narrow as 100 yards. The wet and boggy ground would not have been as much of an obstacle to the soldiers as it would have been to the mules. There was a series of small streams running north to the swamp, they also would not have delayed the soldiers but would have slowed the mules and the *carroballistae.* There was a significant fortification, a turf and soil wall, running round the north facing slopes of the Berg. This wall was around four yards wide at the base and two high. To provide spoil for the wall, and for drainage, there were ditches before and behind the wall and the front and rear faces of the wall were made of turfs. Stripping the turf naturally made the ground the Romans were to march across that bit muddier. There was a small native settlement by the swamp and it is most likely that some tribesmen were stationed in the gap to provide a target for the legions. Presumably the situation was obscured by undergrowth.

It was important to disguise the nature of the threat facing the Romans. Arminius had learned the lesson of Arbalo, his tribesmen could not meet the legionaries head on, so if they could not defeat the fighting men they must defeat their system. The wall was not there to halt the Romans, but it was there to force them into such a situation that they would be vulnerable to a counter-attack.

Unfortunately the reconnaissance did not fully reveal the nature of the German position. Doubtlessly the German cavalry could easily cope with the Roman scouts and only allowed them to see what Arminius wanted them to see and, of course, prevented them taking prisoners. What the Roman scouts did see was the bait of the German warriors on foot waiting to be attacked. This intelligence would have been taken direct to Varus.

The legions are most likely to have come on deployed in vexillations. Fully deployed a cohort would take up around 100 yards and a vexillation 300, so there should have been space, particularly if some of the *posterior* centuries were not deployed. Unfortunately Dio Cassius is difficult to follow in his description of this day's events, but writes '*they had to form their lines in a narrow space, in order that the cavalry and infantry together might run down the enemy*'. [39] The mention of cavalry is surprising and might have referred to the small legionary cavalry detachments. After the humiliating trials of the previous day the soldiers would have been yearning to get at the Germans and would have surged forward through the gap, an irresistible procession of six vexillations, less the baggage escort.

The archaeological record, numbers of coins and pieces of equipment found in this area, shows that there was some fighting here, but the pattern of finds is startling. They fall in a single track as far as a point due north of the Berg, but then there is a split. Some continue due west, but some branch north, into the swamp.[40](*Sketch 2*)

There can be only one explanation for this and it hinges on the formation used by the Romans. If entire legions had been deployed it would be expected that the transport/supply echelons would follow their individual legion, but as vexillations were deployed all the transport/supply echelons, with their escort and various camp followers, formed one large mass, a mass that could not move fast. If there had been the space, and the perceived requirement, the Romans would have formed an *agmen quadratum*, that is a solid wall of cohorts round the transport, but as it was the escort was inadequate. It may be that the formation employed showed a certain lack of subtlety which might have been due to the senior commanders not being present.

When the leading troops came in contact with the Germans they surged through the gap. The wall round the gap would have protected the warriors there who would have showered missiles on the Romans, encouraging them to go faster to get through the beaten zone and any tribesmen in the gap would have fallen back in front of the legionaries, leading them on.

The speed of the advance would have created a gap between the manoeuvre cohorts and the slow moving transport/supply echelon which would naturally, because of the mud, tended to walk to the left close to the German wall. Unfortunately, being close to the wall would have made the mules, and men, more vulnerable to missiles thrown from the wall. As soon as the manoeuvre cohorts had passed Arminius would have put in a counter-attack aimed at the head of the transport echelon, which would have panicked the animals and driven them, their escort, and the crowd of non-combatants northwards away from the fighting echelon and into the swamp. Some might even have tried to return to the last marching camp. This counter-attack could have come from behind the wall, or from mounted warriors concealed to the north. If the latter they would have galloped across the front of the transport to swing round to hit it from the south. The transport animals and their loads would have provided very attractive booty for any Germans and the whole supply echelon would have quickly ceased to exist. This disaster might have been referred to in Dio's garbled account, '*Upon setting out from there they plunged into the woods again, where they defended themselves against their assailants, but suffered their heaviest losses while doing so*'. Meanwhile the fighting troops would have marched on a few hundred yards, exulting in their victory.

This can be the only explanation for the large number of finds in what was swamp at the time of the battle. Certainly the Germans could never have driven the fighting cohorts north into the swamp.

A little rain in this area of Germany, which is only a few feet above sea level and often water-logged, can reduce visibility drastically. It can be expected that Arminius would have organised some Germans to skirmish and generally harass the legionaries, more to give Varus something to think about rather than to inflict real harm, so it is unlikely Varus realised what had happened to his supply echelon until it was too late to do anything about it. Arminius had out-thought him. There would have been a few minutes of perplexed inactivity, the soldiers standing in their ranks, officers consulting with other officers. Some horsemen would have been sent back, probably escorting a senior officer, to investigate the situation. Doubtlessly as soon as it could be organised some cohorts were sent back, but it was too late.

The soldiers had just the clothes, and armour, they stood in. Most would no longer have a *pilum*, their only remaining weapons their sword and shield. There would have been little food available, no tents and few entrenching tools. The future suddenly looked grim.

Varus's first priority would have been an offensive to rescue what was left of his supply echelon, but by the time the troops he sent had reported back, it was too late. He had been wounded and seems, at this point, to have just given up. In fact the only thing he could have done was to turn his legions round and make a forced march back to Minden. This option would have resulted in very heavy casualties, and once back in Minden the survivors would have had to scour the country round to find something to eat before making another desperate march, this time back to the Lippe. The first stage of this march, passing the Kalkrieser Berg, may have been fairly easy as the Germans were totally occupied with searching for booty, but it would have required abandoning the wounded. Whatever his appreciation of the situation, Varus did not act.

The soldiers laid out a camp and made an attempt to build a rampart but achieved little, having no tools. Mostly they just sat in the rain, they would not even have had their cloaks. Their problems were increasing, not only were they hungry but, with the *contubernium* mules missing, they had lost their shield covers. This meant that their shields were getting wet, this weakened their plywood-like structure until they were of little use for defence.

The sequence of events as recounted by Dio is a little vague, but it appears that the next day passed with little change. From the Roman point of view the major event was that the legionary cavalry attempted a break-out. Whether they succeeded or not is not known, similarly whether they had Varus's permission or not is not known, indeed he might have ordered them to go. Either way the legionaries would have regarded this as an act of desertion. Also it is just possible that Varus attempted to negotiate

With Arminius, but naturally no Roman author would ever record such an event. Possibly Varus did not fully understand the part that Arminius had played. The soldiers' defeatism which was brought on by hunger and cold was only increased by seeing, or hearing about, these things. No doubt the Germans were raining missiles into the camp, and as the soldiers' shields were all but useless, as they did not have their sturdy tents, and as the camp ramparts were poor and did not have the usual fence these missiles were much more effective than would normally have been the case.

Arminius and many more Germans could speak Latin. They would have run a day and night propaganda offensive mocking the Romans and suggesting their surrender, the words falling like missiles among the soldiers who were huddled together for warmth and as a protection against slingshot. Doubtlessly the message given was similar to that given seven years later when, during one of Germanicus's campaigns, *'An enemy who knew Latin now rode up to the stockade. In Arminius's name he called out, promising every deserter a wife, some land, and a hundred sesterces a day for the rest of the war. This insulting suggestion infuriated the Roman soldiers'*.[41]

Propaganda and missiles continued till, as Dio put it, *'the fourth day dawned, and again a heavy downpour and violent wind assailed them, preventing them from going forward and even from standing securely, and moreover depriving them of the use of their weapons. For they could not handle their bows or their javelins with any success, nor, for that matter, their shields, which were thoroughly soaked. Their opponents, on the other hand, being for the most part lightly equipped, and able to approach and retire freely, suffered less from the storm. Furthermore, the enemy's forces had greatly increased, an many of those who had at first wavered now joined them, largely in the hope of plunder, and thus they could more easily encircle and strike down the Romans, whose ranks were now thinned, many having perished in the earlier fighting. Varus, therefore, and all the more prominent officers, fearing that they should either be captured alive or be killed by their bitterest foes (for they had already been wounded), made bold to do a thing that was terrible yet unavoidable: they took their own lives.*

'When news of this had spread, none of the rest, even if he had any strength left, defended himself any longer. Some imitated their leader, and others, casting aside their arms, allowing anybody who pleased to slay them; for to flee was impossible, however much one might desire to do so. Every man, therefore, and every horse was cut down without any fear of resistance, and the ...'.[42]

At this point there is a break in Dio's narrative. There is little doubt that the last sentence of this narrative is wrong as it is known that many Roman soldiers did survive. It is more likely that at dawn the Germans assembled for an assault, totally surrounding the camp, and the legionaries, seeing that a further march to the west was impracticable, showed a general unwillingness to fight. There is a further factor which may have affected the soldiers' morale. They may have been, to one degree or another, mutinous, and one of their grievances would have been their years of hard and unprofitable campaigning in Germany. A major mutiny was to break out at Cologne only five years later and the first stirrings of this may have already spread to Varus's legionaries who could have started to resent their officers, and had been losing their habits of obedience. This will not have affected the whole army at the same time, some would have wanted to fight, some to break out, some to give in. Some senior officers, who might have been friendly with Arminius, ordered the soldiers to put up their weapons, as Velleius Parerculus wrote (already quoted) *'nor was as much opportunity as they had wished given to the soldiers either of fighting or of extricating themselves, except against heavy odds; nay, some were even heavily chastised for using the arms and showing the spirit of Romans'.* There was certainly no 'orbs' formed for desperate fights round the eagles. The Germans captured two, and the third was snatched up by the *aquilifer* who ran off towards the swamp in a doomed attempt to preserve it.

A mass surrender, like this, amounted to mutiny and desertion in the face of the enemy and, as in most armies, was a capital offence. This shows the depth of despair felt by both officers and soldiers, and how discipline had broken down.

There is a hint that weakness was shown by some officers in that: '*Some of the prisoners were afterwards ransomed by their relatives and returned from captivity; for this was permitted on condition that the men ransomed should remain outside Italy'*.[43] Presumably the legionaries and *posterior* centurions did not have families that could afford ransoms, nor would the various camp followers, but the senior officers, that might have been negotiating with Arminius, would have had such families. Augustus would have been incensed at their behaviour, not at the ransom.

The Germans swamped into the camp, disarming the soldiers and killing those who resisted. Arminius, who knew the Roman army, knew how to destroy the leadership of a legion. He ordered the tribunes and *prior* centurions separated out and had them massacred.[44] This would for three understrength legions give an approximate number of officers massacred of 66. This total would be reduced for casualties, but increased by adding some senior officers and any surviving officers of auxiliary formations. These officers would have formed the class-based leadership of the legions and witnessing their deaths would have been a salutary experience for the surrendered legionaries.

Archaeology has yet to find the surrender site, which is an indication that there was little fighting there.

A few Romans escaped the surrender. These were most likely from the rearguard, they would have been cut off from the main body of the army by the German counter-attack and could, with some *contubernium* mules have headed initially towards Minden, then south to the Lippe. Others might have escaped in the chaos of the surrender or later while being led away to a life of slavery, and some had been ransomed. Some of the survivors were to return to the Kalkrieser Berg in 15 AD with Germanicus's army, and they pointed out the locations of some of the events of the battle. Some might have felt that they had some difficult questions to answer.

There is no doubt that the loss of three legions, even if they were greatly understrength, was a blow to the Empire, but the reaction to it seems a little extreme. The legions were never reformed (this is not quite true, the 18th Legion was reformed later by Nero, but only existed for a short time) which was unusual. The 14th Legion, whose destruction has been described earlier in this chapter, was reformed as soon as possible. The disaster so upset Emperor Augustus that he was heard to howl '*Vare, redde legiones*', which might have been a theatrical display blaming a safely dead man to divert attention away from German prowess and bad Roman high level policy decisions. Most surprising is that there is so little known about the battle, it is as if news of a mass surrender was suppressed, a possibility which, by its very nature, can never be positively proven, but the break in Dio's narrative is suggestive.

It is a remarkable aspect of the destruction of Varus's army that there was little heavy fighting involved. This impression is confirmed by a comment made during one of the *querelles Allemandes* by Maroboduus, a rival chieftain:

'Arminius, he said, was a senseless inexperienced man who took the credit due to others because he had treacherously trapped three straggling divisions (legions) *and an unsuspecting commander'*.[45] Even so it maybe that the Germans suffered heavily. Certainly there was no immediate assault on the Rhine frontier, so the rear parties of the three legions must have been enough to provide the semblance of an effective defence, presumably calling up reservists and parading around a lot.

The account of the battle given here is the only narrative that fits all the known facts. The driving force of the German actions was Arminius, he had served in the Roman army and had discovered one of its weak points. The legionaries were almost helpless in a hostile country without their transport. Arminius orchestrated an action in the forest to force Varus to organise his transport in a single echelon separate from the legions, then forced the Romans to pass through a gauntlet where the Germans could destroy or capture the whole echelon.

Arminius was to try the same basic tactic again six years later in an action known as the 'Long Bridges' (*Pontes Longi*). The bridges were a corduroy road built fourteen years earlier to cross swampy ground, and the road was an indication that the Romans had had long term plans for Germany. During the fourteen years it had decayed. Passing along the long bridge would be a difficult operation for the Romans, who had an army of four legions, and an opportunity for the Germans. The following action bore certain similarities to the Varus disaster, and certain contrasts.

The greatest contrast was with the commander, Aulus Caecina Severus. As Tacitus put it: *'In his forty years of service as soldier and commander, he had known crisis as well as success'*.[46] He ordered his men to repair the road, and they set about this while under intermittent attack from the Germans, but when the transport started to go along the road the legion posted as rear guard abandoned its post leaving the transport vulnerable. This was not missed by Arminius who '*ordered the Germans to attack. At the head of a picked force, crying that here was another Varus and his army caught in the same trap again, he broke through the Roman column. His chief targets were the horses, which slipped in their own blood and the slimy bog and threw their riders, scattering everyone in their way and trampling on those who had fallen*'.[47]

A large part of the transport was lost, but not as much as at Kalkriese, even so, as at Kalkriese, after the legions had crossed the obstacle the loss of tools made constructing a camp difficult. '*Earthworks had to be constructed, and their material collected; and most of the equipment for moving soil and cutting turf had been lost. Units had no tents, the wounded no dressing. As the muddy bloodstained rations were handed round, men spoke miserably of the deathly darkness, and the end which tomorrow would bring to thousands*'.

But the soldiers had something to eat, still had their weapons, and most importantly had determined leadership. Next morning the Germans assaulted the camp, which would have had poor defences, but, as no doubt Arminius predicted, they were heavily defeated. The Romans could then continue their march to the Rhine, unmolested.

The fighting at the Long Bridges confirms that Arminius's basic tactic was to deprive the legions of their transport, and perhaps he would have had another great success to celebrate if his warriors had not insisted on assaulting the Roman camp. The question returns to Varus and what he could have done to avoid his disaster. The answer must hinge on transport. As soon as he realised that he was in hostile territory he should have ordered all non-essential baggage to be dumped, which he did, then he should have ordered all the freed-up carts and mules to carry the soldiers' personal kit. Then the army should have proceeded with the transport as a central column with legionaries marching on either side. Marching in this formation would have made passing through the bottleneck at Kalkriese difficult, so it might have been best to fall back a march then proceed to the Lippe. Retaining all the carts would have caused difficulty in fitting the whole column in a three legion camp, and might have made feeding the animals difficult, but it would have been better than the alternative.

It is difficult to know to what extent the Romans planned to absorb Germany into the Empire. Roman campaigns in Germany had always been designed as spoiling raids to keep the Germans cowed and uninterested in attacking Gaul.[48] This strategy, overall, was highly successful. The Varus episode was their only attempt at setting up a provincial administration and even then the Romans were returning to the Rhine rather than wintering in Germany. Perhaps the Romans had decided that Germany was not worth the trouble. Ultimately it must be left to the reader to decide if the Varus disaster rates a place as one of 'The Fifteen Decisive Battles of the World'. The defeat was accepted with a dignity probably designed to be seen as a contrast to some of the squalid behaviour seen during the Civil Wars. When a *letter was read in the senate from a chieftain of the Chatti named Adgandestrius, offering to kill Arminius if the poison were sent him for the job. The reported answer was that Romans take vengeance on their enemies, not by underhand tricks, but by open force of arms. By this elevated sentiment Tiberius invited comparison with generals of old who had forbidden, and disclosed, the plan to poison King Pyrrhus*.[49] Despite this Arminius did not last long and was killed by some of his relations.

Some survivors of this disaster were rescued from their

captivity forty years later when some German raiders were intercepted by Roman troops and annihilated.[50]

A Final Speculation. Although it may be repeated that the account of the Varus Disaster given here is the only one to fit all the known facts, there remains the impression that there is something missing, some extra factor that prevented the five or six seemingly triumphant vexillations making a determined effort to reach the Rhine. Their stomachs may have been empty, their shields useless, but they were still Roman soldiers and still had their swords and the alternative was either massacre or slavery. Surely they would show some grit and make the attempt, even if only one in ten succeeded.

But perhaps there was another way of looking at it. Perhaps instead of surrendering, the soldiers were changing sides. Perhaps they were not destined for a life of slavery, but were joining German war bands.

This concept may seem bizarre, legions did not change sides! But Varus's troops were not happy. They resented that they were kept in the army for a longer and longer time. In the reorganisation following Actium the length of a legionary's service was set at sixteen years plus four in the reserve. It had crept up to twenty and five. Also the soldier's pay had not been increased since Caesar's day, but its value had been eroded by inflation. Campaigning in Germans brought in negligible booty and Augustus had reigned for years, so no donatives.

On the other hand the soldiers had been in contact with the German cavalry, many of whom could speak Latin, and these Germans knew that they were going to desert the Romans. Would they not have spoken to the legionaries and said 'come with us'. Perhaps some legionaries listened.

Perhaps the captives freed after 40 years were actually members of a raiding party.

This is, of course, pure speculation, we will never know if it is true.

The Battle of Beth-Horon

In 66 AD the province of Judea revolted against Roman rule and massacred or drove out the Roman garrisons. The Empire could not tolerate this and a counter-attack was inevitable. It would be commanded by Cestius Gallus, the governor of Syria.

Cestius assembled an army of one complete legion, XII *Fulminata*, vexillations of three other legions and the surviving four cohorts of the X *Fretensis*, the original legion that suffered badly in the uprising. He also had four cavalry *alae*, six auxiliary cohorts and 16,000 men, mixed cavalry and infantry, supplied by local client states. The number of Roman army troops was approximately the same as the number of client state troops. This might be a coincidence, but it is likely to be deliberate Roman policy. In view of the poor fighting ability recently shown by the Jews, Cestius could feel confident of victory. Unfortunately the principal source for the ensuing campaign, Josephus, can sometimes be exultantly pro-Jewish, so must be read with care.[51]

After some initial operations to secure his base and communications, Cestius marched his army to Jerusalem and spent six days assaulting the city. He certainly caused some damage but it seems he decided that he had bitten off more than he could chew and on the last day he halted the assault and proceeded to withdraw. Josephus found this decision to retreat inexplicable, but there were two likely causes. One was that it was already late in the year and

Cestius did not want his soldiers to have to endure the cold weather characteristic of winters in the area, so if he could not rush Jerusalem it was sensible to withdraw.

Secondly he was short of supplies and this, regardless of anything else, would have forced his withdrawal. Foraging locally would have brought in little, and his supply line back to Caesarea on the coast was under attack by Jewish guerrillas, a supply column had already been ambushed at the Beth-Horon pass. It is quite possible that he had used his auxiliary cohorts and his allied troops to garrison points on this route, and Jewish assaults could have wiped them out, though it is hard to believe that the Jewish guerrillas were capable of this, certainly Josephus's account does not mention these cohorts as taking any part in the fighting.

The pass at Beth-Horon was the site of a Jewish victory during the Wars of the Maccabees, two centuries earlier and would have been replete with symbolism for the Jews. It was a significant obstacle being narrow and about one-and-a-half miles long. Its history would also have been a warning for the Romans of potential difficulties so these would not come as a surprise and would have been planned for.

When the retreat from Jerusalem started, the legionaries were immediately followed up by the Jewish irregulars who bombarded them with the usual types of missiles. The difficulties for the soldiers were caused by the lack of cavalry and light infantry. The soldiers could double their ranks and raise a shield wall to defend against missiles but this was a purely passive defence, and the Romans would have deployed their *carroballistae*, though this might have been difficult on the rough ground. As Josephus describes their situation: '*they themselves were heavily armed and afraid to open their ranks, while they saw that the Jews were lightly armed and adapted for sudden swoops. This meant that they suffered severely without any corresponding damage to the other side. Throughout the march the battering continued, and men who lost their places in the column were killed*'. He records the deaths of three senior officers, but gives no details. He also says that the army abandoned the bulk of its baggage. The army retreated to its last marching camp at Gibeon, the distance covered would have been around ten miles, normally an easy day's march. It halted there for two days.

Cestius has always received a poor press, yet it is difficult to see what mistakes he made other than finding the defences of Jerusalem stronger than expected. When back at Gibeon, which presumably he had left garrisoned as a depot for his second line transport, he rationalised his baggage train. The retreat so far was a taste of things to come as the Jews became emboldened and more joined the insurgents. It is most likely that he had already lost some siege engines, the Jews would later use these against the Romans, and he would be careful not to lose any more. Also he knew that passing his army with its full compliment of carts through the Beth-Horon pass would not be easy, so he emptied the carts of all non-essentials and loaded the siege engines on them. The leftover carts were destroyed, Cestius wanted as few carts as possible to escort through the pass. All draft animals that were suitable for use as *contubernium* transport he issued for that purpose. They would be essential for transporting the soldiers' packs, as the men would have to march in fighting order. The remaining animals he had slaughtered and turned into something like jerky. This would produce a version of iron rations, his men would not have time to cook anything.

After the two days the army marched out going the same route that it came by, roughly North-West to Beth-Horon. The terrain was open and good for deploying the legionaries for the first few miles but close to the village the countryside became very broken and the road took on the character of a pass. The cavalry, which had kept the Jewish skirmishers back, could no longer operate on the flanks and the infantry were forced into one column with the second line transport. At last light the Jews blocked the road and the Romans could not break through, so they camped at Beth-Horon. They set the watch as if they were going to stay the night, then continued the march to the surprise of the Jews who could not stop them or even catch up with them. There is no doubt that the Jews had been outwitted and the Roman army had functioned smoothly. It had had some casualties but nowhere near the figures given by Josephus of 5,300 infantry and 480 cavalry. Josephus also records that the legionaries were marching so fast that, in utter panic, they abandoned all the siege engines. This is unlikely but it is possible that one or two, or maybe a *carrobalista* or two, were left if a wheel or axle broke on the rough ground.

There is no doubt that this event was a defeat and had to be avenged, but it was not a disaster in the Teutoburg mould. It is true that Suetonius wrote that a legionary eagle was lost,[52] but this may be doubted. The eagle must have belonged to the 12th Legion and the course of the battle would make the eagle's loss highly improbable. Also no other author, particularly Josephus, mentions it. Roman losses were not heavy. Nearly all the fighting was missile action and the most common projectiles used against them were slingshot. For best effect these should be cast of lead, but due to the irregular nature of the Jewish forces most slingshot would have been stones and the Roman shields and armour should have been a good protection against them. Each of the thousands of Jewish fighters might have had a javelin, but it could only be thrown once, the Romans would have broken it to make sure it could not be used again, or they might have used it against its original owners. There seems to have been little hand-to-hand fighting, certainly not enough to have caused major casualties.

There can be little doubt that the Romans had far too few skirmishers. These should have been provided by the auxiliary cohorts and the allies. As Cestius marched on Jerusalem he knew that he would need all his legionaries for the assault, so presumably he left the light troops as garrisons. But if that were the case at least one cohort should have been left at Beth-Horon. Perhaps Cestius was just grossly overconfident. He did, though, keep with him two *alae* of cavalry. When he halted at Gibeon for two days he should have used them to check the Beth-Horon route, and they could have occupied the critical ground, acting as mounted infantry.

Probably the most remarkable aspect of the whole sorry episode was leaving 400 men behind in Beth-Horon to simulate the watch. According to Josephus they were all volunteers and were all killed next morning as soon as the Jews realised that the bulk of the army had left. Like other aspects of the battle there are difficulties with this. It would not have been possible to get 400 volunteers in the time available, perhaps it was a full cohort ordered to stay in place until dawn then to follow on at best speed. The Jewish response might have been fast and the cohort followed, caught and overwhelmed by numbers. This must be judged unlikely, but we will never know.

Comments

The four examples given here show Roman armies coming under attack while marching through enemy territory, and three of them meeting disaster. The examples illustrate four main principles:

The first, and most significant, is that soldiers cannot march, carrying their packs, and fight at the same time. Consequently the *contubernium* mules, or any available carts, must carry the packs.

Secondly there is the importance of marching camps, so, for the construction of these the mules must carry the requisite tools.

Thirdly, the second line transport must be regarded as expendable, it could not easily be accommodated in a marching camp, and would slow the march down.

Finally the troops must march in such a way as to keep the mules protected against both missiles and against being stampeded.

The defeat at Atuatuca may possibly have been inevitable from the moment it was decided to abandon the camp, but by not abandoning the second line transport and by not marching in the correct formation to protect the mules, the legion consigned itself to certain defeat.

The disaster of Carrhae came from not packing the mules correctly, hence not being able to construct marching camps. The result of a night of panic following the battle was the near destruction of the army.

Varus's legions had a very difficult march to make once Varus had decided to follow the route to the north of the Wiehen ridge, but they could have done it if they had marched in such a formation as to prevent the destruction of their baggage train. Once they had lost that there was no alternative to surrender.

Cestius Gallus's march was a success. He may be criticised, at least by Josephus, for putting the troops in such a position that they had to make this very difficult march, but by observing sound principles he conducted the retreat successfully and most of his men fought their way through.

Notes

1. Suetonius, *The Twelve Caesars, Galba*, 6, Penguin Classics, p246

2. As above, Loeb, read on www.penelope.uchicago.edu/Thayer/E/Roman/Texts/Suetonius

3. Polybius, *The Rise of the Roman Empire*, VI.40, Penguin Classics, p335,

4. Josephus, *The Jewish War, Excursus III*, Penguin Classics, p379

5. Josephus, *The Jewish War*, 11, Penguin Classics, p180

6. Tacitus, *The Histories*, 2.40, Penguin Classics, p104

7. Tacitus, *The Histories*, 2.19, Penguin Classics, p92

8. *Plutarch's Lives, Sylla*, Translated by the Revs J & W Langhorne. No date, p323

9. Maj-Gen JFC Fuller, *Julius Caesar*, E&S, 1965, p87

10. Vegetius, *Epitome of Military Science*, I.21, Liverpool University Press, 2011, p23

11. Caesar, *The Conquest of Gaul*, VII.2, Penguin Classics, p187

12. Caesar, *The Conquest of Gaul*, VII.4, Penguin Classics, p219

13. Tacitus, *The Annals of Imperial Rome*, XIII.39, Penguin Classics, p303

14. The Acts of the Apostles, Chapter 23, Verse 23-24. The Bible in general makes little differentiation between javelins and spears, and the Greek terms are very similar. In this case javelineers would be the obvious troops to use.

15. Caesar, *The Conquest of Gaul*, VI.1, Penguin Classics, p141-149

16. Caesar, *The Conquest of Gaul*, glossary, Penguin Classics, p275

17. T Rice Holmes, *Caesar's Conquest of Gaul*, Macmillan, 1903, p79

18. Maj-Gen JFC Fuller, *Julius Caesar*, E&S, 1965, p127

19. HP Judson, *Caesar's Army*, Boston 1902, p45

20. *Plutarch's Lives, Marcus Crassus*, Translated by the Revs J & W Langhorne. No date. p387 and Lucan, *The Civil War*, VIII, Loeb, p459

21. Dio Cassius, *Roman History*, XXXVI.5.2, Loeb Vol III, p11
22. *Plutarch's Lives, Marcus Crassus*, Translated by the Revs J & W Langhorne. No date. p389
23. *Plutarch's Lives, Marcus Crassus*, Translated by the Revs J & W Langhorne. No date. p390
24. Dio Cassius, *Roman History*, XL.22.2, Loeb Vol III, p437
25. *Plutarch's Lives, Marcus Crassus*, Translated by the Revs J & W Langhorne. No date. p390
26. Ammianus Marcellinus, *The Later Roman Empire*, 24.2, 25.1, Penguin Classics, p271, 289
27. Appian, *The Civil Wars*, II,110, Penguin Classics, p128
28. Dio Cassius, *Roman History*, XLIX.26.2, Loeb Vol V, p395
29. Herodian of Antioch, *History of the Roman Empire*, VI.V.9, University of California Press, p163. For commentary – Dr K Farrokh, *Shadows in the Desert*, Osprey, 2007
30. Tacitus, *The Annals of Imperial Rome*, I.60, Penguin Classics, p67
31. Velleius Paterculus, *Compendium of Roman History*, II.cxix, Loeb, p301
32. Dio Cassius, *Roman History*, LVI.18, Loeb vol VII, p39
33. Dio Cassius, *Roman History*, LVI.18, Loeb vol VII, p41
34. Velleius Paterculus, *Compendium of Roman History*, II.cxvii, Loeb, p297
35. Tacitus, *The Annals of Imperial Rome*, I.49, Penguin Classics, p61
36. Tacitus, *Germania*, 6, Penguin Classics, p105
37. Vegetius, *Epitome of Military Science*, III.6, Liverpool University Press, 2011, p73
38. Dio Cassius, *Roman History*, LVI.19-20, Loeb vol VII, p43
39. Dio Cassius, *Roman History*, LVI.21, Loeb vol VII, p45
40. A Rost and S Wilbers-Rost, Weapons at the Battlefield of Kalkriese, Gladius, XXX (2010), p117-135
41. Tacitus, *The Annals of Imperial Rome*, II.13, Penguin Classics, p83
42. Dio Cassius, *Roman History*, LVI.21-22, Loeb vol VII, p47
43. Dio Cassius, *Roman History*, LVI.22, Loeb vol VII, p51
44. Tacitus, *The Annals of Imperial Rome*, I.61, Penguin

Classics, p67

45. Tacitus, *The Annals of Imperial Rome*, II.46, Penguin Classics, p100. The key phrase is '*tres vagas legiones*' which is transated by CH Moore and J Jackson (Loeb) as 'three straggling legions', but by Church and Brodribb (Read on www.sacred-texts.com) as 'three unofficered legions'

46. Tacitus, *The Annals of Imperial Rome*, I.64, Penguin Classics, p69

47. Tacitus, *The Annals of Imperial Rome*, I.65, Penguin Classics, p70

48. EA Oldfather and HV Carter, *The Defeat of Varus and the German Frontier Policy of Augustus*, University of Illinois, 1916

49. Tacitus, *The Annals of Imperial Rome*, II.88, Penguin Classics, p119

50. Tacitus, *The Annals of Imperial Rome*, XII.23, Penguin Classics, p263

51. Josephus, *The Jewish War*, 9, Penguin Classics, p163-165

52. Suetonius, *The Twelve Caesars, X, Vespasian*, Penguin Classics, p276.

Chapter 6: The Two Battles of Philippi

The purpose of this study has been to examine the activity of legionaries in battle, however the previous chapter has shown that in some cases only by considering wider aspects of campaigning can battles be understood. Also battlefield activity can extend further than fighting *ad spathos et ad pila*. To illustrate this, this chapter will consider the Battles of Philippi.

These battles took place in 42 BC in Macedonia. In them the forces of Octavian and Mark Antony, two of the Triumvirs, defeated those of Brutus and Cassius. The Republican troops included 19 legions, in the region of 80,000 men, 20,000 cavalry of various nationalities and 400 mounted archers. This was certainly an impressive force but it was not homogenous, the legions were understrength, and the loyalty of some of them which had served Julius Caesar was suspect. The forces of the Triumvirs were of similar numbers, 19 fully manned legions with two more *en route* and 13,000 cavalry.

The two armies met around two miles to the west of the small town of Philippi which stands on the main east-west Roman road the Via Egnatia which runs parallel to the Mediterranean shore. It is nine miles inland from the coast at Neapolis, the modern Kavala.(*Sketch 3*)

The site was an obvious battlefield. The Via Egnatia ran through a gap of less than two miles between high ground to the north and a swamp to the south. The Republicans arrived first and built two camps, Brutus's to the north, Cassius's to the south. The camps were around a mile apart and were joined by a rampart running continuously with the western faces of the two camps.

The site of the battlefield described here is the generally accepted one but, remarkably, it has not been confirmed by archaeology. In view of the extensive digging of ditches and the quantities of rubble moved to build the causeway, confirmation should not be out of the question. On the map, at least, the battlefield could easily be placed to the south-east of Philippi, on the road to Neapolis. Perhaps in the years to come, archaeology will prove as fruitful as it has done in the case of the Teutoburg Wald.

Brutus and Cassius were in a strong position their two camps being on slight rises. Their fleet had sailed along the coast keeping pace with their army and could land supplies at Neapolis, and there was plenty of water locally. To ensure that the Triumvir's forces could not outflank them and interrupt their communications with Neapolis the southern extension was built, this was an extra rampart running from the south-east corner of Cassius's camp south into the swamp.

The Triumvirs' armies duly arrived under Mark Antony. Octavian was ill and had been left behind, as had all non-essential baggage. They encamped around a mile to the west of the rampart roughly opposite the camps of Brutus and Cassius. Mark Antony, who generally took the lead in military operations, was on the right. This location was not as favourable as that of the Republicans in that there was little water handy and the troops had to sink wells. Also there was little locally to eat and, as the Republican fleet was much the stronger, it would be difficult to bring supplies in, it was natural that the Triumvirs were keen to fight as soon as possible.

There was some light skirmishing and Octavian rejoined the army even though he was still convalescent. He observed events from a litter.

Accordingly, for a few days each morning the Triumvirs

formed up their troops in front of their camp in battle order, but quite reasonably the Republicans would not take the bait. However Mark Antony realised that the Republicans would be forced to fight if he could threaten their communications to the east. Consequently he ordered the construction of a causeway across the swamp to run well to the south of the southern extension. This was a major undertaking, large quantities of rocks and rubble would be required and it all had to be transported to the swamp working mostly at night. So that it would not be noticed that many men were employed in the working parties, Mark Antony ordered that the same number of standards were displayed each morning when the troops formed up for battle.

Work in the swamp was hidden by reeds and continued for ten days, then Mark Antony sent some cohorts along the causeway to set up a redoubt to the rear of the Republican lines. As soon as this was seen by the Republicans Cassius put his men to work extending the southern extension and strengthening it with a palisade, this work would soon block the causeway and cut off any troops working at its eastern end. Naturally a success here for Cassius's troops would have been a massive blow for the Triumvirs' troops after so much toil and short rations, and Mark Antony realised that he could no longer stand on the defensive.

Mark Antony can reasonably be regarded as the foremost soldier of the age and during the ten days his troops were toiling on their earthworks he would have been planning the assault of Cassius's camp, and discussing these plans with his senior officers, so once his decision was made it took only a short time to implement. He probably attacked around midday, 23rd October. The soldiers of both sides were ready for action in the morning but by midday only a thin screen of troops would have been left facing the enemy, the rest would have been assigned to working parties. Mark Antony's troops surged out of their camp, the leading echelon chased away the screen of Republican troops, the second echelon, equipped with '*crowbars and ladders*' assaulted the southern extension while, with the bulk of his troops he faced Cassius's camp to prevent any counter-attack. The fact that the troops were properly equipped shows that this was no *impromptu* action.

Mark Antony's troops took the field before Octavian's, this might have been due to a signalling mishap or perhaps with Octavian being abed his chain of command was not functioning well. As Mark Antony's men advanced, Brutus's men left their camp and, initially, attacked Mark Antony's northern flank probably with cavalry. They scored some success, then as the Republican infantry joined in the fight they switched to attacking Octavian's men issuing from their camp. They defeated these men, cutting up three legions, broke into their camp and set to sacking it, regardless of how the rest of the battle was progressing. Fortunately for Octavian he had already left the camp, forewarned, he said, by a dream.

The rest of the battle was progressing very badly for Cassius's men. As Appian wrote about Mark Antony '*He broke through this line and audaciously reached the wall between the camp and the marsh. His men uprooted the palisade, filled in the ditch, undermined the structure, slaughtered the men guarding the gates, and withstood the rain of missiles from the wall, until Antonius himself forced his way through the gates and the rest came in, some through the breaches in the wall, others by actually climbing on the bodies of the fallen. This all happened so quickly that they had already captured the wall when they confronted the men who had been working in the marsh and were coming to lend support. With a powerful assault they routed these too and after pushing them down into the marsh turned back, this time to Cassius's actual camp. Antonius had with him only those who had surmounted the wall, since all the rest of both forces were fighting each other beyond it.*'[1] This is a little obscure but seems to indicate that Mark Antony had captured and destroyed the southern extension, relieved the cohorts he had earlier sent along the causeway, and broken into Cassius's camp. Some of the obscurity might have been physical. It was a feature of this battle that clouds of dust covered the battlefield, and this might indicate that there was extensive cavalry fighting on the Octavian-Brutus front, but as the fighting was inconclusive and the cavalrymen were not Roman citizens, this fighting was not reported.

At this point Mark Antony seemed to have won the battle, if he could have held Cassius's camp he would have threatened Brutus's communications and would have forced him to retreat. Cassius was dead. He had been fighting outside his camp and was deserted by his cavalry. '*The foot, likewise, began to give way: and though he laboured as much as possible to stop their flight, and snatching an ensign from the hand of one of the fugitives, fixed it at his feet, yet he was hardly able to keep his own praetorian band together: so that, at length, he was obliged to retire, with a very small number, to a hill that overlooked the plain. Yet here he could discover nothing; for he was short-sighted.*'[2] In the chaos of the moment with the situation obscured by dust, he judged the battle lost and committed suicide. The battle, though, was not lost, and Mark Antony was forced to abandon Cassius's camp and return to his own. Why this happened can only be surmised, but seems to have hinged on pillage. Bursting into the camp his soldiers would have stayed with their maniples a short time, but soon the temptation of pillage, particularly of something to eat, would have weakened the units, whereas opposite sentiments were working on Cassius's men. They knew that their enemies were looting their personal kit and were determined to fight.

Soldiers cannot pillage and fight at the same time, and there certainly was a great deal of pillaging. Brutus, the next day, criticised his men: *'You preferred plunder to killing the men you had defeated, for the majority of you went on past the enemy themselves and made for their property'*.[3] The situation had been just as bad for the Triumvirs, and Appian complained that some of Mark Antony's men returning to their camp looked more like porters than soldiers. As a result of this Mark Antony withdrew his troops. This might have been because he wanted to send some troops to assist with the recapture of Octavian's camp, or he might have been accepting that he had generally lost control.

At the end of the day, all four armies had returned to their camps, but the Triumvirs had eliminated the threat to the causeway. As that victory was to be permanent it is most likely that they converted the point of the southern extension into a small redoubt to prevent any further Republican work there.

This concluded the First Battle of Philippi. Casualties had been heavy: 8,000 Republicans and 16,000 of the Triumvirs. It is not known if Cassius's cavalry returned to the army.

Next day Brutus moved his head quarters into Cassius's camp as it was obvious that most of the fighting would be in the south. Because of the loss of personal kit he granted each legionary 1,000 *denarii*, and proportionately more for officers.

For a few days little happened, this was to the advantage of Brutus as news had arrived concerning a disaster at sea for the Triumvirate. Brutus knew that the supply situation for his enemies was becoming desperate, and they had been forced to send a legion away on a foraging expedition. Despite this the morale of the Republican soldiers was declining. There had been desertion among the allies and the Triumvirs had mounted a propaganda campaign getting leaflets into the Republican camps. The Republicans had taken a number of prisoners and some of them were suspected of spreading discontent, so Brutus had them killed.

To increase the difficulties of the Triumvirs' troops, soon after the end of the fighting it started to rain. This was very welcome to parched throats, but it would have halted progress on the causeway. However events were to show that the causeway had gone far enough. Each day the Triumvirs offered battle, but they could not force Brutus to fight, then he made a mistake. Close to what had been Cassius's camp was a small hill. Being close to the camp and within bowshot it would have been difficult for the Triumvirs to approach, even so Cassius had garrisoned it. Brutus withdrew this garrison. The location that best suits the course of the battle is to the south-east of the camp, that is just to the camp's left rear. Brutus had failed to notice that recent changes had made this hill vulnerable.

It was capture at night by some of Octavian's legions. The attacking troops could have assembled at the (conjectured) redoubt on the southern extension, or made their way through the swamp from the causeway. Either way some legionaries occupied the hill, then more came carrying wicker screens which they set up as a protection against arrows while they constructed the ramparts of a four legion camp. A four legion camp was large, approximately 300 yards by 220, far too big to use any defences built by the temporary Republican garrison. The greater part of the camp would have been on the southern slope of the hill, where it could not be seen by Brutus.

The dimensions of the camps given here are based on a formula in a well-known book.[4] However this refers to camps for full-strength units in peacetime, but temporary wartime structures for probably under-strength units may have been significantly smaller.

'*When they had it* (the new camp) *securely in their possession, they shifted the camp of another ten legions more than a thousand yards in the direction of the sea, and the camp of another two nearly a further half-mile*'.[5] Appian's text seems to indicate that this work was done really quickly, but the realities of organising thousands of troops must have extended the time required to at least two weeks.

There can be no doubt that the new camp was a worry for Brutus but he does not seem to have done much about it. It must have been obvious that there were extensive troop movements afoot in the Triumvirs' camps but no attempt was made to take advantage of them.

The next objective, following Appian's sequence of events, of not his time scale, was the new ten-legion camp. This was a major undertaking, such a camp would have sides of around 650 and 1,000 yards and would have to be very carefully, and quickly, marked out. Much work must have been done to improve the communications between the original camps and the new four-legion camp. Presumably the route ran along the causeway, up the southern extension and along the southern edge of the new camp. The route would have to carry heavy traffic, and at night.(*Sketch 4*)

The Triumvirs knew that they could not reconnoitre the site too closely as that would be tantamount to telling Brutus what their next move was going to be, surprise would be essential.

It is possible that the legions involved left a cohort or vexillation behind, partly to disguise the move, and partly to guard the soldiers' kit and the draft animals that were being left behind. Once a date had been settled on the troops would have been assembled as soon as it was dark enough to hide what was happening. The first four legions would have been in fighting order, that is carrying only their weapons and a water bottle. They would have paraded silently and marched off along the causeway then out behind the new camp to the new ten-legion site where experienced officers were hurriedly staking out the site. As the legions arrived they were formed in a solid line presenting a front, one cohort deep, across the 1,000 gap between the two camps, and across the 1,000 yards in front of the camp and across around 500 yards on the eastern side of the new camp to join the northern edge of the swamp. Four legions should have easily managed this. The worry was the Republican cavalry, any units still in motion, or with open flanks, at dawn would have been vulnerable, the Triumvirs knew they could not get their own cavalry through such a difficult night march.

While the troops were marching they were vulnerable, and the march would take a long time. Along the causeway and up the southern extension it would seem reasonable that they could only go two abreast. Marching at night, a maniple would take at least two and a half minutes to pass a point, that is seven and a half minutes for a cohort, and very roughly one hour for an understrength legion, which is presuming a clockwork-type efficiency.

Following the fighting echelon would come the remaining legions. They were more heavily laden, carrying tools for entrenching the camp and stakes for the ramparts. They would have filed into the places reserved for them then rested till dawn when the staking out of the camp would have been checked and work started. No doubt the musicians gave out triumphant peels, no doubt Republican morale sagged.

As the day wore on and it became apparent that the Republicans would not attack, the draft animals would have been brought forward, tents erected and rations cooked.

At this stage it is difficult to understand Brutus's actions. He had built a continuous rampart with a series of small redoubts opposite the new camps of the Triumvirs. Naturally being further away from the swamp, the Republican earthworks were on a higher level than the Triumvirs'. These earthworks was extended a few days later when the Triumvirs built the new two-legion camp. The two lines of earthworks were close, just out of bowshot, probably around 300 yards apart, mobile trench warfare indeed! It stands repeating that none of this has been confirmed by archaeology, and if there was ever a case when archaeology should have been of assistance to the historian, this is it.

It is not known why Brutus held on to his position so long. Falling back towards Neapolis should have been easy. His new position would have been strong and he would be inflicting more labour on the enemy troops. Instead he decided to fight. Perhaps he was worried about being outflanked and cut off from Neapolis, perhaps the rains had extended the swamp and made a retreat more difficult, or perhaps he gave in to the urging of his troops who were tired of the travails of the campaign and wanted to end it.

Regardless of why the battle was fought, the constricted nature of the battlefield caused certain difficulties. The fighting was mainly between the two fortified lines, these being roughly 3,000 yards long. A cohort would usually deploy on a front of 100 yards, so the main battle may have been carried out by four understrength legions on each side. There may have been an opportunity for manoeuvre on the eastern, open, flank but it is not mentioned.

A maniple before deploying would require a depth of 32 yards for its sixteen ranks. If the legions were deployed in two lines of cohorts they would require a theoretical depth of 64 yards, but in reality this must be at least 80 yards or crowding would result in a loss of control, as it did at Cannae.

It can be seen then, that as the troops deployed their front ranks were very close to each other. This made deployment difficult and the battle did not start till midday. Before the start of the battle it was reported that two eagles were seen fighting above the battlefield, but this is such a trope that it is difficult to believe, but the suspense must have been acute and the armies suddenly detonated into action. *'There came a piercing shout from the enemy, the standards were raised on both sides, and the charge was violent and harsh. They had little need of volleys of arrows or stones or javelins according to the custom of war, since they made no use of the other techniques and manoeuvres of battle, but came to grips with drawn swords, inflicting and receiving thrusts, and trying to push each other out of formation'.*[6]

The Republicans, having the high ground could be expected to have lined their ramparts with archers, but if they did the press of man against man made missile action useless. It may be that the continuous entrenchment, *vallum* and ditch, of the Republicans became a great hindrance. The Triumvirs' men drove the Republican front line back, but the second line could not pull back with it because of the entrenchment and soon the cohorts of the second line became mixed up with those of the first line. *'Their opponents were pushed back foot by foot, gradually and with deliberation; but once their formation had been disrupted, they retreated more rapidly, and as the reserves of the second and third lines joined in the retreat they all became chaotically mixed up and were squeezed by their own men and the enemy, who gave them no respite from attack, until they were in open flight'.*[7]

There followed a general collapse of the Republican troops which ended the Second Battle of Philippi. The casualties are not known, but around 14,000 Republican soldiers surrendered and were incorporated into the Triumvirs' army.

This account of the two Battles of Philippi has shown that, on occasion, the legionary's ability as a navvy was every bit as important for battlefield success as was his ability in fighting *ad spathos et ad pila.*

To quote Sextus Julius Frontinus, '*Domitius Corbulo used to say that the pick* (dolabra) *was the weapon with which to beat the enemy*'.[8]

Notes

1. Appian, *The Civil Wars*, IV,111, Penguin Classics, p264
2. *Plutarch's Lives, Marcus Brutus*, Translated by the Revs J & W Langhorne. No date, p686
3. Appian, *The Civil Wars*, IV.117, Penguin Classics, p267
4. The approximations of camp sizes are derived from a formula given in A Harkness, *The Military System of the Romans*, reprinted by Leonaur. The formula is, width in feet = 200 x square root of number of cohorts, and length = width x 1.4
5. Appian, *The Civil Wars*, IV.121, Penguin Classics, p269
6. Appian, *The Civil Wars*, IV,128, Penguin Classics, p272
7. Appian, *The Civil Wars*, IV.128, Penguin Classics, p273
8. Frontinus, *Stratagems*, VII.2, Loeb, p309

Chapter 7: Campaigning at the High Point of Empire

Under the reign (98 to 117 AD) of Marcus Ulpius Nerva Traianus Caesar, usually known as Trajan, the empire reached its greatest extent. It may be taken, then, that his two main offensive wars, with Dacia and Parthia, showed the legions at the final point of their evolution for this type of warfare. Unfortunately the surviving accounts of the Parthian War are too sparse to provide any details of how the soldiers fought although they do seem to indicate an increased appreciation of the importance of archery by the Romans. More information can be gleaned from the Dacian Wars.

Trajan's Dacian Wars

The importance of these wars lies more with the chief source of information about them, Trajan's Column, than their place in the history of the Roman Empire. The column gives a fair representation of the army on campaign even if it is vague geographically.

The wars started in 101 AD when Trajan's forces crossed the Danube and invaded Dacia, the modern Romania. It is not known how large his army was, nine legions could have been involved, and more could have sent vexillations. There was also a roughly equal number of auxiliary troops.

The army advanced slowly as the country was rough and the Dacians adopted a scorched earth policy. The legionaries seem to have spent most of their time on construction tasks. They were aiming at the Dacian capital Sarmizegethusa. Finally there was a battle, presumably the

Dacians felt confident enough to attack the Romans, but it was inconclusive and the Roman troops constructed a camp to pass the winter in. In order to distract the Romans, the Dacian commander, Decebalus, mounted a raid across the Danube in the region of Nicopolis, but this on the whole was unsuccessful.

Next year Trajan decided to attack on a different axis but it is not clear if he withdrew all his troops from their winter camp for the new campaign or left some there. He attacked up the river Oltul. On this axis were several forts covering Sarmizegethusa, in order to besiege them he had to form two cavalry commands to scour the countryside to ensure that the siege troops were not attacked from their rear. After these forts fell, Decebalus surrendered to save Sarmizegethusa from a siege. So ended the 1st Dacian War.

From the legionary's point of view the important military fact of the war would have been the Falx, the 'national' weapon of the Dacians which looked more like an agricultural tool, a kind of sickle, than a weapon. It was around three feet long with a long wooden handle and a forward curving blade, a bit like a medieval billhook or halberd. No doubt these weapons could inflict a serious wound but would be less useful the closer the owner was to a Roman soldier. A panel in the Tropaeum Traiani, a triumphal monument built by the army at Adamklissi in Romania to commemorate the Dacian wars, shows a Roman soldier hitting a Dacian with his shield while stabbing him with his sword, the unfortunate Dacian not being able to use his weapon at such close quarters.[1] However, either out of respect for the Dacian weapons or as a part of an on-going trend, the legionaries' helmets seem to have been reinforced with iron plates or bars, and some soldiers, shown at Adamklissi, wore armour on their legs and sword arms (greaves and vambraces). There are no representations of falx on Trajan's Column, presumably there were but were in metal and, like the soldiers' *pila,* have been stolen. The column does show some short one-handed scimitar-type swords, but these should not have caused the Romans much trouble.

One remarkable aspect of the representations of legionaries on Trajan's Column is that their shields are much smaller than would be expected. This has been put down to artistic effect, in that correctly sized shields would have dominated the scenes to a far too great extent. However it is not impossible that the shields are correctly shown, that a decision had been made to reduce their size to increase the soldiers' mobility. Perhaps as missile troops became more important so shields shrank as the soldiers were less dependant on passive defence. Also it must be noticed that when the large shield was in vogue the legionaries had little need of armour, but the column shows almost obsessively the legionaries in near perfect *lorica segmentata*. This might just be a justification for the smaller shields. It might also be that, in the real world, only the centurions, having a much higher pay than the legionaries hence able to afford armour, and having much smaller shields hence the incentive to buy it, were the only ones wearing body armour, but the Column was a propaganda statement and the citizens would want to see that all the Roman soldiers were as well protected as possible, so all were shown wearing armour. The column is correct in so many other points but not even very fortunate archaeology will be able to prove this point.

There is nothing further to learn about the legion at war from the 2nd Dacian War. At least three more legions were deployed and Sarmizegethusa was captured, Decebalus became a fugitive and finally committed suicide. However Trajan's Column does invite some analysis.

In considering the images of the wars shown by drawings of scenes on the column [2] it will be seen that there are 40 separate representations each of both legionaries and auxiliary troops, but there are significant differences between the activities being undertaken in these scenes. The 40 legionary pictures include 14 where the soldiers are involved in construction work, two where they are attacking fortifications and four where they are fighting in the field.

These figures may be compared with the 40 representations of auxiliary troops. These include no cases of construction work, one assault on fortifications – assisting legionaries – and 14 fighting in the field, three of these cases in mounted action.

These figures fit well with the basic concept of the legions being the solid core of the army, relentlessly driving to their objective and being unbeatable in close quarter combat. Conversely the auxiliary troops are shown as being employed in frequent skirmishing and pursuits.

Notes
1. Sir I Richmond, *Trajan's Army on Trajan's Column*, British School at Rome, 1982, plate 20
2. Drawings by S Reinach, *Repertoire de Reliefs grecs et romains*, reproduced in *The Imperial Roman Army* by Yann Le Bohec, Routlege 2000.

Chapter 8: Changing the Strategy of Empire

Roman frontier policy changed dramatically after the death of the Emperor Trajan. His successor Publius Aelius Hadrianus, 117 to 138 AD, known as Hadrian, ended the steady expansion of empire, he even permitted it to shrink a little by withdrawing from Mesopotamia and some other regions. He then fortified the frontiers of the empire, most notably in Britain, and deployed the army to maintain these defences.

This system of defence worked well until the reign of Marcus Aurelius Antonius, 270 to 275 AD, known as Aurelian, when in a series of desperate wars thousands of barbarians crossed the Danube and even made their way into northern Italy. Roman forts and walled cities were like islands in a sea of barbarians whose main object was plunder. The resulting military situation robbed the legions of their effectiveness, the legions excelled in defensive fighting, but the invaders had no reason to attack them, rather the opposite. Instead of hurling themselves on the points of the Roman swords they would collect their wives and children and move on, and only in exceptional circumstances could the legions force them to fight. The change of emphasis caused by this is hinted at by Ammianus Marcellinus. He frequently mentioned centuries and maniples in the same sentence, indicating that the fundamental difference between legions and auxiliary troops was still maintained, but despite that the bulk of the fighting was now being done by the auxiliaries, particularly cavalry, with the legionaries becoming more and more like construction troops. The auxiliaries, he wrote, '*always think such work beneath them*'.[1] Also possibly bearing on the auxiliaries' view of the legion was that the legions, since the reign of Caracalla, no longer had a monopoly of Roman citizenship with the advantages in civil life that would have provided.

As most of the campaigning was now done within the Empire and troops could be billeted in cities and move quickly on good roads, there was a reduced requirement for the construction of marching camps, so much a part of the old Roman warfare. Even so the legions in general maintained the discipline to construct such camps as necessary up until the Battle of Adrianople, after that so many barbarians were incorporated into the legions that the old discipline could not be maintained.

The Romans had lost the initiative and could no longer anticipate being able to put together armies in which the legions and auxiliary forces balanced each other, consequently the legions had to become more flexible. Three things happened. One was that they reduced in size. Secondly the legionaries had to become better at attacking, and finally they had to supply their own firepower.

The first was achieved during the restructuring of the army into frontier troops (*limitanei*) and the mobile army (*comitatenses*). The *limitanei* were important for general policing and intelligence gathering duties, but the *comitatenses* may be assumed to have been the better soldiers and the following comments apply mostly to them. To facilitate this restructuring, and to allow greater flexibility, the legions shrank to 1,000 to 1,200 men. This is close enough to the strength of a vexillation to suggest that that was the basis of the new organisation.

Secondly the legionaries had to become better at attacking and fortunately the column, built 180 to 192 AD, of Marcus Aurelius, not to be confused with Aurelian, makes plain how this was done.[2] Quite simply, to make them more mobile, the majority of the legionaries' main offensive armament was changed to a spear and they no longer used a *pilum*, and their curved rectangular shield was replaced by a flat oval or round one which they carried in the usually way holding a hand grip with forearm through a loop. They now slung their swords on their left which they were able to do now that the new shield did not clash with their sword and scabbard. It was necessary to sling the sword on the left as it was now longer, being the *spatha* with a blade well over two feet long, so it could not be drawn if slung on the soldier's right. Illustrating these changes the Arch of Constantine, 312 to 315 AD, shows Roman infantrymen looking much like the hoplites of 700 years earlier.[3]

The third requirement, that of firepower, was met when a significant percentage of the soldiers, probably the younger and more active ones, were converted to *lanciarii*. They were to be basically skirmishers and fought with javelins, though retaining swords and shields for hand-to-hand fighting. According to Vegetius, one in three or four of the youngest and fittest soldiers became archers and all were taught to use the sling. These light infantry were classified as *antisignani*.[2] During this period most wars were with barbarians who did not wear armour, thus making missile action more effective.

There are endless discussions about the origins of these troops, but by Trajan's time the need for such troops was acknowledged and there is an argument that some of these are shown on his column. As time marched on so the percentage of such troops increased, and the legions came to consist of two types of soldiers, *lanciarii* and spearmen (hoplites), light and heavy infantry. If the *lanciarii* were termed shield-and-javelin men, it would seem superficially that the legions were evolving backwards towards something similar to the Polybian model but, with the difference in enemies and different challenges, this was unlikely.

Unfortunately the drills for the deployment of these two troop types are difficult to reconstruct, but on balance it seems that both types of soldier were incorporated within the *contubernia*. This would be necessary for the great flexibility shown during the fourth century. It is, though, possible that occasionally units consisting solely of *lanciarii* were formed. For the mixed *contubernia* to work, they would have formed up on the battlefield with the spearmen in front followed by the *lanciarii*, with a spearman file closer.

The heavy legionary, then, had become a later version of the targeteer of the Republican armies. These troops had shown excellent offensive capability, but this change meant that the legions lost their great defensive strength. The soldier was no longer backed up by the *pilum* of the man behind him, though it is possible this was done with *plumbatae* (or *mattiobarbuli*) which were heavy, lead-weighted, darts well known to archaeology. Vegetius wrote that the soldiers '*usually carried five* mattiobarbuli *each, slotted inside their shields. If soldiers throw them at the right moment, it seems almost as if shield-bearing infantry are imitating the role of archers. For they wound the enemy and his horses before they can get not merely to close quarters, but even within range of javelins.*'[5] A rack of five *plumbatae* on a shield is difficult to believe, shields are heavy enough without lumps of lead being attached to them. Probably one or two may have been carried like this, with the rest in some kind of quiver. Modern reconstructions indicate a maximum range of between 32 and 70 yards.

The soldier could not so easily shoulder barge the enemy and, if not given enough space in a melee, his sword would be hard to swing, it being too long to use for stabbing. As shown below, the disaster at Adrianople was caused by this lack of personal space. There is no reason to believe that the quality of the legionaries declined in any way, but if it did, this fact was hidden by the improving co-operation of arms, as the number of archers and cavalry increased so the legionaries became less important.

Adopting the spear, which was a more difficult weapon to use in a close-quarter melee than the short sword, may have resulted in the Romans showing increasing interest in parade ground drill (*campicursio*) which Vegetius hinted at. This interest is illustrated by the Emperor Julian, who found that '*being a prince as well as a philosopher he had to practise the rudiments of military training, and when he found himself learning the Pyrrhic march-step to the sound of the fife he would often call out the name of Plato and repeat the old proverb: "Pack-saddles are put on the ox: they are no fit burden for me".*'[6] The Pyrrhic dance, which seems to have been a stylised display of skill-at-arms, was very old and was mentioned by Xenophon in the *Anabasis*.

Naturally this change in weaponry and tactics took a long time to complete and some rectangular shields would have lingered on in stores for a long time after oval shields had become standard. The column of Marcus Aurelius shows large numbers of legionaries with oval shields but also some with rectangular ones. The column shows a tortoise in action, the drill being carried out with rectangular shields, essential for this drill. It is a possibility that this scene was a cameo copied from Trajan's column, but whether this is true or not under the new strategic situation the Romans would have had few places to besiege, so little use for a tortoise. The conversion back to spearman was recognised by the Emperor Caracalla (211-217 AD) who boasted to the King of Parthia of the skill of the Roman infantry in close-quarter combat with spears,[7] but perhaps the change-over was not complete until 218 AD when the Emperor Macrinus relieved the praetorians of '*their grooved shields and had thus rendered them lighter for battle*'.[8]

The praetorians seem to have retained their traditional *pilum* and *scutum* weaponry long after the legions had abandoned them. There are two third-century gravestones showing praetorians holding a *pilum*, in both cases the wooden shaft of the *pilum* has some sort of binding wrapped round its entire length.[9] The only possible use for this binding would have been to improve the soldier's grip, which shows that these weapons were still being taken very seriously.

The *lanciarii* were not the complete answer to the firepower requirement and for this an existing trend was extended. For many years archers and other missile troops had been deployed behind the legionaries but now this trend was extended and some legionaries were told off to act as missile troops. Vegetius describes the new deployment of the *contubernia* thus: '*In two lines are posted those older in years, confident and experienced, and protected by heavy armour. Their role is to act like a wall; at no time should they be made to retreat or pursue lest they disturb their ranks. They should receive oncoming adversaries and repel or rout them by standing their ground and battling it out.*

'*The third line is formed from very fast light infantry, young archers and good javelinmen…The fourth line is similarly constructed from very light "shield-bearers", young archers and those who fight briskly with light javelins and lead-weighted darts called* plumbatae…*It should be noted that whereas the front two lines stand their ground, the third and fourth lines always go out to challenge the enemy with missiles and arrows, in the forward position…*

'*In a fifth line were sometimes placed carriage-ballistas, and* manuballistarii, "*sling-staff men" and slingers…*

'*The sixth line behind all the others was held by very reliable warriors, armed with shields and every type of arms. These the ancients called* triarii'.[10] Put simply, Vegetius's *contubernium* consists of two spearmen, followed by two *lanciarii*, then a missile man and a file-closer. He has made a mistake in placing a *carroballista* within the century. He may have confused it with a *manuballista*, an early crossbow. The *carroballistae*, of course, would form up behind the century and fire over the soldiers' heads.

The legionary organisation described by Vegetius shows a startling similarity to that of the Macedonian phalanx after a large number of Persian troops had been recruited into it. This is covered in Appendix One.

Vegetius was writing in the 390s, and could well be describing the standard legionary form of the time of Adrianople. It is worth emphasising that this formation had evolved under the control of senior officers who had shown themselves to be highly competent professionals. No doubt the third and fourth of Vegetius's ranks were the later version of the *antisignati*, with the fifth rank providing the longer range firepower. This was a flexible system but it had two obvious weak points. One was that the new *contubernium* was only six men, indicating a 25% reduction since the time of the old legion. Secondly, only the first two, and possibly the last, men were equipped for hand-to-hand fighting, this meant that the weary or wounded could not file to the rear, as had been the case earlier. This would indicate that the legionary troops of the late fourth century no longer had the staying power for sustained hand-to-hand fighting that the old legions had. This may have been fatal at Adrianople.

Vegetius described the troops of the Western Empire. In the East there were threats from cataphracts and elephants that the westerners did not have to content with and it is possible that in the East there was a greater requirement for missile troops which may have reduced the number of spearmen even more. The increasing effectiveness of the Roman missile troops may be the reason that the legions did not evolve into phalanxes of pikemen.

During the third and fourth centuries, because of the increasing complexity of warfare, there may well have been a general improvement in the quality of officers. During the early empire officer appointments were year long stepping stones in Roman political careers, but this almost amateurish system broke down and the army became a career open to talents and quality men rose to the top, even some emperors started as private soldiers. It is only a pity that ancient sources do not record the military triumphs of the later empire as well as they do those of the early.

It is possible that the legion itself was changing from being a fighting organisation to being an administrative and training one. This change is hinted at by the existence of legions of *lanciarii* and *ballistarii* which might have been difficult to deploy as single units. The truth, or otherwise, of this supposition, however, was soon to be rendered irrelevant.

The Battle of Adrianople

In the years before 378 AD large numbers of Visigoths had been allowed to settle within the empire to the south of the Danube. The Romans had a system for accepting such immigrants, breaking them up into small packets and sending them to allocated areas or inducting them into the army. Unfortunately this year more Goths arrived than were expected, they set to plundering to stay alive, and refused to disperse. The Emperor of the East, Flavius Valens, realised that he would have to mount a campaign to drive them out.

Valens had been emperor since 369 and had conducted many hard campaigns, he knew that this one would not be easy. Consequently he asked Gratian, his colleague in the West and also his nephew, to send reinforcements, and this Gratian did, leading them himself.

The Visigoths were in the vicinity of Adrianople, a town in Thrace, now modern European Turkey. Valens and his army approached from the east. The Visigoths were at their most vulnerable, in small columns, moving slowly weighed down with booty. Sebastianus, the general commanding the Roman advanced guard, detached 300 men from each of his legions, and pursued and defeated a large band of Visigoths, retrieving vast quantities of plunder.

The easy success must have convinced Valens that the Visigoths would not be that much of a challenge, though there are hints that he wanted to win the war without seeming to be dependent on aid from Gratian, and even that he was jealous of Sebastianus. Whatever the motivation, Valens's actions were to display rashness that would be fatal to his army.

Valens, with the main army, reached Adrianople and constructed a fortified camp as a firm base, then marched out looking for the Visigoths. His marching force has been estimated as 15,000 to 20,000 strong. The Roman scouts had located the main body of the Visigoths a few miles away where they had formed a large circle of wagons on some high ground and within the circle were the cattle they had stolen. Unfortunately the scouts badly underestimated the number of Visigothic fighting men there.

It must have seemed to Valens that he now held a winning hand. He knew that the Visigoths would have to fight to defend their wagons and the Romans would easily win a heavy hand-to-hand battle.

The day was very hot and the ground rough, so when the infantry came close to the Visigoths they were already feeling the strain. At this stage an earlier generation of Romans would have started to construct a marching camp so that they could spend the night in security and the next day fight fully refreshed. Unfortunately Valens did not hesitate but formed his legions into line and ordered his cavalry to the flanks. Also unfortunately the cavalry that were to cover the left flank arrived late and went straight into the attack. Predictably they could make little impression on a wall of wagons but this action seems to have had a knock-on effect and some the infantry advanced without orders which would have resulted in a loss of order. Then, just as the main attack got under weigh, thousands of Visigoth cavalry that had been out foraging appeared on the battlefield and assaulted the Roman flanks. This came as a complete surprise, and one of the very few examples of the failure of Roman tactical intelligence, perhaps the premature start of the fighting did not allow time for the reports to come in. The best quality legions were posted in the middle of the line, those towards the flanks did not have the experience or discipline to handle the new situation and face to the flank and so were forced into fighting while not in files, consequently they bunched up and retreated towards the centre. Once the infantry had lost its formation the superior numbers of the Visigoths were bound to tell, as Ammiamus Marcellinus put it: *'This left the infantry...so closely huddled together that a man could hardly wield his sword or draw back his arm once he had stretched it out.'*[11] He also mentioned the lethal effects of battle-axes, and he credited both sides with the use of them, so they were a late addition to the legionary's weapons, probably a result of the increasing 'barbarianisation' of the army. They might have been handy infantry weapons in a crush like this one.

It is impossible to be sure of the form the infantry fighting took, but there are indications which may be considered. If the legions consisted of a mix of *lanciarii* and targeteers, and advanced with the *lanciarii* deployed to the front, then probably the targeteers, hit from a flank, could not fight in file and were massacred as the Romans were at Cannae. Also the *lanciarii*, being skirmishers, would not be able to stand against the Visigoth infantry and could not fall back behind the targeteers.

For some time Valens held out defended by his two elite legions, the *Lanciarii* and the *Mattiarii*. Their names imply that they were javelineers (*matara* = celtic javelin), but in the end either inappropriate weapons of weight of numbers defeated them. Perhaps old-style legionaries fighting *ad spathos et ad pila,* in front of an entrenched camp, might have turned the tide.

The Battle of Adrianople cost the Romans around 10,000 men. This figure includes not only the Emperor but a large number of senior officers, which speaks well of their hands-on approach to command.[12] How bad a disaster it was is difficult to gauge. A new emperor was put in place and the campaign continued to a successful conclusion, but to replace the casualties to the field army some *limitanei* were withdrawn from the frontier garrisons and added to it and this resulted in the frontier becoming more porous. The significance of this, however, is beyond the range of this study.

The brief account of the Battle of Adrianople offered here concludes this study of Roman tactics.

Notes

1. Ammianus Marcellinus, *The Later Roman Empire*, 18.2, Penguin Classics, p144
2. Iain Ferris, *Hate and War, The Column of Marcus*

Aurelius, The History Press, 2009

3.   Iain Ferris, *The Arch of Constantine*, Amberley, 2013

4.   One of the panels at Mainz shows a Roman soldier equipped like this. He is usually described as an auxiliary, but if this were so he would be the only auxiliary shown on these panels. He certainly wears a legionary-type helmet. The viewer will reach his own conclusion, but this writer believes him to be an *antisignanus*. This chapter relies heavily on *The Framework of an Imperial Legion*, by MP Speidel, a chapter in *The Second Augustan Legion and the Roman Military Machine,* ed RJ Brewer, National Museums & Galleries of Wales, 2002

5.   Vegetius, *Epitome of Military Science*, I.17, Liverpool University Press, 2011, p17

6.   Ammianus Marcellinus, *The Later Roman Empire*, 16.5, Penguin Classics, p93

7.   Herodian, *History of the Roman Empire*, IV.X, University of California Press, p 125

8.   Dio Cassius*, Roman History*, LXXIX.37.4, Loeb Vol IX, p426

9.   MC Bishop & JCN Coulston, *Roman Military Equipment*, Oxbow Books, 2006, p153, and
S James, *Rome and the Sword*, Thames & Hudson, 2011, p201, this illustration is also given as colour print 26 in
Guy de la Bedoyere, *Praetorian,* Yale University Press, 2017.

10.   Vegetius, *Epitome of Military Science*, III.14, Liverpool University Press, 2011, p93

11.   *Ammiamus Marcellinus*, 31.13, Penguin Classics, p435

12.   TS Burns, *Barbarians within the Gates of Rome*, Indiana UP, 1994, p33

Conclusion

This short study has followed the evolution of the Roman army from its early days, when it was similar to the hoplite phalanx of the Greeks, to its fully developed state at the height of Empire. The main subject covered has been the legionary tactics during that period. The legion, at its best, functioned in battle with a system which made the most efficient use of the fighting capacity of every legionary, putting him in contact with the enemy for a short time, appropriately armed and trained, and backed up by the *pilum* of the man behind him. These tactics were highly successful but only when used in the correct strategic situation and this situation existed when the Romans were following an offensive strategy, forcing their enemy to attack them on a tactical level. Further the study has covered, as far as sources allow, the breakdown of the legionary system.

The Romans believed that only long service regulars could be efficient soldiers but, although such considerations are really beyond the scope of this study, it must be mentioned that the weakness of this system was that the peacetime army was the same size as the wartime army, and the under-employed peacetime army was an indirect cause of many of the civil wars that were so disastrous for the Empire. It is difficult to understand why the Romans did not develop some sort of short term enlistment whereby soldiers could be dismissed after the conclusion of a war but retained as a reserve.

Once the empire had reached its greatest extent it was found that its frontier defences could not withstand the various barbarian assaults and the legions were used to counter-attack the hordes that had penetrated and were pillaging their way through the Empire. In this situation the legions could no longer rely on their enemies attacking them, so the legionaries had to become more mobile for the tactical offensive and change their battle techniques. All the while cavalry and light infantry were becoming more important. The end result was that the legionary organisation of the Caesar to Trajan period ceased to exist and the legions returned to being composite units of spearmen and missile troops. Unfortunately the evolution of the Roman infantry was interrupted by two major disasters, the Battles of Adrianople, 378 AD (Eastern Empire), and Frigidus, 394 AD (Western Empire). After these battles the Roman infantry started to lose its distinctive Roman nature, particularly as more and more use was made of barbarian units, either from outside the empire or from barbarian enclaves within the empire. Consequently this study ended at Adrianople.

There are two main deductions to be drawn from this study. One is that, although the legionaries with their big shields and swords, and the phalangites with their pikes, might be important in specific circumstances, the best general purpose heavy infantrymen of the classical world were a combination of shield-and-javelin men and targeteers with their small shields and long spears.

The second conclusion is that because hand-to-hand fighting is so exhausting, the soldiers must fight in file so that when weary or wounded, the leading soldier could fall back to the rear of the file. To be caught in a situation where the soldiers could not fight in file could be disastrous, as at Cannae or Adrianople.

Appendix 1: The Macedonian Phalanx

Chapter Two has shown that hoplites were first supported, then replaced, by a combination of targeteers and shield-and-javelin men. For the Roman army the shield-and-javelin men were the most important and provided the basis for Roman infantry development. The Greek and Macedonian experience was different and was based on the targeteers, that is soldiers armed with small shields and spears so long that they required the use of both hands.

This type of soldier seems to have come into existence almost spontaneously and had two functions. Firstly they cooperated with skirmishers to provide a defence against cavalry. Secondly as the skirmishers were driven back and the hand-to-hand clash approached, the targeteers would form up on the flanks of the hoplite phalanx. They were first organised as a regular type by Iphicrates early in the fourth century BC and, though evidence is a little vague, targeteers won their first and most famous victory under Chabrias in 378 BC. This fight was against the Spartans, and the Spartan phalanx was confronted with a phalanx of targeteers, the first rank of which was on one knee with their shields propped up against the other. If the soldiers were shoulder-to-shoulder and the second rank was close behind the first then there would have been a thick hedge of spear points facing the Spartans who backed off.

The advantage of the long spears/pikes was that, working in pairs, one man could jab his spear into his opponent's shield, thereby making it difficult for him to defend himself, while his mate could easily attack the man. Targeteers were not highly regarded in Greece, but their potential was quickly seized upon in Macedon, where Iphicrates had contacts, and which did not have a hoplite tradition. It was in Macedon, most likely during the reign of Philip II, the father of Alexander the Great, or possibly earlier, that the decision was taken to make a phalanx of targeteers the main heavy infantry component of the army. Once that decision had been taken it was inevitable that spears would increase in length until they became unmanageable because, due to the smallness of their shields and the need to use both hands to control the spear, when a phalanx of targeteers met another the soldiers could not fence with their spears as hoplites could, but would hold their long spears at waist level and jab with them, and victory went to those with longer spears. The spears soon reached maximum manageable length becoming pikes termed '*sarissai*'. The result was the Macedonian Phalanx which was to dominate warfare for 200 years. This was because if its enemies were not themselves phalangites, and could not retreat then they could be stabbed to death almost with impunity, as was the fate of the Theban elite, the 'Sacred Band', which was trapped against the River Cephissus and totally massacred at the Battle of Chaeronea (338 BC). However when a phalanx fought against another phalanx, the result tended to be inconclusive.

The length of the *sarissa* is difficult to ascertain, this is partly because ancient authors used cubits and the length of the cubit varied across the ancient world, and partly because *sarissai* tended to grow longer throughout the Hellenistic period. It is generally agreed, after studies of ancient authors, that the lengths of useable *sarissai* peaked at around eighteen feet.[1] However it is not always obvious how much these authors actually knew, or if they had even seen a *sarissa*, consequently it is worthwhile considering the words of Sir James Turner, an experienced English soldier of the seventeenth century, who wrote of the pike that: '*In our modern wars it is order'd by most Princes and States to be eighteen foot long, yet few exceed fifteen; and if Officers be not careful to prevent it, many base Soldiers will cut some off the length of that, as I have oft seen it done*'.[2]

The appearance of a phalanx was described by Plutarch: '*First of all marched the Thracians, whose very aspect struck the beholders with terror. They were men of a prodigious size; their shields were white and glistering; their vests were black, their legs armed with greaves: and as they moved their long pikes, heavy-shod with iron, shook on their right shoulders*'.[3]

Because of the lack of freedom of movement of the individual phalangites it was necessary that they should wear armour. When he was convincing the Achaeans to form a phalanx and replace their light shields and spears '*Philopoemen altered both; persuading them instead of the buckler and lance, to take the shield and pike; to arm their heads, bodies, thighs, and legs; and, instead of a light and desultory manner of fighting, to adopt a close and firm one. After he had brought the youth to wear complete armour, and on that account to consider themselves as invincible, his next step was to reform them with respect to luxury and love of expense.*'[4]

The phalangites of Alexander the Great were only lightly armoured, Polyaenus says that '*Philip accustomed the Macedonians to constant exercise, as well in peace, as in actual service: so that he would frequently make them march three hundred furlongs, carrying with them their helmets, shields, greaves, and spears; and, besides those arms, their provisions likewise, and utensils for common use*'.[5]

Polyaenus does not mention any kind of breastplate or corselet. Perhaps helmet and light armour were enough to keep arrows out, but not javelins at a short range. This was shown, in 327 BC, in a small but desperate battle: '*the battle was a scene of horror. They fought hand to hand, and as the contestants engaged each other every form of death and wounds was to be seen. The Macedonians thrust with their long spears through the light shields of the mercenaries and pressed the iron points on into their lungs, while they in turn flung their javelins into the close ranks of their enemies and could not miss the mark, so near was the target'.*[6] The unfortunate mercenaries had been surrounded and could not escape.

Actions such as this should have provided a serious warning of things to come, but it seems not because when lightly equipped phalangites came into contact with Roman legionaries, the result was a disaster. It has been seen how the casualties caused by such a clash, in 200 BC, had a depressing effect on the other soldiers as described by Livy (see Chap 3, note 5). This was also described by Florus whose account, if briefer contains an interesting detail. *'Nothing caused the Macedonians greater fear than the sight of their wounds, which, having been dealt not with darts or arrows or any Greek weapon but by huge javelins and no less huge swords, gaped wider than was necessary to cause death'.*[7] This gives the impression that the Roman *pila*, with their long iron shanks, could pierce the phalangites light shields and reach the unarmoured bodies behind them. Consequently the phalanx would have been easily destroyed by the legion. The legionaries would have marched up to within a yard or so of the points of the *sarissai* and, one after the other, thrown their *pila* until the phalanx crumbled.

Armour prevented this and there must have been something of a scramble to armour the phalanx and make it fit for the coming battles with the Romans. Some soldiers, at least, were well equipped by the time of the assault of Atrax in 198 BC (see Chap 4, note 1).

The phalangite's shield was not as large as that of the hoplite and in the phalanx it was slung on the left shoulder and supported on the left forearm in such a way that the phalangite could use both hands to handle his pike.

However the phalangite could be employed in other roles so his shield must have been reasonably large with the general purpose loop and grip of the hoplite's *aspis*. The phalangite's shield is sometimes mentioned as being covered in metal, no doubt a thin sheet but enough to make it more resistant to the weather. As the shield was smaller than the hoplite's it may well have been a little thicker and more proof against missiles, this was important as missile action became progressively more important throughout the Hellenistic period.

All the above is generally agreed upon, however there is a good deal of argument on the subject of how the individual phalangite actually fought. As was standard in the ancient world the phalangites fought in file. The standard file was sixteen men long and contained two half-files, each of eight men. Each half-file had a leader and file closer, and the troops were all in pairs, 'Front-rank-men' and 'Rear-rank-men'.[8]

The phalanx would manoeuvre with the troops in the sixteen-man files, but once they had taken up their fighting positions the rear half-files would move forward on the left of the front half-file, a process called 'doubling'. While they were manoeuvring the ranks were in open order, that is each file had a front of six feet, after doubling this was reduced to three, the intermediate order. The phalangite was now in contact with the enemy and it is necessary to consider how he used his *sarissa*.

An excellent recent book, based on re-enactment,[9] has estimated the weight of the shaft of a *sarissa* as 9.4lbs. For a 'ball park' estimate its length is taken as 12 cubits (18 feet). In order for the *sarissa* to be manageable its centre of gravity should be no further forward than the soldier's left hand, and the location of this will be shown to be very important. Most modern accounts show him holding the *sarissa* right at the rear, as if it were a fishing rod, his left hand about two cubits along. If this were the case there must be a counter-balancing butt weight of over 18lbs, giving a total weight for the *sarissa* of over 28lbs.[9.1] This is unrealistically heavy.

If, on the other hand, as Polybius says, the soldier's left hand was four cubits from the rear end which would project about a yard behind the soldier, the butt weight would be only 4.7lbs, giving a total weight for the *sarissa* of 14.1lbs. [9.2] This is reasonable, though not light. By way of comparison a Lee-Enfield No 4, the standard British rifle of the Second World War, weighed 9lbs 3oz. One consequence of the weight of the *sarissa* was that a thrust with it, using both hands, would generate enough momentum to smash through nearly any shield or armour. Another consequence was that the butt end of the *sarissa* would project about a yard behind the soldier and this would, in the squash of a closely deployed phalanx, be a factor limiting the use of the *sarissa*.

It must be written, though, that this estimate of the weight of the shaft is based on one of diameter of 1.4-inches, with a short front section narrowed a little to fit into the socket of the spearhead. In view of the occasional reports of attacking soldiers hacking the heads off *sarissai*, as at Atrax, these figures seem a little high. Frontinus gives a similar example when, during the Battle of Pydna, Paulus Aemilius '*commanded the cavalry on the left wing to ride at full speed past the front of the phalanx, covering themselves with their shields, in order that the points of the enemy's spears might be broken by the shock of their encounter with the shields. When the Macedonians were deprived of their spears, they broke and fled.*'[10] Either this, and similar cases, are fantasy or the *sarissa* shafts were thinner, less robust and lighter than assumed.

As observed above pikemen were most effective when working in pairs and the organisation of the files reflects this. The soldiers were paired off and the 'front-rank-man' was probably the most heavily armoured of the two, his function was to immobilise the enemy soldier by stabbing his shield. The 'rear-rank-man', who was right behind and to the left of the leader, who might have been stooping a little, could jab his *sarissa* over him, or round his left side, to wound if not kill the enemy. It has been seen that the phalangite engaging the enemy must have around a yard of open space behind him for the butt end of his *sarissa*. Consequently behind the first two men came a gap. The third soldier, who was also the second 'front-rank-man', might just have been able to deploy his *sarissa*. If he could it would be to defend the first man against an enemy who had managed to get inside the row of pike heads to attack with a sword. To defend the front man the third soldier would have to hold his *sarissa* high, at least at shoulder height, in the manner of how renaissance-period pikemen are often depicted, otherwise he would have been a nuisance to the front pair.

The action of fixing the enemy's shield was demonstrated at the Battle of Pydna: '*As soon as the attack was begun, Aemilius, advancing to the first ranks, found that the foremost of the Macedonians had struck the heads of their pikes into the shields of the Romans, so that it was impossible for his men to reach their adversaries with their swords. And when he saw the rest of the Macedonians take their bucklers from their shoulders, join them close together, and with one motion present their pikes against his legions, the strength of such a rampart and the formidable appearance of such a front struck him with terror and amazement. He never, indeed, saw a more dreadful spectacle, and he often mentioned afterwards the impression it made upon him*'.[11]

The concept that only the leading two soldiers of any file were able to do serious fighting is illustrated in one of Polyaenus's Stratagems. At the siege of Edessa,

Cleonymus's phalanx was attacked by a phalanx carrying 24 foot *sarissai*. He '*ordered the front line to use no arms; but with both hands to seize the enemy's spears, and hold them fast; while the next rank immediately advanced, and closed upon them. Their spears thus seized, the men retreated; but the next rank, pressing on them, either took them prisoner, or slew them*'.[12] This might show that 24 foot *sarissai* were too long to be useful, but it certainly shows that the rear ranks could not bring their *sarissai* into action.

The yard-long gaps in the files, necessary for the rear ends of the *sarissai*, are the reason that the phalanx could function in battle. Fighting with the *sarissa* would be every bit as tiring and dangerous as fencing with the hoplite's spear, but with the phalanx in intermediate order there would have been little or no space between the files to allow the wounded or weary leading pairs of soldiers to file to the rear. So when these men signalled that they were going back and moved their *sarissai* to the vertical, the men in the left hand file would slot into the gaps in the right hand file to let them pass, then step back out after they had passed.

Holding the *sarissa* vertical was also a sign of surrender, but like all such signs it has to be understood by the enemy. Roman soldiers, who presumably were ignorant of this convention, massacred large numbers of phalangites who were trying to surrender at Cynoscephalae (197 BC).

Now that the functioning of the phalangites has been considered, it will be worthwhile to consider Polybius's opinions: '*There are a number of factors which make it easy to understand that so long as the phalanx retains its characteristic form and strength nothing can withstand its charge or resist it face to face. When the phalanx is closed up for action, each man with his arms occupies a space of three feet. The pike he carries was earlier designed to be twenty-four feet long, but as adapted to current practice was shortened to twenty-one, and from this we must subtract the space between the bearer's hands and the rear portion of the pike which keeps it balanced and couched. This amounts to six feet in all, from which it is clear that the pike will project fifteen feet in front of the body of each hoplite when he advances against the enemy grasping it with both hands. This also means that while the pikes of the men in the second, third, and fourth ranks naturally extend further than those of the fifth rank, yet even the latter will still project three feet in front of the men in the first rank.'*[13]

Polybius was a man of substantial military knowledge and a good deal of common sense, and is an essential primary source of information for the times he wrote about. Consequently few will argue with his comments about the Macedonian phalanx. However they cannot be accepted in their entirety.

The obvious point is that, if the phalanx was in the intermediate order with the soldiers effectively shoulder-to-shoulder only the first two, and possibly the third, soldiers in a file could level their *sarissai*.

To some extent the situation was clarified by referral to Asclepiodotus, '*The needs of warfare have brought forth three systems of intervals: the most open order, in which the men are spaced both in length and depth four cubits apart, the most compact, in which with locked shields each man is a cubit distant on all sides from his comrades, and the intermediate, also called a 'compact formation', in which they are distant two cubits from one another on all sides.*'[14] The space taken by the soldier was included in these intervals, so in the open order each soldier was around a yard away from his neighbour. It was in this order that the pikes of the second, third and fourth ranks could be deployed in the manner described by Polybius.

The open order, with all its pikes, was an impenetrable defence against cavalry and if a very difficult one to make mobile, this was easier than with the other orders. Presumably when marching the phalangites would have held their pikes vertically, either advanced or shouldered.

'From these facts we can easily picture the nature and the tremendous power of a charge by the whole phalanx, when it advances sixteen deep with levelled pikes. Of these sixteen ranks those who are stationed further back than the fifth cannot use their pikes to take an active part in the battle. They therefore do not level them man against man, but hold them with the points tilted upwards over the shoulders of the men in front. In this way they give protection to the whole phalanx from above, for the pikes are massed so closely that they can keep off any missiles which might clear the heads of the front ranks and strike those immediately behind them. Once the charge is launched, these rear ranks by the shear pressure of their bodily weight greatly increase its momentum and make it impossible for the foremost ranks to face about.'[15] It may be possible that holding the *sarissa* low over the heads of the phalangites in front could have been some protection against projectiles coming from a flank, but it would certainly have been exceptionally tiring for the soldiers holding their *sarissai* in such a position.

The *sarissa*-armed phalanx had to advance *en bloc* so that the phalangites would be mutually supporting. They could not mount a wedge assault, which would disrupt their front and be suicidal. This resulted in phalanx tactics becoming generally sterile and unimaginative.

It seems that there was a degree of faith in the concept of the soldiers following each other so closely that each would drive the man before him forward, or at least prevent his flight. As Asclepiodotus, reflecting Polybius, wrote: *'the men in the lines behind the fifth, though they cannot extend their spears beyond the front of the phalanx, nevertheless bear forward with their bodies at all events and deprive their comrades in the front ranks of any hope of flight.*'[16] This may be the origin of the *othismos* error but it is an error none-the-less. It was impossible for the third rank to push forward against the backs of the leading pair of phalangites. This was because there had to be a space for the projecting rear yard or so of their *sarissai*. Any attempt to apply *othismos*-type pressure would prevent the phalanx functioning.

If the assault failed then the phalanx would have to return to the open order to stand on the defensive, this order being necessary to allow the best use of the pikes. If the phalanx, being in open order, was assailed by missiles, then the front rank of the phalanx would adopt the close order. This order Asclepiodotus called '*with locked shields*'. In this order the front rank phalangites, having but eighteen inches per man, would have had to stand sideways so could not stoop or level their *sarissai*, but their shields overlapped to give them excellent protection against missiles. Only the front rank adopted this order because it was important that the formation could be quickly opened up as soon as there was any threat of hand-to-hand combat which the phalangites could not, in this formation, handle. It is possible, but with no evidence to support the idea, that in the close order alternate phalangites could have dropped to one knee making the shields alternately high and low to give better coverage, and allow some of the following rank men to use their *sarissai*.

Phalangites were not totally helpless in terms of sword fighting. Their swords, though still secondary weapons, were an improvement of the insignificant swords of the earlier hoplites. This was shown at the Battle of Cynoscephalae when the Macedonian commander, Philip, '*gave orders that the Macedonians of the phalanx should put down their spears, whose length was a hindrance, and rely on the swords'.*[17]

As can be seen it was vitally important that the files were correctly spaced one from the other, but maintaining this spacing was easier said than done. The decision to double from files of sixteen soldiers to files of eight would usually be taken by the file leader when he noticed that the gap between his file and the next to his left was becoming too large. Conversely if the files were becoming squashed up the commander of two 16 man files would convert them into one 32 man file. At each stage as the number of files was doubled, there was a new commander. In theory a whole phalanx could be reduced to one long single file of soldiers, but in practice the most important tactical unit was the *syntagma*, a unit of 256 men. This was, of course, 16 sixteen man files. It had an alternate title, that of '*speira*', which Oxford Classical Greek Dictionary translates as 'a body of soldiers' or 'anything coiled'.

There was a number of extra personnel allowed at *syntagma* level, these included a second-in-command, standard bearer, trumpeter and herald. This implication is that the *syntagma* could rotate through a right angle to change from a column of march into a fighting formation, and the *syntagma* commander would be responsible for it being in the correct order. Consequently the phalangites would be trained to obey orders conveyed by flag and trumpet, as well as shouting. It was a matter of great importance that the *syntagma* retained contact with its adjacent units, failure to do this, particularly when fighting Romans, could be disastrous. The result of this was that assaults would be delivered at a stately march with frequent halts to check the dressing.

The importance of maintaining the correct spacing between individual phalangites and between sub-units was commented on by Frontinus: '*Manius Curius, observing that the phalanx of King Pyrrhus could not be resisted when in extended order, took pains to fight in confined quarters, where the phalanx, being massed together, would embarrass itself'.*[18]

This constant fear of disorder meant a poor offensive capacity and no pursuits. It also meant that the phalanx was vulnerable to being out-flanked. The corners were obvious weak points and if an opposing phalanx managed to overlap, even by just a few yards, the unsupported flank of a phalanx, the result would be disaster. Phalanxes were surprisingly vulnerable to being out-flanked by cavalry. The front of a well-ordered phalanx was totally proof against cavalry and it would seem reasonable that if cavalry surrounded it then it was just a matter of the rear few ranks turning about and presenting their *sarissai* at the horsemen, but there are several examples of phalanxes being surrounded and not being able to cope because the very fact of enemy cavalry being behind them meant that they no longer had any light infantry protection against missiles and most cavalry of the time fought with javelins. The probably root cause of the problem was that when fighting infantry the phalangites would be holding their *sarissai* at waist level, but when threatened by cavalry the front rank would stoop, or kneel, down and set the butt of their *sarissai* in the ground. This is presuming that they would follow the procedure of renaissance period pikemen. Unfortunately this drill would halt the sub-unit. If the whole phalanx halted this would not matter, but if some other sub-units kept moving the phalanx could fall apart.

Probably the most well known example of the effect of cavalry on a phalanx occurred during the Battle of Gabene (317 BC), where the phalanx of Eumenes was driving back that of Antigonus and the battle seemed won till Antigonus sent some of his cavalry round to the rear of Eumenes's key unit, the 'Silver Shields'. These were the finest troops of the day, the successors of Alexander the Great's hypaspists. The Silver Shields were without cavalry and light infantry support so they halted and adopted an all-round defence. That halted the battle and proved fatal to Eumenes, as the Silver Shields observed that Antigonus's troops had captured their baggage train and their families, so they mutinied.

In ideal circumstances the phalanx's two vulnerabilities, missiles and disorder, would be planned for and avoided by the army commander. He would not have deployed the phalanx unless it was covered and supported by light infantry and cavalry so that it need not fear missiles. Also he would have deployed the phalanx on as flat and open ground as possible. The phalanx was much better at fighting over rough terrain than might be thought, but broken ground could result in the sub-units advancing at differing rates and becoming separated. When fighting against Romans, this could be fatal.

As can be seen the standard of drill required for a phalanx to be efficient would have been pretty impressive. This was shown in the description of the phalanx as given by Curtius: '*The Macedonian line is certainly coarse and inelegant, but it protects behind its shields and lances immovable wedges of tough, densely-packed soldiers. The Macedonians call it a phalanx, an infantry column that holds its ground. They stand man next to man, arms interlocked with arms. They wait eagerly for their commander's signal, and they are trained to follow the standards and not break ranks. To a man they obey their orders. Standing ground, encircling manoeuvres, running to the wings, changing formation – the common soldier is no less skilled at all this than the officer* '.[19]

The actual process of drill was illustrated by Asclepiodotus with a list of drill commands, some of which have a distinctly modern sound: '*Stand by to take arms! Baggage-*

men fall out! Silence in the ranks! Shoulder arms! Take distance! Shoulder spear! Dress files! Dress ranks! Dress files by the file-leader! File-closer, dress file! Keep your original distance! Right face! Forward march! Halt! Depth double! As you were! Depth half! As you were! Length double! As you were! Laconian counter march! As you were! Quarter turn! As you were! Right half turn! As you were! Etc'.[20]

The deployment of phalanxes evolved over time. The Macedonian phalanx was created by Philip II and fully instituted by Alexander the Great. It came to consist of a maximum of seven *taxies*, each of a theoretical strength of 1,540 men. Separate were the hypaspists. There is some argument, but it seems that these were shield-and-javelin men, and there were 3,000 (two *taxies*) of them. After the Battle of Arbela (or Gaugamela, 331 BC) the clear distinction between the two types of infantry began to fade, both types adopting spears or *sarissai* as the situation demanded. The hypaspists, though, retained their status as an elite and this continued throughout their evolution as the Silver Shields right up to the end of the Hellenistic period.

To win his major battles Alexander used his phalanx as his defensive wing, and his cavalry and hypaspists for the offensive. By the time that Hellenistic armies were clashing with the Romans they were relying almost entirely on the phalanx. In the first of these battles the Hellenistic troops were commanded by Pyrrhus who must have been the best of the Hellenistic generals. He appreciated the problem caused by the rigidity of the phalanx and tried to overcome this by deploying the phalanx in subunits and filling the gaps between them with targeteers. He defeated the Romans twice.

For reasons that are not obvious other Hellenistic generals did not follow Pyrrhus's lead and, although the traditional Macedonian phalanx, with its *sarissai*, could deliver a sharp shock which the legions found hard to counter, as the initial fighting at Pydna showed, it could not sustain an offensive beyond a couple of hundred yards without falling into disorder and making itself vulnerable. If the Macedonian army at Pydna had been a balanced force with a cavalry and hypaspist wing it could very well have won the battle.

Disorder need not have been fatal to a phalanx, well drilled troops could recover if not pressed too hard. At least this is the impression given by Polybius in his account of the Battle of Sellasia.[21]

There is an aspect of the development of the phalanx which is worth noting. Arrian, in his account of how Persians were enlisted into the Macedonian army, wrote: '*The Persians were then enrolled into the various Macedonian units, so that the 'decad' – or section – now consisted of a Macedonian leader, two of his compatriots, one of them a 'double-pay' man, the other a 'ten-stater' man (so called from the pay he received, which was less than that of the 'double-pay' soldiers but more than that of the ordinary rank and file), twelve Persians, and, last, another 'ten-stater'. Four Macedonians, that is – the section-leader and three others on extra pay – and twelve Persians. The Macedonians wore native equipment; the Persians were armed either with bows or light javelins.*'[22] As this excerpt shows the soldiers involved were not armed with the *sarissa* so the unit can no longer be regarded as a phalanx, although the soldiers could be seen as substitute hypaspists. Even so it was still important to be able to very quickly double the ranks and this organisation may have been adopted to overcome any potential language problem.

Arrian's file is led by the file leader, followed by the leader of the rear half-file, followed by an experience soldier. These were all Macedonians. The last man in the file was also a

Macedonian, the rest were Persians. This organisation may seem cumbersome but was well designed for its task. The file leader decides to double his file and tell the half-file leader who steps forward and to his left. The next soldier runs back past six Persians, tells the rear half-file to move forward and takes up his post as front half-file closer. The rear half-file forms up behind its leader.

It may be noted that there is no hint in literature that enlisting Persians into Macedonian formations reduced their effectiveness in any way.

After the Battle of Magnesia, the last great Roman clash with a phalanx, the Hellenistic rulers started to reorganise and re-equip their armies in imitation of the Romans, and the phalanx's day had passed.[23]

Pike phalanxes were to enjoy a brief renaissance in sixteenth century Europe where they provided the backbone of most armies for a short while before gunpowder blew them away. Even despite firearms the European phalanxes were much more fluid and flexible that the Hellenistic ones because of the wider range of weaponry available. The front few ranks of the European phalanxes wore armour and carried pikes much as the Hellenistic phalangites did, but behind them came some ranks of halberdiers and other troops equipped for the close hand-to-hand fighting which would result if any enemy managed to fight their way through the hedge of pikes. Also, when attacking another pike phalanx, European pikemen were often preceded by some heroes armed with two-handed swords (*zweihander*), up to six feet long, which were used to beat aside the enemy's pikes and open up a break in the ranks. Hellenistic blacksmithery did not run to producing such weapons, and so the Hellenistic phalanx never quite developed the flexibility required to cope with the legions.

Notes

1.   AM Snodgrass, *Arms and Armour of the Greeks*, Thames and Hudson, 1967, p118

2.   Sir James Turner, *Pallas Armata*, III.5, 1683, reprinted by EEBO editions, p176

3.   *Plutarch's Lives, Paulus Aemilius*, Translated by the Revs J & W Langhorne. No date, p194

4.   *Plutarch's Lives, Philopoemen*, Translated by the Revs J & W Langhorne. No date, p260

5.   Polyaenus, *Stratagems of War*, IV.II.10, Ares Publishers, p136

6.   Diodorus Siculus, *The Library of History*, XVII.84, Loeb Vol VIII, p363

7.   Florus, *Epitome of Roman History*, I.XXIII, Loeb, p117

8.   Asclepiodotus, II.3, *Aeneas Tacticus, Asclepiodotus, Onasander*, Loeb, p255

9.   CA Matthews, *An Invincible Beast*, Pen & Sword, 2015

9.1   p91 gives the total weight of the shaft as 4,270g (9.4lbs). Taking the length of the *sarissa* as 12 cubits and ignoring the weight of the spearhead, which is small, the counter-balancing butt weight, W, can be calculated   by balancing the turning moment round the centre of gravity. If this is two cubits along the shaft:

$$Wx2=4x9.4$$

W=18.8. This, added to the weight of the shaft gives a total *sarissa* weight of 28.2lbs

9.2   If the centre of gravity were four cubits along the shaft, then:

$$Wx4=2x9.4$$

W=4.7. Which, added to the weight of the shaft gives a total *sarissa* weight of 14.1lbs

10.   Frontinus, *Stratagems*, II,iii,22, Loeb, p121

11.   *Plutarch's Lives, Paulus Aemilius*, Translated by the Revs J & W Langhorne. No date, P194

12.   Polyaenus, *Stratagems of War*, II.XXIX.2, Ares Publishers, p85

13.   Polybius, *The Rise of the Roman Empire*, XVIII.29, Penguin Classics, p509-510

14.   Asclepiodotus, III.5, *Aeneas Tacticus, Asclepiodotus, Onasander*, Loeb, p267

15.   Polybius, *The Rise of the Roman Empire*, XVIII.30, Penguin Classics, p510

16. Asclepiodotus, V.2, *Aeneas Tacticus, Asclepiodotus, Onasander*, Loeb, p273

17. Livy, *Rome and the Mediterranean*, XXXIII.8, Penguin Classics, p115

18. Frontinus, *Stratagems*, II,ii,1, Loeb, p99

19. Quintus Curtius Rufus, *The History of Alexander*, 3.2.13, Penguin Classics, p29

20. Asclepiodotus, XII.11, *Aeneas Tacticus, Asclepiodotus, Onasander*, Loeb, p333

21. Polybius, *The Rise of the Roman Empire*, II.65, Penguin Classics, p170

22. Arrian, *The Campaigns of Alexander*, 7.23, Penguin Classics, p388

23. N Sekunda, *Hellenistic Infantry Reform in the 160's BC*, Gdansk University, 2006.

Appendix 2: The Legionary Shield

The large rectangular shield is, in modern times, the most well known piece of the Roman legionary's equipment and yet it was in service for only a comparatively short time. There is general agreement about the broad outline of the nature and evolution of the shield, however it is the view of this writer that the detailed description given in many books, and the reproduction shields carried by re-enactors, are wrong and would not have been serviceable on the battlefield.

The problem centres on how the shields were carried. Apart from Trajan's Column there are few representations of legionary shields being carried, and none show the back, or inside, of the shields. This in itself is remarkable, Greek art shows many illustrations of both front and back of the *aspis*, and Trajan's Column and other sculptures such as the Arch of Orange, show both back and front of auxiliaries' shields. It can only be concluded that there was something about the way the legionaries' shields were carried that made seeing their backs difficult.

The Roman legions were certainly aware of the necessity of good shields. Polybius's comments on the superiority of the Roman shields at the Battle of Telamon, in 225 BC, has already been quoted, but the earliest representation of a legionary shield dates from 168 BC, it is on the Aemilius Paulus monument celebrating the Battle of Pydna. The image is badly damaged and shows a total of seven Roman infantrymen in a variety of poses. If the reconstruction of this monument [1] is viewed it can be seen that the left hands of the Romans hold the shields substantially further than half-way down where there must have been a hand grip. This would indicate that the forearm was through a loop above, and to the left of, the central boss. Some of the shields shown are oval, and some have the tops and bottoms truncated.

The next oldest representation of shields is the Altar of Domitius Ahenobarbus, 122 BC, currently in the Louvre. Although at first sight this monument seems well preserved and accurate, the method of carrying the shield is ambiguous though likely to have been the same as for the Aemilius Paulus monument. In both sculptures the shields approximate to Polybius's figure of four feet high. The width is harder to gauge.

Interestingly Aemilius Paulus ordered his sentries not to carry a shield while on watch because of the temptation for the soldier to lean forward and rest his head on the shield, and lapse into a doze. So the top of the shield must have been fairly flat.[2]

The evolution of the shield is made harder to follow by a relief at Praeneste, which is usually dated as late First Century BC and shows a warship crewed by Roman legionaries. They carry the usual oval shields, and the back of one is plainly shown. It has one handgrip which is vertical and looks as if it was attached to the central spine. Of course it may be that this was a special sea pattern shield, but it is of interest in that it illustrates the fact that if a hand grip were set into the interior of the central boss then it would be vertical.

The conclusion to all this must be that during the Republican era the Roman shields were tall, hence thin, and held by a hand grip and loop close to the middle. This pattern worked well while the Roman infantry were shield-and-javelin men and their tactics were based on missile warfare, but as the wars with the Gauls began it was found that the shields did not provide a proper defence against the brutal hand-to-hand fighting of the barbarians. Not only were the shields penetrable but the soldiers could not control their shields when Gauls seized them and dragged them forward and down, exposing their owners to attack.

It must have been obvious that the swords and shields were not being used to best effect when Rutilius Rufus, in 105 BC, had a gladiatorial instructor make recommendations. The result, which would have been merged into what are generally known as the Marian Reforms, was the classic panoply of the Roman legionary and the most significant changes were to the shield, the outside face of which was altered in that the top and bottom were truncated, making the shield roughly rectangular. It was also curved inwards from the central spine. There is no evidence that the shield was convex before this time.

Also there can be no doubt that the hand grip was changed but, despite history and common sense, a general belief has grown that the shield was carried by a single grip which was horizontal and fitted across the hollow of the central boss. This cannot be right. There are many representations of legionaries carrying their shields and there can be no doubt that the boss of the shield is significantly above the left hand, which is to say that the shield is a minimum of six inches higher than it would have been if the legionary was carrying it by the grip on the inside of the boss.

From a practical point of view the single grip half-way up the shield would not have worked in any hand-to-hand contacts, the shield would have tended to spin around the hand grip. There are two cases on Trajan's Column of legionaries, attacking defended walls, holding their shields almost horizontally in front of them. With a single hand grip the shields would have been impossible to control.

The same can be said of the left hand figure in the sculptured relief at the fortress of Mainz, referred to in Chapter Three. He holds his shield up horizontally to cover the soldier in front of him from missiles.[3]

All these objections to the single, central, hand grip are met by positing the existence of hand grips in the form of two bars, running horizontally as chords across the curved inside of the shield, in the region of eighteen inches from the top and bottom of the shield. The soldier would carry the shield with his forearm between the top bar and the back of the shield, and gripping the lower bar. Holding the shield like this would result in it being flat against the body, so the back of the shield would not be seen. The best illustration of this is the Praetorian Relief, of 51/52 AD, in the Louvre. Remarkably there is in illustration of the back of a legionary shield on Trajan's Column and this certainly shows a hand grip well below the central boss.[4]

There was an obvious need to alter the handgrips to give the soldiers greater control of their shields, particularly when barbarians were trying to wrench their shields off them. Another reason was that the shield was becoming heavier and thicker to cope with arrows, and it has been estimated as weighting 22 lbs. Altering the hand grips as suggested here would solve these problems. A panel at Adamklissi shows a soldier holding his shield high so that the central boss would have been level with his chin. With the suggested hand grips doing this would have been easily done by upending the shield, not difficult to do as the horizontal shields on Trajan's Column show, but impossible without the hand grips.[5]

There is no archaeological evidence for such bars, but then the archaeological evidence for shields in general is a bit sparse, so there is no evidence against their existence. However some reinforcing strips, up to twenty inches long, have been found and these could have formed a framework that could have supported both the material of the shield and the bar-like handgrips. Some such framework, with the bars, might be thought necessary to maintain the curvature of the shield and prevent it warping flat in the sun and rain of campaigning.

Such bars would seem to be a necessity for the tortoise drill, without them the horizontal 'roof' shields would 'concertina' in and out to such an extent that control would soon be lost. Also the 'roof' of the tortoise had to be supported strongly enough to bear the weight of not only the rocks and other such items as the defenders might drop on it, but also the weight of other soldiers climbing on to it, as in the description by Tacitus of the assault of the camp near Cremona. *'Henceforward bloodshed and wounds could not check the troops' determination to undermine the rampart and shatter the gates. Climbing on one another's shoulders and mounting on top of the re-formed 'tortoise', they clutched at the enemy's weapons and shoulders'*.[6] Plainly loads like this could not be carried with one hand even with the shield resting on the shoulder, so the proposed bars would be necessary.

In the case mentioned above of the legionaries holding their shields almost horizontally before them, the difficulty disappears as with the bars the weight of the shield is now resting stably on the forearm. The shield as now described would be ambidextrous, as illustrated by Polyaenus when he instanced Caesar's troops passing through a defile, *'on the sea side, Pompey's fleet, that attended him on his march, with their darts and javelins heavily galled him. Against this attack Caesar ordered his men to carry their shields on their right hands: which had the desired effect.'*[7]

However, despite the posited existence of the two bars, the grip on the inside of the boss was retained. The bulk of the shield was made of a kind of plywood, with layers of wood glued together with what Polybius called *'bull's hide glue'*. It was protected from the weather by a cover of either canvas or leather. It may be that wet weather, by causing the plywood to disintegrate, helped seal the fate of Varus's men, as Dio Cassius wrote: '*For they could not handle their bows or their javelins with any success, nor, for that matter, their shields, which were thoroughly soaked'*.[8] Rain could be a major problem for the Romans. Once when Sulla was campaigning in Italy his army was caught in a violent rain storm and his officers begged him for a break in operations '*shewing him how his men were beaten out with fatigue, and seated upon the ground with their shields under them*', no doubt they were keeping their shields dry.[9]

The plywood parts of the shield tended to decay with time, Lucan comments how the citizens of Ariminum, being suddenly alarmed, snatched down their arms: '*such arms as the long peace supplied: they lay hold on shields that are falling to pieces with framework exposed, javelins with their points bent, and swords roughened by the bite of black rust.*'[10] This quote is interesting in that it mentions a framework probably similar to that just suggested.

Also the plywood would be hacked to pieces in battle, and it has been shown how easily phalangites' *sarissai* could penetrate Roman shields. To counter this there was a trend for the boss to increase in size until it was a large metal plate and made a reasonable buckler in the event of the plywood parts of the shield being no longer serviceable, and the grip behind the boss was needed to wield it. Lucan describes such a case: '*All the host and all the weapons make him their sole object; no hand misses its aim, no lance failed of its mark; and Fortune sees a new pair meet in combat – a man against an army. The stout boss of his shield rings with repeated blows; his hollow helmet, battered to pieces, galls the forehead which it covers; and nothing any longer protects his exposed vitals except the spears which stick fast when they reach his bones.*'[11]

Having some sort of unit identification on the shield was

an obvious requirement, but not one currently fully understood, despite some rather optimistic claims. Similarly during the Civil Wars it was common to write the general's name on the shields so that the soldiers would have some idea of whose side they were on.[12]

There was a certain symbolism attached to the shield, and the drama of a general seizing a shield of a hesitating or retreating soldier so that he could plunge into the fray, may have been a trope as popular as that of snatching up a legionary eagle to lead an assault. Florus, who was just repeating other historians, gave two examples:

'In this, while there were many notable exploits on the part of Roman soldiers, a remarkable feat was performed by the general himself; for when his troops were wavering and on the point of retiring, snatching a shield out of the hand of a retreating soldier, he rushed to the front line and by his own efforts restored the battle',[13] and

'Caesar (ie Augustus) *himself undertook an expedition against them and gave orders for the building of bridges. It was here that, in the confusion caused by the water and the enemy, he snatched a shield from the hand of a soldier who was hesitating to mount the bridge, and was the first to cross'.*[14]

There may have been many more such cases.

The shield, being such a prominent item, could be used to signal a wish to surrender by raising it above the owner's head.[15]

This appendix will conclude with a quote from Dio Cassius in which he describes the use of a tortoise by Mark Antony, an event already referred to, with a Plutarch quote, in Chapter Three:

'One day, when they fell into an ambush and were being struck by dense showers of arrows, they suddenly formed the testudo *by joining their shields, and rested their left*

knee on the ground. The barbarians, who had never seen anything of the kind before, thought that they had fallen from their wounds and needed only one finishing blow; so they threw aside their bows, leaped from their horses, and drawing their daggers, came up close to put an end to them. At this the Romans sprang to their feet, extended their battle-line at the word of command, and confronting the foe face to face, fell upon them, each one upon the man nearest him, and cut down great numbers, since they were contending in full armour against unprotected men, men prepared against men off their guard, heavy infantry against archers, Romans against barbarians. All the survivors immediately retired and no one followed them thereafter.

'This testudo and the way in which it is formed are as follows. The baggage animals, the light-armed troops, and the cavalry are placed in the centre of the army. The heavy-armed troops who use the oblong, curved, and cylindrical shields are drawn up around the outside, making a rectangular figure; and, facing outwards and holding their arms at the ready, they enclose the rest. The others, who have flat shields, form a compact body in the centre and raise their shields over the heads of all the others, so that nothing but shields can be seen in every part of the phalanx alike and all the men by the density of the formation are under shelter from missiles. Indeed, it is so marvellously strong that men can walk upon it, and whenever they come to a narrow ravine, even horses and vehicles can be driven over it. Such is the plan of this formation, and for this reason it has received the name testudo, with reference both to its strength and to the excellent shelter it affords. They use it in two ways: either they approach some fort to assault it, often even enabling men to scale the very walls, or sometimes, when they are surrounded by archers, they all crouch together – even the horses being taught to kneel or lie down – and thereby cause the foe to think that they are exhausted; then, when *the enemy draws near, they suddenly rise and throw them into consternation.* '[16]

No doubt Dio exaggerated the strength of the tortoise when thinking in terms of driving horses over it, but this quote does illustrate the importance of the 'oblong, curved, and cylindrical shields' to Roman warfare.

Notes
1.   Ancient Warfare, Vol VIII, issue 6
2.   Livy, *Rome and the Mediterranean*, XLIV.33, Penguin Classics, p584
3.   www.livius.org/mo-mt/mogontiacum/mainz_pedestals.html
4.   YL Bohec, *The Imperial Roman Army*, Routledge,2000. Illustration 86 shows handgrip, 30,31 and 86 show shields held horizontally.
5.   Sir I Richmond, *Trajan's Army on Trajan's Column*, British School at Rome, 1982, plate 20
6.   Tacitus, *The Histories*, 3.28, Penguin Classics, p162
7.   Polyaenus, *The Stratagems of War*, VIII,XXIII,13, Ares Publishers, p328
8.   Dio Cassius, *Roman History*, LVI.21, Loeb, Vol VII, p47
9.   *Plutarch's Lives, Sylla*, Translated by the Revs J & W Langhorne. No date, P331
10. Lucan, *The Civil War*, I. Line 243, Loeb, p21
11. Lucan, *The Civil War*, VI. Line 189, Loeb, p319
12. Dio Cassius, *Roman History*, XLVIII.301, Loeb, Vol V, p283
13. Florus, *Epitome of Roman History*, I.XLV, Loeb p 201see also Appian, *The Civil Wars*, II.104, Penguin Classics, p124
14. Florus, *Epitome of Roman History*, II.XXIII, Loeb p329
15. Appian, *The Civil Wars*, II.42, Penguin Classics, p91
16. Dio Cassius, *Roman History*, XLIX.29, Loeb, Vol V, p401-403

Sketch Maps

Sketch 1: The Battle of Leuctra

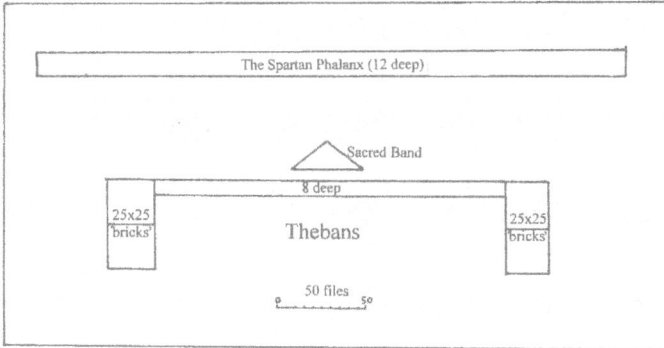

Sketch 2: The Varus Disaster

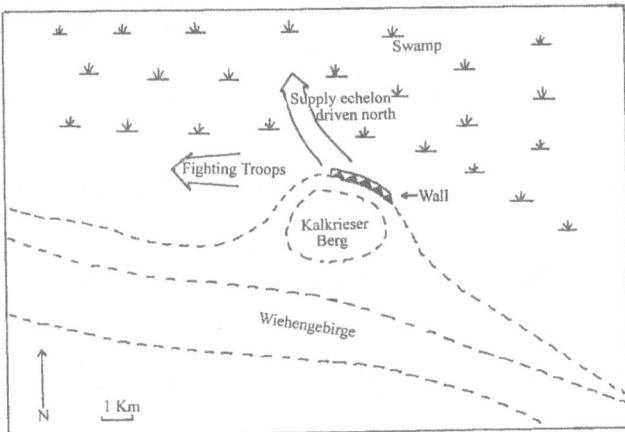

Sketch 3: The First Battle of Philippi

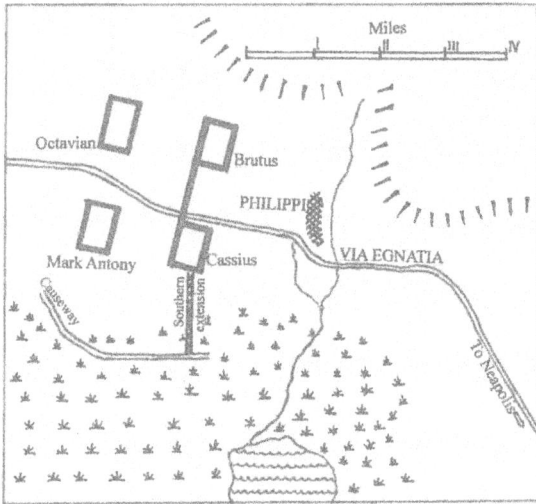

Sketch 4: The Second Battle of Philippi

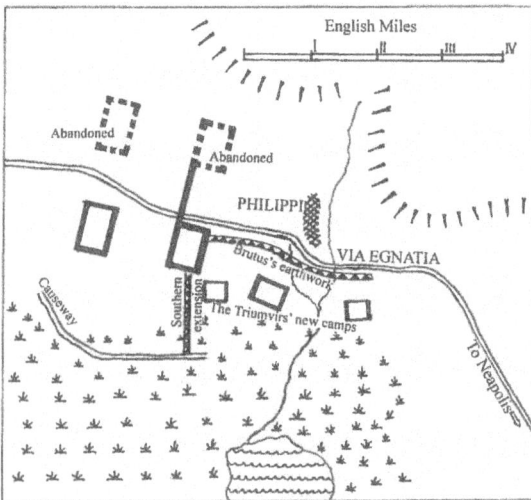

The Author and his Books

As the author of the books listed here I wish to write a few words about them, but first I should give some personal background.

I was born in 1945 and have been fascinated by warfare ever since I found out that people were killed in wars. I graduated in Metallurgy at Sheffield University and after that followed my real interest by soldiering with the 13th/18th Royal Hussars.

Most of my books are about tanks, or anti-tank warfare. These books are of a similar format, covering manuals, vehicles and battles. In writing them I benefited greatly from personal experience and contact with veterans, spin-offs of military service. These books are based on facts, whereas my other two books, 'War' and 'Roman Legionary' are, to a large extent, my opinions. Naturally I am proudest of these two.

My books are all Print-on-Demand, they are available on www.amazon.co.uk and several other sites. They are advertised at £7.99 or less.

Writing military books is my hobby, and I'm always interested to hear what readers think of them. So if you read one, please either leave a comment on Amazon or contact me via the publishers.

Cruiser Tank Warfare
This is the term used to describe the British concept of armoured warfare based on fast, thinly armoured tanks. The book traces the history of this concept from the publication of 'Mechanised and Armoured Formations' in 1929 up to the end of the Second World War. It does this

by following the British understanding of the subject in manuals, 'Modern Formations' being extensively quoted, by considering the development of Cruiser tank design, and by looking at the major actions that Cruisers were involved in. The conclusion drawn is that the Cruiser Tank Warfare concept was fundamentally flawed.

It is important to note that the book restricts itself to a detailed investigation of the British experience of tank warfare, only occasionally referring to foreign armies and then purely for comparison. The book is 70,500 words long.

Infantry Tank Warfare
This is the term used to describe the use of armoured vehicles to support infantry in the attack. Although there are chapters covering the experience of armour in the Great War, and inter-war developments, the greater part of the book covers the Second World War. Within the main theme there are three topics: infantry tanks, specialised armour and armoured personnel carriers. Each topic is studied separately by considering the vehicles involved, the manuals for their use, and the actions they were involved in. The result is an appreciation of the fine achievements of the British armoured forces.

As with Cruiser Tank Warfare, this book restricts itself to a detailed investigation of the British experience, only occasionally referring to foreign armies and then purely for comparison. The book is 58,500 words long.

British Anti-Tank Warfare
This book is an attempt to describe the British army's approach to Anti-Tank Warfare from its inception during the Great War until 1945.

During the Great War the army found little reason to study anti-tank warfare and after the war what little anti-tank awareness there was slowly faded away. This was inevitable because of the 'ten year rule' which proclaimed that there would be no major war in that period, and it was only in the second half of the thirties that the British army started to take the subject seriously.

In 1939 the British anti-tank armament and tactics were inadequate, this became a major worry after Dunkirk and this book gives particular emphasis to the anti-tank defences built in England against the expected German invasion. Under the pressure of necessity tactics and equipment improved reaching a high point of effectiveness at Medenine in 1943. After that, although equipment improved slightly, the threat was never again so great and the British army could confidently handle whatever Axis armour came its way.

There must be some doubt if anti-tank warfare should be regarded as a subject in its own right, mostly because it is purely a reaction to the invention and progress of the tank. The writer of this book believes it should be, and this book should support this view. The book is 72,000 words long.

German Anti-Tank Warfare
This short study follows German Anti-Tank Warfare from 1916 to 1945. During its early days in the Great War German Anti-Tank Warfare quickly achieved a surprising degree of sophistication but throughout most of the inter-war period it was largely ignored. As the Second World War approached it was regarded as a matter for specialist teams but as it progressed though the desert campaigns it became a matter for AT guns, with mines increasingly important. In its final stage in Europe every soldier was expected to play his part, with mines and Panzerfausts, in the fight against tanks. The book looks at the equipment

available, particularly self-propelled guns, and at trends in permanent fortification. In particular it considers the Mareth Line and the Siegfried Line and the British and American assaults of these Lines.

The book is not long, being 55,000 words. As with any subject as vast as the subject of this study, it is impossible to guarantee a proper balance and proportion in the way it is described, but an attempt has been made and it is hoped that the reader will find this study informative and useful.

Although this book has been written to stand alone, it also forms a companion piece to the author's 'British Anti-Tank Warfare' and a kind of counterpoise to some of his other books about tanks.

The 1st Armoured Division
This division saw more action than any other British armoured division from its deployment in France in 1940 until its disbandment in Italy in 1944. Despite its impressive record this division has been almost ignored by historians and this book is an attempt to rectify this. It follows the division through its disastrous campaign in France, then to North African to follow its retreat to Gazala and its part in that defeat. It looks closely at the division's actions around Ruweisat Ridge where the reputation of British armour reached an all-time low. This is followed by an account of the division's part in Alamein and its triumphant march across North Africa to Tunisia. Finally the division's part in the Italian campaign, specifically the assault of the Gothic Line, is studied, then the circumstances of its disbandment.

Hopefully the publication of this book will go some way to reinstating the reputation of this fine division. The book is 50,000 words long.

War

This book is the result of its author's determination to understand the phenomenon of war, a determination which has been one of the driving forces of his life for over half a century. It has taken well over ten years to write.

In this book two basic types of conflict are defined, primary and secondary warfare. The study mostly covers secondary warfare which is considered in terms of the army/government/people triad, both in the context of conventional war between countries, and guerrilla insurrections within countries.

Each aspect of warfare is illustrated, and each conclusion is backed up, with copious examples.

The final conclusion of the endemic nature of warfare will not please many people who read it, but if it has the effect of causing them to be much more critical of various government policies then this book can be regarded as a success. The book is 73,000 words long.